STREET TALK·2

SLANG USED IN POPULAR AMERICAN TELEVISION SHOWS

(PLUS LINGO USED BY TEENS, RAPPERS, & SURFERS!)

STREET TALK -2-

is now...

available on cassette!

See the coupon on the back page for details

STREET TALK·2

SLANG USED IN POPULAR AMERICAN TELEVISION SHOWS

(PLUS LINGO USED BY TEENS, RAPPERS, & SURFERS!)

David Burke

Optima Books

Los Angeles   San Francisco

Publisher: Optima Books
Editor: Robert Graul
Managing Editor: Debbie Wright
Editing, Design, and Production: Optima PrePress
Front Cover Illustration: Jim Graul
Inside Illustrations: Jim Graul

This publication is designed to provide accurate and authoritative information in regard to the subject matter covered. It is sold with the understanding that the publisher is not engaged in rendering legal, accounting, or other professional services. If legal advice or other expert assistance is required, the services of a competent professional person should be sought. FROM A DECLARATION OF PRINCIPLES JOINTLY ADOPTED BY A COMMITTEE OF THE AMERICAN BAR ASSOCIATION AND A COMMITTEE OF PUBLISHERS.

Library of Congress Preassigned Catalog Card Number: 92-81410
ISBN 1-879440-06-7
Printed in the United States of America
92 10 9 8 7 6 5 4 3 2

This book is dedicated to my sister Nancy...
a babe magnet, a fly girl, a betty, a cheeky mama, a robo babe,
nectar, taste, nasty, the bomb, hot to trot!

preface

For years, parents have had the same complaint: *"I can't understand what my teenagers are saying!"* which is exactly how they want it. But parents are relentless. They keep trying to decipher their teen's jargon in order to bridge the communication gap and simply to be kept out of the dark. But it may seem easier than it looks.

The parent, desperate to unravel this mysterious teen lingo, overhears a conversation that his/her offspring is having on the phone:

> *"Hey, **brah**! You looked way **dope** in that **fly** hat when we were out **cruisin'** today. Oh, no! I'm late for class! I'm **breakin' out**!"*

That wasn't so hard. Having comprehended every word, the unsuspecting parent walks away smugly pleased to have finally broken through the language barrier, believing to have understood:

> *"Hey, my **bra**! You looked like an **idiot** in that **pilot's** hat when we were out **sailing** today. Oh, no! I'm late for class! **My skin is erupting**!"*

What the teen really said was:

> *"Hey, **friend**! You looked really **great** in that **fantastic** hat when we were out **looking for girls** today. Oh, no! I'm late for class! I'd **better leave right away**!"*

To further complicate the parent's burden of comprehension, there are two other types of slang that are becoming increasing popular among teens; *rap slang* and *surfer slang*. Rap and surfer slang are heard not just in daily conversations between members of the younger generation, but on prime time American television and radio as well. In fact, television besieges the viewers with this type of slang every Saturday morning when the majority of its viewers are youngsters and teenagers.

STREET TALK -2 takes a close look at teen, rap, and surfer slang, as well as everyday slang used consistently in popular American television shows, traffic reports, news broadcasts, television weather reports, and sports broadcasts, which are of special importance to non-native speakers who are trying to integrate into our culture.

STREET TALK -2 is a self-teaching guide divided into four parts:

- **DIALOGUE**

  Twenty to thirty new American expressions and terms (indicated in boldface) are presented as they may be heard in an actual conversation. A translation of the dialogue in standard English is always given on the opposite page followed by an important phonetic version of the dialogue as it would actually be spoken by an American. This page will prove vital to any non-native since, as previously demonstrated, Americans tend to rely heavily on contractions and shortcuts in pronunciation.

- **VOCABULARY**

  This section spotlights all of the slang words and expressions that were used in the dialogue and offers more examples of usage, synonyms, antonyms, and special notes.

- **PRACTICE THE VOCABULARY**

  These word games include all of the new terms and idioms previously learned and will help you to test yourself on your comprehension. (The pages providing the answers to all the drills are indicated at the beginning of this section.)

- **A CLOSER LOOK**

  This section offers the reader a unique look at common words used in slang expressions pertaining to a specific category such as *Rhyming Slang, Exclamations Used in Cartoons and Comic Books, Foreign Words Used in Everyday Speech, Popular College Slang, etc.*

Whether you're a parent who wants to understand the most popular slang used by the youth of today, a non-native speaker who is lost everytime he/she turns on the television, or even a teen who has been accused of being *"uncool"* or *"square,"* **STREET TALK -2** will quickly unravel the "inside language" of slang that has always been reserved for specific groups...*until now!*

David Burke
Author

acknowledgments

A special thanks goes to Janet Graul and Vivian Margolin for making the copyediting phase of this book so enjoyable. Their patience, expertise, and attitude are, as always, so appreciated.

I am especially grateful to Bob Graul for his contribution in the technical end of this book's production. His commitment to quality, accuracy, and detail are absolutely unsurpassed.

I am particularly thankful to Jim Graul, our cover and illustration artist. His creativity, professionalism, and ability to produce exceptional images were astounding.

I owe a special debt of gratitude to all of the people throughout the U.S. that I hounded for information regarding slang, idioms, and gestures. I was always met with kindness and an eagerness to offer a total stranger some, oftentimes bizarre, information.

legend

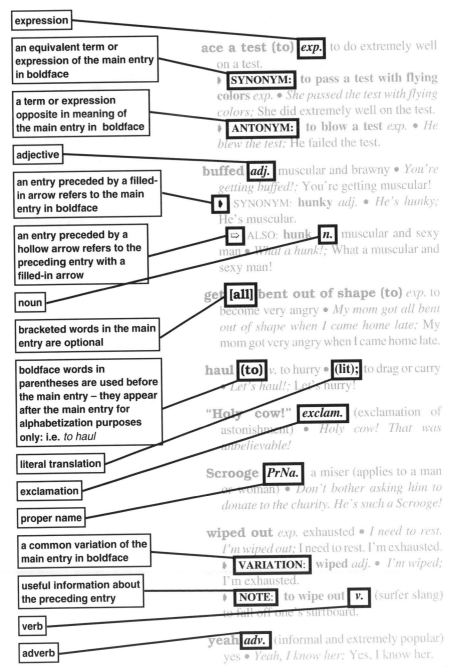

expression

an equivalent term or expression of the main entry in boldface

a term or expression opposite in meaning of the main entry in boldface

adjective

an entry preceded by a filled-in arrow refers to the main entry in boldface

an entry preceded by a hollow arrow refers to the preceding entry with a filled-in arrow

noun

bracketed words in the main entry are optional

boldface words in parentheses are used before the main entry – they appear after the main entry for alphabetization purposes only: i.e. *to haul*

literal translation

exclamation

proper name

a common variation of the main entry in boldface

useful information about the preceding entry

verb

adverb

ace a test (to) *exp.* to do extremely well on a test.
  ▸ **SYNONYM:** to pass a test with flying colors *exp.* • *She passed the test with flying colors;* She did extremely well on the test.
  ▸ **ANTONYM:** to blow a test *exp.* • *He blew the test;* He failed the test.

buffed *adj.* muscular and brawny • *You're getting buffed!;* You're getting muscular!
  ▸ SYNONYM: hunky *adj.* • *He's hunky;* He's muscular.
  ⇨ ALSO: hunk *n.* muscular and sexy man • *What a hunk!;* What a muscular and sexy man!

get [all] bent out of shape (to) *exp.* to become very angry • *My mom got all bent out of shape when I came home late;* My mom got very angry when I came home late.

haul (to) *v.* to hurry • **(lit);** to drag or carry • *Let's haul!;* Let's hurry!

"Holy cow!" *exclam.* (exclamation of astonishment) • *Holy cow! That was unbelievable!*

Scrooge *PrNa.* a miser (applies to a man or woman) • *Don't bother asking him to donate to the charity. He's such a Scrooge!*

wiped out *exp.* exhausted • *I need to rest. I'm wiped out;* I need to rest. I'm exhausted.
  ▸ **VARIATION:** wiped *adj.* • *I'm wiped;* I'm exhausted.
  ▸ **NOTE:** to wipe out *v.* (surfer slang) to fall off one's surfboard.

yeah *adv.* (informal and extremely popular) yes • *Yeah, I know her;* Yes, I know her.

contents

STREET TALK · 2
SLANG USED IN POPULAR AMERICAN TELEVISION SHOWS
(PLUS LINGO USED BY TEENS, RAPPERS, & SURFERS!)

Slang used in T.V. Comedies

– At the Nightclub –

Lesson One- SLANG USED IN T.V. COMEDIES

Dialogue In Slang

At the Nightclub

DIALOGUE

Neil brings his younger brother, John, to a nightclub for the first time.

Neil: What are you wearing that **getup** for? You really look **geeky**.

John: **That tears it! Catch ya later**.

Neil: Okay, okay! Don't **flip out**. Look, we'll just **hang** here for a while… this is the best spot to **pick up chicks**.

John: What do I do if one **gives me the eye**?

Neil: **Get with the program**! Just go up and **dialogue** her. **No biggy**!

John: **No way, José**! I'd **chicken out**. Don't you ever get scared of girls?

Neil: Never! Okay, I'm getting you a drink… a vodka **rocks**. How does that **sound**? I guarantee it'll **do the trick**. Actually, maybe you should have it **straight up**. I think you need to get yourself **faced**.

John: Oh, great. I'll get totally **plastered**, walk right up to her then **toss my cookies** right on her foot. Do we have **to stick around** here?

Neil: **Mellow out**! We're staying here all night.

John: Hey, Neil… isn't that the girl who had a **mad crush** on you? You know, the one you **blew off** in order to take out her roomate? I never saw anyone so **teed off** before. Man, has she ever gotten big!

Neil: She's a weight lifting **buff**. If she **spots** me here, **my goose is cooked**. Hey, she's coming this way! **Yike**! Let's get out of here!

John: **Hold on**! What was that about never being scared of a girl?

Neil: Only the kind that can't **knock my block off**. Come on, let's **beat it**!

Lesson One- SLANG USED IN T.V. COMEDIES

At the Nightclub

DIALOGUE

Neil brings his younger brother, John, to a nightclub for the first time.

Neil: What are you wearing that **outfit** for? You really look **ridiculous**.

John: **That's all I can tolerate! See you later**.

Neil: Okay, okay! Don't **get upset**. Look, we'll just **pass time** here for a while... this is the best spot to **look for women**.

John: What do I do if one **flirts with me**?

Neil: **Get up-to-date**! Just go up and **talk to** her. **It's not a big problem**!

John: **Absolutely not**! I'd **lose my courage**. Don't you ever get scared of girls?

Neil: Never! Okay, I'm getting you a drink... a vodka **with ice**. How does that **appeal to you**? I guarantee it'll **have a positive effect**. Actually, maybe you should have it **plain, without anything to dilute it**. I think you need to get yourself **intoxicated**.

John: Oh, great. I'll get totally **drunk**, walk right up to her then **vomit** right on her foot. Do we have **to stay** here?

Neil: **Calm down**! We're staying here all night.

John: Hey, Neil... isn't that the girl who **liked you romantically**? You know, the one you **abandoned** in order to take out her roomate? I never saw anyone so **angry** before. Man, has she ever gotten big!

Neil: She's a weight lifting **fanatic**. If she **finds** me here, **I'm dead**. Hey, she's coming this way! **Oh, no**! Let's get out of here!

John: **Wait**! What was that about never being scared of a girl?

Neil: Only the kind that can't **beat me up**. Come on, let's **leave**!

Dialogue in slang as it would be heard

At the Nightclub

DIALOGUE

Neil brings 'is younger brother, John, to a nightclub fer the firs' time.

Neil: Whaddya wearing that **gedup** for? You really look **geeky**.

John: **That tears it. Catch ya lader.**

Neil: Okay, okay! Don't **flip out**. Look, we'll just **hang** here fer a while… this is the best spot ta **pick up chicks**.

John: Whad do I do if one **gives me the eye**?

Neil: **Get with the program**! Jus' go up 'n **dialogue** 'er. **No biggy**!

John: **No way, José**! I'd **chicken out**. Don'chew ever get scared of girls?

Neil: Never! Okay, I'm gedding you a drink… a vodka **rocks**. How's that **sound**? I guarantee it'll **do the trick**. Actually, maybe you should have it **straid up**. I think you need ta get cherself **faced**.

John: Oh, great. I'll get todally **plastered**, walk right up to 'er then **toss my cookies** right on 'er foot. Do we have **ta stick around** here?

Neil: **Mellow out**! We're staying here all night.

John: Hey, Neil… isn't that the girl who had a **mad crush** on you? Ya know, the one you **blew off** in order ta take out 'er roomate? I never saw anyone so **teed off** b'fore. Man, 'as she ever gotten big!

Neil: She's a weight lifting **buff**. If she **spots** me here, **my goose's cooked**. Hey, she's coming this way! **Yike**! Let's ged oudda here!

John: **Hold on**! What was that about never being scared of a girl?

Neil: Only the kind that can't **knock my block off**. C'm on, let's **bead it**!

Vocabulary

beat it (to) *exp.* to leave • *We'd better beat it before they come home;* We'd better leave before they come home.
  ‣ SYNONYM: **to scram** *exp.* • *Let's scram!;* Let's leave!

blow someone off (to) *exp.* to jilt someone • *Did you hear that Jim just blew off his girlfriend?;* Did you hear that Jim just jilted his girlfriend?
  ‣ SYNONYM: **to shine someone** *exp.* • *He shined his girlfriend;* He jilted his girlfriend.

buff • **1.** *n.* devotee, fanatic • *Tom's a real music buff;* Tom's a real devotee of music. • **2.** *adj.* muscular • *Your brother's buff!;* Your brother's muscular! • buffed, buffed out *adj.* muscular.
  ‣ SYNONYM: **freak** *n.* • *He's a real movie freak;* He's a real movie enthusiast.

catch someone or something later (to) *exp.* to see someone or something later • *I'll catch you later;* I'll see you later. • *I'll catch the movie next week;* I'll see the movie next week.

chicken out (to) *exp.* to become scared • *I was going to ask her out but I chickened out at the last minute;* I was going to ask her out but I got scared at the last minute.
  ‣ SYNONYM: **to wuss out** *exp.* • *He was going to ask his boss for a raise but he wussed out;* He was going to ask his boss for a raise but he got scared.

dialogue someone (to) *exp.* to talk to someone • *There's my favorite movie star! I'm gonna go dialogue her;* There's my favorite movie star! I'm gonna go talk to her.
  ‣ SYNONYM: **to chew the fat with someone** *exp.* to chat with someone • *We chewed the fat for an hour;* We chatted for an hour.

do the trick (to) *exp.* to have a positive effect • *I'm sorry you don't feel well. Here, drink this tonic. It'll do the trick;* I'm sorry you don't feel well. Here, drink this tonic. It'll have a positive effect.

flip [out] (to) *exp.* to become uncontrollably upset • *My mother flipped [out] when I wrecked her car;* My mother became uncontrollably upset when I wrecked her car.
  ‣ SYNONYM: **to wig [out]** *exp.* • *She wigged [out] when I told her the news;* She became uncontrollably upset when I told her the news.

geeky *adj.* foolish • *Why are you wearing that geeky hat?;* Why are you wearing that foolish hat?

  ◗ ALSO: **to be geeked out** *exp.* to be foolish looking • *Do I look geeked out in this dress?;* Do I look foolish in this dress?

  ◗ SYNONYM: **nerdy** *adj.* • *Those glasses are really nerdy;* Those glasses are really foolish looking.

get faced (to) *exp.* to get extremely intoxicated • *We got faced at the party;* We got extremely intoxicated at the party.

  ◗ NOTE: This expression is a euphemistic and shortened version of *"to be shitfaced."*

get with the program (to) *exp.* to become aware, to become current • *Didn't you know this was a formal dinner? Get with the program!;* Didn't you know this was a formal dinner? Get current!

  ◗ SYNONYM: **to get a clue** *exp.*

getup *n.* clothing, outfit • *What kind of getup is she wearing?;* What kind of outfit is she wearing?

  ◗ NOTE: The term *"getup"* may be used both derogatorily and favorably, depending on the context and delivery of the speaker: *Nice getup!;* Nice outfit!

give someone the eye (to) *exp.* to look at someone with romantic interest • *I think that guy is giving you the eye;* I think that guy is looking at you with romantic interest.

  ◗ SYNONYM: **to check someone out** *exp.* • *She's been checking you out ever since you came in;* She's been looking at you romantically ever since you came in.

goose cooked (to have one's) *exp.* to be in severe trouble • *If I forget her birthday again this year, my goose is cooked;* If I forget her birthday again this year, I'm going to be in severe trouble.

  ◗ SYNONYM: **to have one's butt in a sling** *exp.* • *My butt's gonna be in a sling if I don't get home by 9:00;* I'm going to be in severe trouble if I don't get home by 9:00.

hang (to) *v.* to pass the time idly • *Let's hang here for a while until it stops raining;* Let's just pass the time here for a while until it stops raining.

  ◗ NOTE: This is a common shortened version of the expression *"to hang out."*

  ◗ SYNONYM: **to kick back** *exp.* • *Let's kick back at my house;* Let's pass the time idly at my house.

hold on (to) *exp.* to wait • *Hold on! Don't go without me!;* Wait! Don't go without me!

  ◗ SYNONYM: **to hold the phone** *exp.* • *Hold the phone! That was a really mean thing you just said;* Wait! That was a really mean thing you just said.

"How does that sound?" *exp.* "Does that appeal to you?"
  ▸ SYNONYM: **"How does that grab you?"** *exp.*

knock someone's block off (to) *exp.* to punch someone in the face • *If you don't give me that, I'm gonna knock your block off!;* If you don't give me that, I'm going to punch you in the face!
  ▸ NOTE: **block** *n.* face, head.
  ▸ SYNONYM: **to punch someone's lights out** *exp.* • *She punched his lights out in front of everyone!;* She knocked him unconscious in front of everyone!

mad crush on someone (to have a) *exp.* to have great romantic interest in someone • *I can't believe she has a mad crush on me!;* I can't believe she has romantic interest in me!
  ▸ NOTE: In this expression, the adjective *"mad"* which literally means "angry," takes on the slang meaning of "intense," having nothing to do at all with anger.
  ▸ SYNONYM: **to have the hots for someone** *exp.*

mellow out (to) *exp.* to calm down • *Would you mellow out? There's no need to get so upset!;* Would you calm down? There's no need to get so upset!
  ▸ SYNONYM: **to chill [out]** *exp.*

"No biggy!" *exp.* "No problem!"

"No way, José!" *exp.* "Absolutely not!"

pick up chicks (to) *exp.* to look for girls for romantic encounters • *This bar is great for pickin' up chicks;* This bar is great for finding girls for romantic encounters.
  ▸ SYNONYM: **to cruise chicks** *exp.*

plastered (to be) *adj.* to be extremely intoxicated • *Don't let her drive. She's plastered!;* Don't let her drive. She's extremely drunk!
  ▸ SYNONYM: **to be blitzed** *adj.*

rocks (on the) *adv.* served with ice • *Would you like your drink on the rocks?;* Would you like your drink served with ice?

spot someone (to) *v.* to find someone • *I had trouble spotting you in this crowd;* I had trouble finding you in this crowd.

stick around (to) *exp.* to stay • *Stick around. The fun is about to begin!;* Stay here. The fun is about to begin!

straight up *adv.* pure and undiluted (said of alcoholic drinks) • *I had a hard day today. I think I need a vodka straight up;* I had a hard day today. I think I need some undiluted vodka.

teed off (to be) *exp.* to be angry • *He got teed off at me 'cause I was 20 minutes late;* He got angry at me because I was 20 minutes late.
  ♦ NOTE: This is a common shortened version of *"to be ticked off."*
  ♦ VARIATION: **to be T'd off.**

"That tears it!" *exp.* "That's all I can tolerate!"
  ♦ VARIATION: **"That rips it!"** *exp.*

toss one's cookies (to) *exp.* to vomit • *He tossed his cookies in the bus;* He vomited in the bus.
  ♦ SYNONYM: **to blow chunks** *exp.*

"Yike!" *exclam.* exclamation denoting surprise • *Yike! What was that?!*
  ♦ VARIATION: **Yikes!**

PRACTICE THE VOCABULARY

[Answers to Lesson One, p. 209]

A. Underline the definition of the expression in boldface.

1. **to chicken out**:
    a. to be a vegetarian   b. to become scared   c. to run quickly

2. **buff**:
    a. fool   b. fat person   c. devotee

3. **geeky**:
    a. foolish   b. happy   c. intelligent

4. **getup**:
    a. alarm clock   b. coffee   c. outfit

5. **to hang**:
    a. to eat voraciously   b. to pass time idly   c. to drink

6. **to hold on**:
    a. to hurry   b. to walk slowly   c. to wait

7. **"No biggy!"**
    a. "Absolutely not!"   b. "This is terrible!"   c. "No problem!"

8. **on the rocks**:
    a. free of charge   b. served with ice   c. expensive

9. **to stick around**:
   a. to laugh   b. to stay   c. to leave

10. **to be teed off**:
    a. to be angry   b. to be sleepy   c. to be hungry

11. **to toss one's cookies**:
    a. to vomit   b. to bake   c. to juggle

12. **"No way, José!"**
    a. "That's great!"   b. "Absolutely not!"   c. "Absolutely!"

B. Fill in the blank with the words that best completes the phrase.

1. We'd better _____ it before they come back home.
   a. **beat**   b. **repeat**   c. **eat**

2. She didn't even talk to me at the party. She just _____ me off!
   a. **flew**   b. **grew**   c. **blew**

3. There's that guy you like! Go _____ him!
   a. **monologue**   b. **dialogue**   c. **log**

4. Don't _____ out. Just relax.
   a. **tumble**   b. **turn**   c. **flip**

5. If you don't stop drinking that, you're gonna get _____ .
   a. **faced**   b. **traced**   c. **booted**

6. If your mother sees what you're doing, your _____ is cooked.
   a. **moose**   b. **cow**   c. **goose**

7. If you don't beat it, I'm gonna knock your _____ off!
   a. **brick**   b. **wood**   c. **block**

8. _____ out. We'll talk care of the problem.
   a. **Flip**   b. **Mellow**   c. **Chicken**

9. Don't let her drive. She's _____ !
   a. **plastered**   b. **cemented**   c. **flipped**

10. I think I want to have Italian food tonight. How does that _____ ?
      a. **sound**   b. **round**   c. **ground**

11. _____ ! What was that?!
      a. **Bike**   b. **Hike**   c. **Yike**

12. He borrowed my shirt without asking? That _____ it!
      a. **slices**   b. **dices**   c. **tears**

C. Match the two columns.

☐ 1. His glasses look foolish.

☐ 2. She found her husband at a bar with another woman!

☐ 3. Do you want to go pass the time at my house for a while?

☐ 4. I'll contact you later.

☐ 5. Leave!

☐ 6. I think she is very interested in you romantically.

☐ 7. This drink should have a positive effect.

☐ 8. I think I'm going to vomit.

☐ 9. Let's go look for girls for romantic encounters.

☐ 10. I want to stay here and see what happens.

☐ 11. Do you want your drink with or without ice?

☐ 12. You look really angry!

A. **You look really teed off!**

B. **I think I'm gonna toss my cookies.**

C. **You want your drink straight up or on the rocks?**

D. **She spotted her husband at a bar with another woman!**

E. **Let's go pick up chicks.**

F. **I think she has a mad crush on you.**

G. **I wanna stick around and see what happens.**

H. **His glasses look geeky.**

I. **Wanna go hang at my house for a while?**

J. **Catch ya later.**

K. **Beat it!**

L. **This drink should do the trick.**

D. Step 1: Complete the boxes by choosing the appropriate words from the list below.

Step 2: Transfer the letters in the bold boxes in order of appearance to the crossword grid on the next page to reveal a popular American expression which means, "to become extremely angry."

WORD LIST

beat	chicken	sound
flip	geeky	faced
program	mad	hang
way	mellow	cookies

1. to become aware

T	O	■	G	E	T	■	W	I	T	H
T	H	E	■			☐				

2. to become uncontrollably upset

T	O	■	☐			■	O	U	T

3. to get extremely intoxicated

T	O	■	G	E	T	■	☐			

4. to leave

T	O	■			☐	■	I	T

5. to become scared

T	O	■	☐					■
O	U	T						

6. foolish

7. to pass the time idly

T	O	█			

8. "Absolutely not!"

N	O	█		█	J	O	S	É

9. "Does that appeal to you?"

H	O	W	█	D	O	E	S	█	T	H	A	T

10. to have great romantic interest in someone

T	O	█	H	A	V	E	█	A	█			
C	R	U	S	H	█	O	N					
S	O	M	E	O	N	E						

11. to calm down

T	O	█					█	O	U	T

12. to vomit

T	O	█	T	O	S	S	█	O	N	E	'	S

Fill in the boxes to find the expression which means…
"to become extremely angry."

	T	O	█	F	L	Y	█			
			█							

A CLOSER LOOK:
Entertainment Slang

The entertainment industry has given birth to a wide variety of slang expressions and jargon that are common to everyone since watching television is such a popular pastime.

The following is a list of terms and expressions familiar to anyone in or out of the entertainment industry.

angel *n.* one who backs a show financially • *The show isn't going to close after all! We found an angel!;* The show isn't going to close after all! We found a backer!

back a show (to) *exp.* to support a show monetarily • *Be nice to him. He's backing the show!;* Be nice to him. He's supporting the show monetarily!
  ‣ NOTE: **backer** *n.* one who supports a show monetarily.

bit *n.* skit • *What did you think of his comedy bit?;* What did you think of his comedy skit?

biz (the) *n.* the entertainment industry • *Is he in the biz?;* Is he in the entertainment industry?

blockbuster *n.* an extremely successful movie or show • *You've got to see this movie. It's a blockbuster!;* You've got to see this movie. It's a huge success!

blooper *n.* a filmed mistake, usually comical, made by a performer •

Did you see the television program last night where they showed bloopers from the top shows?; Did you see the television program last night where they showed filmed mistakes made by performers from the most popular shows?
  ‣ SYNONYM: **out-take** *n.*

blow a line (to) *exp.* to blunder while speaking the words in the script • *He blew a line on stage;* He blundered while speaking the words in the script.

bomb *n.* failure • *The movie was a bomb;* The movie was a failure.

boo (to) *v.* to disapprove of a performer by yelling "Boo!"

"Break a leg!" *exclam.* "Good luck!"
  ‣ NOTE: Due to superstition common to the entertainment industry, it was believed that to wish a performer good luck was sure to bring disaster. Since one of the worst occurrences that

could happen to a performer, especially a dancer, is to break a leg, this exclamation is commonly used in order to manifest the contrary.

bring the house down (to) *exp.* to cause such enthusiasm in the audience during a performance that the *"house"* or "theater" may tumble due to the applause or laughter • *She really brought the house down tonight!;* She really caused unbelievable enthusiasm in the audience tonight!

business *n.* actor's performing routine • *The director wants me to do some comedic business as soon as I enter;* The director wants me to do some comedic routines as soon as I enter.

cliffhanger *n.* an unresolved ending of extreme suspense and intrigue • *The scene ended just as someone broke into her bedroom. What a cliffhanger!;* The scene ended just as someone broke into her bedroom. What a suspenseful ending!
♦ NOTE: This term denotes a scene which ends with someone hanging from a cliff, creating a mood of extreme suspense.

comp *n.* complimentary ticket • *My sister gave me a comp to her performance tonight;* My sister gave me a complimentary ticket to her performance tonight.
♦ ALSO: **to comp** *v.* to give a complimentary ticket • *I got*

comped to tonight's show; I got a complimentary ticket to tonight's show.
♦ SYNONYM: **freebie** *n.* • *My ticket didn't cost me a thing. It was a freebie!;* My ticket didn't cost me a thing. It was free!

dark (to be) *adj.* to be closed (said of a theater) • *Traditionally, theaters are dark on Mondays;* Traditionally, theaters are closed on Mondays.

deadpan (to) *v.* to react facially in a completely unexpressive manner • *Whenever anything absurd happens to him, he always deadpans. It's hysterical!;* Whenever anything absurd happens to him, he always reacts with absolutely no facial expression. It's hysterical!

die (to) *v.* to fail miserably during a performance • *He died last night;* He failed miserably during last night's performance.

double feature *n.* two movies which are shown one after the other • *I saw a great double feature yesterday;* I saw two great movies one after the other yesterday.

double take (to do a) *exp.* to look at something nonchalantly for an instant, turning away, and then, upon realizing its impact, quickly turning back with astonishment • *I did a double take when I saw her kissing him!;* I looked at them for an instant, turned away, then when I suddenly realized what was happening, I turned back in astonishment!

dry run *n.* rehearsal • *Let's do a dry run before the performance tomorrow;* Let's do a rehearsal before the performance tomorrow.

"Encore!" *exclam.* "More!"
◆ NOTE: This is a common cry by the audience to see more.
As a noun, an *"encore"* is "an additional brief performance" • *The singer did two encores;* The singer did two additional brief performances.

extra *n.* performer who is seen in the background but never heard • *He makes a good living at being an extra;* He makes a good living at being a performer who is seen in the background but never heard.
◆ ALSO: **to do background** *exp.* to perform silently in the background.

fake it (to) *exp.* to improvise • *I forgot what to say during my speech so I just faked it;* I forgot what to say during my speech so I just improvised.

flick *n.* movie • *Wanna go see a flick tonight?;* Do you want to go see a movie tonight?

floor show *exp.* performance presented in an entertainment arena • *The floor show at the cabaret was great!;* The

performance presented at the cabaret was great!

flop *n.* complete failure (said of anything) • *The show was a flop;* The show was a complete failure. • *My dinner is a flop;* My dinner is a complete failure.

full house *exp.* a locale (such as a theater, club, nightclub, etc.) which is filled to capacity • *This play must be popular. It's a full house here tonight;* This play must be popular. It's filled to capacity here tonight.
◆ ANTONYM: **empty house** *exp.*
◆ NOTE: The term *"house"* traditionally refers to the "theater" or "performing arena."

gag *n.* quick comic routine • *The comedian did a funny gag on the show;* The comedian did a funny quick comic routine on the show.

get the hook (to) *exp.* to get the performer off the stage (due to a poor performance) • *Get the hook!;* Get the performer off the stage!
◆ NOTE: In the early years of theater, a long hook was used to literally pull the performer off the stage if the audience's response was extremely negative. This action was prompted by the audience's plea to *"Get the hook!"* or *"Give 'm the hook!"*

get the show on the road (to) *exp.* to begin the event • *Let's get the show on the road!;* Let's begin the event!

♦ NOTE: This can be said of anything, for example: *Everyone is expecting to eat dinner at 5:00. I'd better get the show on the road!;* Everyone is expecting to eat dinner at 5:00. I'd better begin preparing it!

go out with a bang (to) *exp.* to end a performance in an extraordinary way • *He went out with a bang!;* He ended the performance in an extraordinary way!

green room *exp.* waiting room for actors • *Please wait here in the green room and when we need you, we'll let you know;* Please wait here in the waiting room and when we need you, we'll let you know.

♦ NOTE: All actors have the same question: "Why is it called the green room when the room is practically never green?" There has been a great deal of speculation regarding this. One of the theories is that the color green was originally thought to inspire energy and creativity.

ham *n.* flamboyant and pretentious performer • *What a ham!;* What a flamboyant and pretentious performer!

♦ SYNONYM: **ham bone** *n.*

has-been *n.* performer who has lost popularity, one who "has-been" popular in the past • *She used to be famous but now she's a has-been;* She used to be famous

but now she's a performer who has lost popularity.

hit *n.* extremely successful show • *The movie was a hit;* The movie was extremely successful.

improv (to) *v.* a common abbreviation for "to improvise" • *Let's improv the scene;* Let's improvise the scene.

industry *n.* abbreviation for "entertainment industry."

"Let's hear it for..." *exp.* "Let's have some applause for..."

"Lights, camera, action!" *exp.* (used by directors in the movie and television industry) "Turn on the lights, start the camera, begin the scene!"

lines *n.pl.* the actor's words that are to be performed • *I don't know my lines!;* I don't know what words I'm supposed to say!

♦ ALSO: **to go over one's lines** *exp.* to rehearse one's words that are to be performed.

M.C. *n.* common abbreviation for "Master of Ceremonies" • *She's the M.C. of the show;* She's the Master of Ceremonies of the show.

mug (to) *v.* to make overly expressive faces in order to get laughs • *That actor does nothing but mug;* That actor does nothing but make overly expressive faces in order to get laughs.

♦ ALSO: **mug** *n.* face • **mug shot** *exp.* photo taken of a prisoner.

number *n.* musical or theatrical selection • *For my next number, I will sing my favorite aria;* For my next selection, I will sing my favorite aria.

on (to be) *adj.* • **1.** to be on stage • *I'm on in five minutes;* I'm on stage in five minutes. • **2.** a performer who carries his/her flamboyant theatrical behavior into his/her personal life • *He's always on!;* He's always performing even in his personal life!

one-liner *exp.* a complete joke that is told in one sentence • *Every time I try and have a serious conversation with him, he gives me a one-liner;* Every time I try and have a serious conversation with him, he tells jokes.

open for someone (to) *exp.* to be the opening act before the main show • *Who's opening tonight?;* Who's the opening act before the main show tonight?

overact (to) *v.* to act using artificial and exaggerated emotions • *Stop overacting. Just pretend you're actually the character that you're portraying;* Stop acting with artificial and exaggerated emotions. Just pretend you're actually the character that you're portraying.

pan a show (to) *exp.* to criticize brutally a show or performance • *The critics totally panned the show;* The critics totally criticized the show.

pit *n.* abbreviation for the "orchestra pit" which is the large hole in front of the stage from which the orchestra plays.

plug something (to) *exp.* to publicize something • *Authors commonly plug their books on television;* Authors commonly publicize their books on television.

pull out all the stops (to) *exp.* to do something with full force, dedication, and expense • *We're gonna pull out all the stops to make this the best performance!;* We're going to do everything in our power to make this the best performance!

punch line *exp.* the closing line or resolution of a joke • *Your joke is so long! Can you get to the punch line?;* Your joke is so long! Can you get to the closing line?
♦ VARIATION: **punch** *n.*

rep company *exp.* a common abbreviation of "repertory company."

road show *exp.* a group of actors touring a production • *She only sees her boyfriend every few months because he's doing a road show;* She only sees her boyfriend every few months because he's doing a show that's touring the country.

‣ ALSO: **to take it on the road** *exp.* to take a show from city to city.

"Roll 'em!" *exp.* (used by directors in the movie and television industry) "Turn the camera on!"

round of applause *exp.* clapping • *Let's have a round of applause for our performers!;* Let's clap for our performers!

run-through *n.* rehearsal • *Let's do a quick run-through before the performance tomorrow;* Let's do a quick rehearsal before the performance tomorrow.

scalp tickets (to) *exp.* to purchase tickets in order to resell them for a profit • *He's making money illegally by scalping tickets;* He's making money illegally by purchasing tickets in order to resell them for a profit.

‣ ALSO: **scalper** *n.* one who purchases tickets in order to resell them for a profit.

sellout *n.* a successful show whose tickets have all been sold • *It's a sellout tonight!;* All the tickets for tonight's show have been sold!

shelve a project or show (to) *exp.* to postpone a project or show • *We had to shelve the project due to lack of funds;* We had to postpone the project due to lack of funds.

show girl *exp.* a burlesque performer or background dancer in a show • *She used to be a show girl and now she's a star;* She used to be a background dancer and now she's a star.

shtick *n.* (Yiddish) an actor's performing routine • *I don't like his shtick;* I don't like his routines.

sight gag *exp.* a visual comedic routine • *When she came out dressed like a clown, it was a sight gag that made everyone laugh;* When she came out dressed like a clown, it was a visual comedic routine that made everyone laugh.

sitcom *n.* an abbreviation for "situation comedy" • *Did you see the new sitcom on T.V. last night? It was hysterical!;* Did you see the new situation comedy on television last night? It was hysterical!

sitdram *n.* an abbreviation for "situation drama" • *He just got an acting part on a new sitdram;* He just got an acting part on a new situation drama.

skin flick *exp.* a movie whose plot revolves around explicit sexual acts • *You went and saw a skin flick?;* You went and saw a movie that revolves around explicit sexual acts?

‣ SYNONYM: **X-rated movie** *exp.*

slap stick *exp.* physical comedy • *She's a genius at slap stick;* She's a genius at physical comedy.

sleeper *n.* a film with an unexpected success • *That movie was a real sleeper!;* That movie was a real unexpected success!

slot *n.* a time period in television programming • *Early evening is a great slot for any television show because everyone is at home watching at that time;* Early evening is a great time period for any television show because everyone is at home watching at that time.

smash *n.* an extremely successful show • *The movie was a smash;* The movie was extremely successful.
◗ ALSO: **smash hit** *exp.* a tremendously successful show

special *n.* a television program which is not part of the ordinary schedule • *There's a special about computers on T.V. at 8:00;* There's a television program which is not part of the ordinary schedule about computers on T.V. at 8:00.

spoof *n.* satire • *On the comedy show last night, they did a spoof on television commercials;* On the comedy show last night, they did a satire on television commercials.
◗ SYNONYM: **takeoff** *n.*

spot *n.* a brief announcement or advertisement broadcast between television or radio shows • *I saw you acting in a commercial spot yesterday!;* I saw you acting in a commercial broadcast yesterday!

stand-up comic *exp.* a comedian who performs alone, usually standing, telling humorous stories and jokes • *He's a great stand-up comic;* He's a great comedian who performs alone.
◗ ALSO: **to do stand-up** *exp.* to perform comedy alone in front of an audience • *I've always wanted to do stand-up;* I've always wanted to perform comedy alone in front of an audience.

straight man *exp.* a comedian's partner who is always serious even during the most uproarious moments • *He's a great straight man;* He's great at being serious while his partner is doing hilarious antics.

take *n.* **1.** a successfully filmed scene • *That's a take. Now let's move on to the next scene;* That's an acceptably filmed scene. Now let's move on to the next scene. • **2.** the immediate filming of a scene after a final rehearsal • *Quiet everyone! This is a take!;* Quiet everyone! We're going to film now!
◗ ANTONYM: **retake** *n.* the refilming of a scene due to technical or performance problems • *Let's do a retake on that scene;* Let's refilm that scene.

trades *n.pl.* term which refers to *Variety* or *Hollywood Reporter,* the primary magazines of the entertainment industry • *I read a good review today in the trades about the movie;* I read a good review today in *Variety* (or *Hollywood Reporter*) about the movie.

turkey *n.* a bad or losing show • *The movie was a real turkey;* The movie was really bad.

upstage (to) *v.* to take the focus from other performers • *She keeps upstaging the actor by standing in front of him all the time;* She keeps taking the focus from the actor by standing in front of him all the time.

walk-on *n.* a short performance by an actor that consists of walking onto the stage or movie set, speaking a few words, and then leaving • *I'm going to be in my first movie! It's just a walk-on but I'm still excited!;* I'm going to be in my first movie! It's just a short performance but I'm still excited!

wrap it up (to) *exp.* to close production for the day • *That was a good job today. Let's wrap it up;* That was a good job today. Let's close production for the day. ♦ NOTE: In the movie and television industry, the director commonly yells, *"That's a wrap!"* meaning, "Let's close production for the day!"

write-up *n.* review • *The show got a good write-up;* The show got a good review.

More Slang Used in T.V. Comedies

– The New Neighbors –

Dialogue In Slang

The New Neighbors

DIALOGUE

Nancy and Tessa are talking about the new neighbors.

Nancy: Looks like you **landed** yourself some new neighbors! Okay, let's **get down to brass tacks**. What's the **dirt** on them? I mean, you did go over and **break the ice** already, didn't you?

Tessa: **I'll say**. I **popped in** on them right after the last **stick of furniture** was lugged into the house. I **sized them up** real fast. **Take it from me**, they're kind of **off-the-wall**. He's okay but as for her, **the lights are on but nobody's home**. I don't mean to **put her down**, but the lady's a **trip**! She's sort of a **cold fish**, too.

Nancy: Well, try to **go easy** on her. She was probably pretty **crazed**. I mean, moving is no **picnic**. Once they've had a chance to **pull it together**, I bet they **turn out** to be real nice. All right. Let's **cut to the chase**. What do they look like?

Tessa: I have to admit it. She's a **knockout**. I'm telling you. She's got a figure **that won't quit**. She's **stacked**. And you should see him...a total **hunk**. He looks like your typical **jock**.

Nancy: You know, I'm starting to **hate their guts**.

Translation of dialogue in standard English

The New Neighbors

DIALOGUE

Nancy and Tessa are talking about the new neighbors.

Nancy: Looks like you **found** yourself some new neighbors! Okay, let's **talk about the essentials**. What's the **inside information** on them? I mean, you did go over and **introduce yourself** already, didn't you?

Tessa: **Absolutely. I went over to visit without notice** right after the last **piece of furniture** was brought into the house. I **evaluated them** real fast. **Believe me**, they're kind of **different**. He's okay but as for her, **she's not very bright**. I don't mean to **criticize her**, but the lady's **rather strange**! She's sort of **unfriendly**, too.

Nancy: Well, try to be **tolerant** of her. She was probably pretty **agitated**. I mean, moving is not **easy**. Once they've had a chance to **get organized**, I bet **you discover that they're** real nice. All right. Let's **get to the most important issue**. What do they look like?

Tessa: I have to admit it. She's **gorgeous**. I'm telling you. She's got a figure **that's fantastic**. She's very **big-breasted**. And you should see him...a total **masculine man**. He looks like your typical **athlete**.

Nancy: You know, I'm starting to **completely despise them**.

Dialogue in slang as it would be heard

The New Neighbors

DIALOGUE

Nancy 'n Tessa 'r talking about the new neighbors.

Nancy: Looks like ya **landed** jerself s'm new neighbors! Okay, let's **get down ta brass tacks**. What's the **dird** on 'em? I mean, you did go over 'n **break the ice** already, didn' chew?

Tessa: **I'll say**. I **popt in** on 'em ride after the las' **stick of furniture** was lugged inta the house. I **sized 'em up** real fast. **Take it from me**, they're kinda **off-the-wall**. He's okay bud as fer her, **the lights 'r on but nobody's home**. I don' mean ta **put 'er down**, but the lady's a **trip**! She's sort of a **cold fish**, too.

Nancy: Well, try ta **go easy** on 'er. She was prob'ly preddy **crazed**. I mean, moving's no **picnic**. Once they've had a chance ta **pull it tagether**, I bet they **turn out** ta be real nice. Awright. Let's **cut ta the chase**. Whaddo they look like?

Tessa: I haf ta admid it. She's a **knockout**. I'm telling you. She's godda figure **that won't quit**. She's **stact**. An' you should see him...a todal **hunk**. He looks like yer typical **jock**.

Nancy: Ya know, I'm starding ta **hate their guts**.

Vocabulary

break the ice (to) *exp.* to make the first move in establishing communication • *I'm going to break the ice with the new employee;* I'm going to make the first move in establishing communication with the new employee.

cold fish (to be a) *exp.* to be an unfriendly person • *How can she be such a cold fish when her parents are so friendly?;* How can she be such an unfriendly person when her parents are so friendly?

crazed (to be) *adj.* to be agitated as a result of being very busy • *I have so much work to do today, I'm a little crazed;* I have so much work to do today, I'm a little agitated.
♦ NOTE: This adjective comes from the expression *"to be going crazy."*
♦ SYNONYM: **to be bouncing off the walls** *exp.* to be so busy and moving that it appears that one is literally propelling from one end of the room to the other.

cut to the chase (to) *exp.* to go directly to the most essential part or culmination of a story • *I don't care about the details. Just cut to the chase. Are they really going to get a divorce?;* I don't care about the details. Just go directly to the culmination of the story. Are they really going to get a divorce?
♦ NOTE: This expression was derived from the movie industry. Audiences used to commonly fill the theaters to watch westerns which would typically culminate in an exciting chase scene. If a director felt that it was taking too long to get to this part of the movie, he would instruct the editor to "cut to the chase" to keep the viewers from getting bored.
♦ SYNONYM: **to cut to the juicy part** *exp.*
⇨ NOTE: **the juicy part** *exp.* the most interesting, and usually shocking, part of a story.

dirt *n.* • **1.** gossip, scandal • *Got any new dirt to tell me?;* Do you have any new gossip to tell me? • **2.** material which causes corruption, pornography • *What is this dirt you're reading?;* What is this corruption you're reading?
♦ ALSO: **dirty** *adj.* pornographic, obscene • *I found my little brother looking at dirty magazines!;* I found my little brother looking at pornographic magazines! • *My parents don't tolerate dirty language spoken in their home;* My parents don't tolerate obscene language spoken in their home.

get down to brass tacks (to) *exp.* to discuss the essential matters • *I would love to continue talking about my vacation but we really should get down to brass tacks;* I would love to continue talking about my vacation but we really should discuss the essential matters.

go easy on someone (to) *exp.* to be lenient with someone • *I don't know why the judge went so easy on the criminal;* I don't know why the judge was so lenient with the criminal.
  ▸ ANTONYM (1): **to throw the book at someone** *exp.* to give someone the maximum punishment (said only of the court system) • *The judge really threw the book at him!;* The judge really gave him the maximum punishment!
  ▸ ANTONYM (2): **to come down on someone** *exp.* to criticize someone severely • *Her parents are always coming down on her;* Her parents are always criticizing her.

hate one's guts (to) *exp.* to despise someone intensely right down to the core of his/her being • *I hate his guts!;* I despise him right down to the core of his being!

hunk *n.* an extremely muscular and virile man • *What a hunk!;* What an extremely muscular and virile man!
  ▸ ALSO: **hunky** *adj.* extremely muscular and virile • *Your brother's so hunky!;* Your brother's so muscular and virile!

"I'll say" *exp.* "Absolutely!"
  ▸ SYNONYM: **"You said it!"** *exp.*
  ▸ ANTONYM: **"No way!"** *exp.* "Absolutely not!"

jock *n.* athlete • *My father used to be a real jock when he was in school;* My father used to be a real athlete when he was in school.

knockout (to be a) *adj.* to be a stunning beauty • *Your mother's a knockout!;* Your mother is a stunning beauty!
  ▸ SYNONYM: **to be a ten** *exp.* to be rated the highest on a scale of 1-10.

land oneself something (to) *exp.* • to acquire something after a great deal of effort • *I heard you just landed yourself a great job!;* I heard you just acquired a great job! • *I just landed a big contract with a national company!;* I just acquired a big contract with a national company!

◆ NOTE: The verb "to land" is commonly used in regards to fishing: *to land a fish;* to catch a fish and bring it to shore.

off-the-wall (to be) *adj.* to be highly unusual and bizarre • *You really like him? He's so off-the-wall;* You really like him? He's so unusual and bizarre. • *Her sense of humor is really off-the-wall;* Her sense of humor is really bizarre.
◆ SYNONYM: **to be out there** *exp.* • *She's really out there!;* She's really bizarre!
  ⇨ NOTE: The expression *"to be out there"* refers to "out there in space" or "in another world."

picnic (to be a) *adj.* enjoyable experience (usually used in the negative *"to be no picnic"*) • *You think I like having to tell him he's fired? Believe me. This is no picnic for me;* You think I like having to tell him he's fired? Believe me. This is not an enjoyable task for me.
◆ SYNONYM: **to be a snap** *exp.* • *The math homework was a snap;* The math homework was extremely easy.

pop in (to) *exp.* to arrive without notice • *I wish she wouldn't just pop in on us all the time. Why doesn't she ever call us first?;* I wish she wouldn't just arrive at our house without notice all the time. Why doesn't she ever call us first?
◆ ALSO: **to pop over** *exp.* to arrive unceremoniously (or without notice) • *Why don't you pop over after the movie?;* Why don't you come over after the movie?
◆ SYNONYM: **to drop in** *exp.* • *You'll never believe who dropped in today!;* You'll never believe who arrived without notice today!

pull it together (to) *exp.* to become organized • *How am I possibly going to be able to pull it together before they arrive?;* How am I possibly going to be able to get organized before they arrive? • *How'd you pull the dinner together so fast?;* How did you organize the dinner so fast?
◆ VARIATION: **to get it together** *exp.*

put someone or something down (to) *exp.* to criticize someone • *Why do you put me down for everything I do?;* Why do you criticize me for everything I do? • *Stop putting down her performance! I thought it was terrific;* Stop criticizing her performance! I thought it was terrific.

▸ SYNONYM: **to jump all over someone** *exp.* • *Quit jumping all over me about it!;* Quit criticizing me about it!

size someone or something up (to) *exp.* to evaluate someone or something • *I sized him up and just don't like him;* I evaluated him and just don't like him. • *After sizing up the situation, I don't think we should proceed any further;* After evaluating the situation, I don't think we should proceed any further.

stacked (to be) *exp.* to have large breasts • *She says she doesn't like being stacked because it puts too much weight on her shoulders;* She says she doesn't like having such large breasts because it puts too much weight on her shoulders.

stick of furniture *n.* single piece of furniture • *After the fire, they don't have a stick of furniture left;* After the fire, they don't have a single piece of furniture left.

"Take it from me" *exp.* "Believe me."

"...that won't quit" *exp.* "...that is exceptional" • *She has a face that won't quit!* She has a beautiful face!"
▸ SYNONYM: **for days** *exp.* • *He has a body for days!;* He has a fantastic body!

"The lights are on but nobody's home" *exp.* said of someone who appears to be awake yet is hopelessly oblivious and slow.
▸ SYNONYM (1): **not to be cooking on all four burners** *exp.* not to be using one's entire brain.
▸ SYNONYM (2): **not to have both oars in the water** *exp.*
▸ SYNONYM (3): **"The elevator doesn't go all the way to the top"** *exp.*

trip (to be a) *exp.* to be rather strange • *I've never met anyone so bizarre. She really is a trip!;* I've never met anyone so bizarre. She really is strange.
▸ SYNONYM: **to be screwy** *exp.* • *He's screwy!;* He's crazy!

turn out (to) *exp.* to conclude • *They turned out to be great friends;* They concluded by being great friends.
▸ SYNONYM: **to end up** *exp.* • *They ended up by compromising;* They concluded by compromising.

PRACTICE THE VOCABULARY

[Answers to Lesson Two, p. 210]

A. Complete the sentence by filling in the blanks with the appropriate word(s) from the list below.

ice	**fish**	**dirt**
tacks	**knockout**	**guts**
wall	**size**	**pull**
stacked	**that won't quit**	**turn**

1. She's got a beautiful figure. Is she ever _____ !

2. I've been trying to _____ up the situation for the past hour, but I still don't know what's happening!

3. You actually like her? I think she's such a cold _____ !

4. I hate his _____ !

5. So, what did you find out about her? Give me the _____ .

6. After our fight, I tried to go over and break the _____ , but she wouldn't talk to me.

7. Let's get down to brass _____ . How much money do you think she makes?

8. She's gorgeous! What a _____ !

9. How did your predicament finally _____ out?

10. He has a strange sense of humor. He's really off-the- _____ .

11. Look at her! She's got a body _____ !

12. I only have ten minutes to _____ it together before the guests arrive.

B. **Underline the word that best completes the phrase.**

1. Have you met her? She's a real (**journey, trip, vacation**).

2. I know you're angry about what happened, but try to go (**simply, hard, easy**) on him.

3. I hate her (**guts, colon, pancreas**)!

4. You're always criticizing me! Why do you feel it's necessary to keep putting me (**up, in, down**)?

5. I just thought I'd pop (**in, up, down**) and say hi!

6. Life isn't always a (**breakfast, dinner, picnic**).

7. (**Cut, Slice, Dice**) to the chase! What really happened?

8. I heard you're about to (**hover, takeoff, land**) a big job!

9. Look at that guy's muscles! What a (**block, clock, jock**)!

10. Got any new (**sand, dirt, mud**) to tell me?

11. She's really strange. I'm telling you, the (**lights, lamps, flashlights**) are on, but nobody's home.

12. They're so poor, they don't have a single (**brick, trick, stick**) of furniture.

C. **Fill in the crossword on the opposite page by using the words from the list below**

knockout	**size**
dirt	**cut**
jock	**off-the-wall**
crazed	**cold**
land	**tacks**

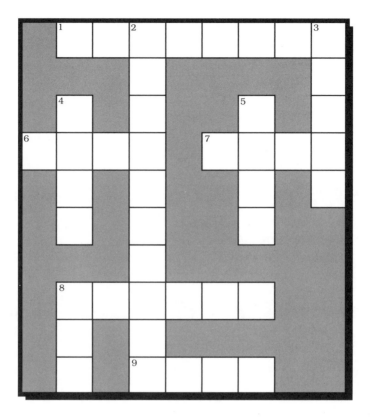

ACROSS

1. _____ **(to be a)** *adj.* to be a stunning beauty.

6. _____ *n.* gossip, scandal.

7. _____ *n.* athlete.

8. _____ **(to be)** *adj.* to be agitated as a result of being very busy.

9. _____ **oneself something** *exp.* to acquire something after a great deal of effort.

DOWN

2. _____ **(to be)** *adj.* to be highly unusual and bizarre.

3. **get down to brass** _____ **(to)** *exp.* to discuss the prevailing essential matters.

4. _____ **someone or something up (to)** *exp.* to evaluate someone or something.

5. _____ **fish (to be a)** *exp.* to be an unfriendly person.

8. _____ **to the chase (to)** *exp.* to go directly to the most essential part or culmination of a story.

D. Choose the appropriate slang synonym of the italicized word(s). Write the corresponding letter of the correct answer in the box.

☐ 1. He's such a *muscular and virile man.*

    A. **crazed**

☐ 2. What a *beauty!*

    B. **hunk**

☐ 3. *Absolutely!*

    C. **puts me down**

☐ 4. He's always *agitated as a result of being so busy.*

    D. **Take it from me**

☐ 5. Got any new *gossip* to tell me?

    E. **popped in**

☐ 6. Look who just *arrived without notice!*

    F. **turn out**

☐ 7. She always *criticizes me.*

    G. **break the ice**

☐ 8. I'll go *establish communication* with them.

    H. **I'll say**

☐ 9. He has a body *that's exceptional.*

    I. **knockout**

☐ 10. *Believe me.*

    J. **dirt**

☐ 11. How did your dinner party *conclude?*

    K. **that won't quit**

☐ 12. He's *highly unusual and bizarre.*

    L. **off-the-wall**

A CLOSER LOOK:
Exclamations & Sounds Used in Comic Books and Cartoons

Anyone who has ever watched a cartoon or read a comic book has undoubtedly encountered an array of colorful exclamations. On occasion, cartoons quickly flash exclamations on the screen during climactic fight scenes to give a comic-book-like effect. These whimsical interjections are commonly used in daily speech to add impact and excitement to a descriptive story or simply to express an entire thought or feeling with just one sound.

After exploring the following list, you'll certainly agree that a single sound is worth a thousand words.

Argh! *exclam.* used to indicate extreme frustration • *Argh! I can't believe she's going to make us sit through another one of her songs!*

Blah! *exclam.* used to indicate dislike for someone or something • *You actually like her? Blah!*

Blech! *exclam.* a response to having tasted or seen something unpleasant • *Blech! I've never tasted anything so revolting!* ◆ NOTE: The *-ch* in *blech!* is pronounced "-ck" or simply as a guttural sound.

Boom! *exclam.* used to describe an explosive sound • *He was driving home at midnight when boom! He was suddenly hit by another car!* ◆ NOTE: This term may also be used as a noun: *Did you hear the loud boom outside?*

Crash! *exclam.* used to describe the sound of two or more objects colliding • *The baseball went crash! Right through the window!* ◆ NOTE: This term may also be used as a noun: *I heard a crash in the kitchen!*

Eek! *exclam.* used to denote fear • *Eek! There's a mouse running around on the floor!*

Eww! *exclam.* a response to having tasted, smelled, or seen something unpleasant • *Eww! That smells horrible!*

Gee! *exclam.* • **1.** used to denote disappointment • *Gee! Every time I try and bake a cake, it burns!* • **2.** used to indicate admiration • *Gee! He's so muscular!* • **3.** used to indicate disapproval • *Gee! I'd never* *wear a dress like that!*

♦ VARIATION: **Gee wiz!** *exclam.*

Geez! *exclam.* used to denote exasperation and disbelief • *Geez! Why did you tell her our secret?*

♦ NOTE: This exclamation is a euphemism for *"Jesus!"*

Gosh! *exclam.* used to indicate surprise • *Gosh! I wonder why he suddenly hit him!*

Grrrrr! *exclam.* used to indicate playful anger • *Don't talk to me today. I'm in a bad mood! Grrrrr!*

♦ NOTE: *Grrrrr!* is a humorous imitation of the sound an enraged animal makes when provoked.

Gulp! *exclam.* used to denote impending doom • *My mother's gonna be so mad when she comes home and finds out what we did. I think she just pulled up in the car! Gulp!*

♦ NOTE: *"Gulp!"* is usually said somewhat quietly.

I-I-I-I-I! *exclam.* used to denote disbelief • *I-I-I-I-I! Look what she's wearing!*

♦ NOTE: Pronounced: *eye-y'eye-y'eye-y'eye-y'eye!*

Kaboom! *exclam.* used to describe a sudden explosion • *That bomb is gonna go kaboom! any second.*

Ow! *exclam.* used to denote pain • *Ow! That hurt!*

Pew! *exclam.* used to describe a repulsive smell • *Pew! I think we*

just passed a skunk!

♦ VARIATION: **P.U!** *exclam.* • *P.U! Do you smell that?*

Phew! *exclam.* used to express great relief after experiencing high anxiety • *Phew! What a relief! I thought the boss was gonna fire me but instead, he gave me a raise.*

Piuck! *exclam.* a response to having tasted, smelled, or seen something unpleasant • *Piuck! What smells so horrible!*

Pow! *exclam.* used to describe a sudden attack • *The victim was just standing on the sidewalk when pow! this big guy punches him in the face!*

Sigh! *exclam.* used to denote disappointment and resignation • *I like her so much but I know she's not interested in me at all. Sigh!*

♦ NOTE: *"Sigh!"* is said quietly in resignation.

Smash! *exclam.* used to describe the sound of two or more objects colliding with such force that breakage or damage occurs• (breakage) *As I was cleaning the glass vase, I lost my grip on it and smash! It hit the floor and broke into a million little pieces!* • (damage) *The other driver went though the red light and smash! He dented my car!*

♦ NOTE: This term is also commonly used as a verb: *My*

brother bought a new car last week and already smashed it.

Thwack! *exclam.* used to describe the quick dry sound of two or more objects colliding but causing no breakage • *Her mother slapped her right in the face. Thwack!*

Whack! *exclam.* used to describe the quick dry sound of two or more objects colliding but causing no breakage • *It was the first time I've seen an actual birth. The doctor first slowly pulled the baby out, then whack! He slapped her on the buttocks and she started screaming.*
♦ NOTE: This term is commonly used as a verb: *She whacked him in front of all the guests!;* She hit him in front of all the guests!

Wham! *exclam.* • **1.** used to describe the sound produced by a fast moving object stopped abruptly by a stationary object • *She was so angry as she left the room, she slammed the door as hard as she could. Wham! I thought the whole house was going to fall down!* • **2.** used to describe a quick action • *It didn't take long for the plumber to fix the pipes. He just tightened something and wham! He was done!* • **3.** used to describe a quick sexual action • *Our anniversary wasn't at all romantic. I thought we were going to spend a nice quiet evening making love. Instead, it was just wham! and then he went to sleep!*
♦ NOTE: A common and humorous rhyming expression describing quick love-making is: *Wham! Bam! Thank you, ma'am!* For example: *With him it's just 'Wham! Bam! Thank you, ma'am!';* With him it's just 'Let's have quick sex! Thank you and good-bye!'

Whew! *exclam.* used to express great relief after experiencing high anxiety • *Whew! What a relief! I thought the policeman was gonna give me a ticket!*

Whoa! *exclam.* (pronounced: *woh*) • **1.** used as a way to tell the other person to stop an action • *Whoa! I don't want to hear about that anymore!* • **2.** used to indicate complete confusion • *Whoa! Did you understand what our math teacher was talking about?* • **3.** used to indicate sexual enthusiasm • *Whoa! Look at her! She's beautiful!*

Whoops! *exclam.* • **1.** used to indicate sudden recall of a duty • *Whoops! I forgot to go to the store today.* • **2.** used to indicate an accident • *Whoops! I accidentally dropped my glass of water on the floor!*
♦ ALSO: **Oops!** *exclam.*

Whoosh! *exclam.* used to demonstrate the sound made by a fast moving object • *Did you see*

how fast he drove by us?
Whoosh!
▶ NOTE: This term is commonly used as a verb: *Did you see him whoosh by us?*

Wow! *exclam.* • **1.** used to indicate surprise • *Wow! What was that?!* • **2.** used to indicate excitement • *Wow! Your new car is beautiful!*

Yike! *exclam.* used to indicate surprise and concern • *Yike! Look at the size of that bee!*
▶ VARIATION: **Yikes!** *exclam.*

Yipe! *exclam.* used to indicate surprise and concern • *Yipe! Look what your little brother is doing!*

Yuck! *exclam.* a response to having tasted, smelled, or seen something unpleasant • *Yuck! That tastes terrible!*

Yum! *exclam.* a response to having tasted, smelled, or seen something that excites the appetite • *Yum! That chocolate cakes looks fantastic!*

Zap! *exclam.* used to indicate a quick and sudden attack • *I took a can of insect repellant and zap! I killed the fly instantly.*
▶ NOTE: This term is commonly used as a verb: *I took a can of insect repellant and zapped the fly!*

Zowie! *exclam.* **1.** used to indicate a physical attack • *He insulted her and zowie! She hit him right in the face!* • **2.** used to indicate enthusiasm and surprise • *Zowie! Look at that gorgeous guy!*

Slang Used in T.V. Dramas

– In the Hospital –

Dialogue In Slang

In the Hospital

DIALOGUE

Our **soap** begins with Eric talking to the doctor.

Eric: **Give it to me straight**, doc. Is she gonna **pull through**?

Doctor: Well, it was **touch and go** in **O.R.** for a while. Your wife's a **tough cookie**. It's a good thing she's got a strong **ticker**. She'll be back **in full swing** in **no time**. Just make sure she **takes it easy**. She finally **came to** just an hour ago. Why don't you **go peek your head in**. I think it'll **lift her spirits**.

(Moments later, Eric visits his wife's room)

Eric: **Yoo hoo**! I thought I'd **stop by** and **check up** on you.

Monica: **Hi there**. So, do I look like **death warmed over**?

Eric: No, I don't think we'll have **to pull the plug** this time.

Monica: Well, that's a **load off my mind**. So, tell me. How was the wedding? I can't **get over** that I had to miss the day my little sister got **hitched**.

Eric: I don't know how **to break this to** you, but I know you'd want me to **come clean** with you. Your sister got **dumped** at the altar yesterday. The **upshot** is that her fiancé, Gregory, was having a **fling** that'd been **dragging on** for quite a while with your sister's best friend, Rebecca. It was also a **double whammy** because Gregory **knocked her up** three months ago.

Monica: That little **slut**! I'm gonna find them and **blow them both off the face of the earth**!

Lesson Three - SLANG USED IN T.V. DRAMAS

Translation of dialogue in standard English

In the Hospital

DIALOGUE

Our **soap opera** begins with Eric talking to the doctor.

Eric: **Be frank with me**, doctor. Is she going to **survive**?

Doctor: Well, it was **unpredictable** in the **operating room** for a while. Your wife's a **hardy person**. It's a good thing she's got a strong **heart**. She'll be back **to normal very quickly**. Just make sure she **rests**. She finally **revived** just an hour ago. Why don't you **go say hello**. I think it'll **make her happy**.

(Moments later, Eric visits his wife's room)

Eric: **Hi**! I thought I'd **come over** and **verify your condition**.

Monica: **Hi**. So, do I look like **I've been dead for a while**?

Eric: No, I don't think we'll have **to disconnect the life support** this time.

Monica: Well, that's a **relief**. So, tell me. How was the wedding? I can't **believe** that I had to miss the day my little sister got **married**.

Eric: I don't know how to **disclose** this to you, but I know you'd want me to **tell you everything**. Your sister got **abandoned** at the altar yesterday. **In short**, her fiancé, Gregory, was having an **affair** that'd been quite **prolonged** with your sister's best friend, Rebecca. It was also a **double shock** because Gregory **got her pregnant** three months ago.

Monica: That little **prostitute**! I'm gonna find them and **kill them both**!

Dialogue in slang as it would be heard

In the Hospital

DIALOGUE

Our **soap** b'gins with Eric talkin' ta the doctor.

Eric: **Give it ta me straight, doc**. Ishi gonna **pull through**?

Doctor: Well, it was **touch 'n go** 'n **O.R.** fer a while. Yer wife's a **tough cookie**. It's a good thing she's godda strong **ticker**. She'll be back **'n full swing** 'n **no time**. Jus' make sher she **takes id easy**. She fin'ly **came to** just 'n hour ago. Why don' cha **go peek yer head in**. I think id'll **lift 'er spirits**.

(Moments lader, Eric visits 'is wife's room)

Eric: **Yoo hoo**! I thod I'd **stop by** 'n **check up** on you.

Monica: **Hi there**. So, do I look like **death warmed over**?

Eric: No, I don' think we'll have **ta pull the plug** this time.

Monica: Well, that's a **load off my mind**. So, tell me. How was the wedding? I can't **ged over** thad I had ta miss the day my liddle sister got **hitched**.

Eric: I don' know how **ta break this ta** you, bud I know you'd want me da **come clean** with you. Yer sister got **dumped** at the altar yesterday. The **upshod** is that 'er fiancé, Gregory, was having a **fling** that'd been **dragging on** fer quite a while with yer sister's best friend, Rebecca. It was also a **double whammy** b'cause Gregory **knocked 'er up** three months ago.

Monica: That little **slut**! I'm gonna find 'em 'n **blow 'em both off the face 'a the earth**!

Vocabulary

blow someone off the face of the earth (to) *exp.* • **1.** to shoot someone with extreme force • *I'm gonna get my gun and blow him off the face of the earth!;* I'm going to get my gun and shoot him! • **2.** to reprimand someone severely • *I can't believe my sister lied to me! When I see her again, I'm gonna blow her off the face of the earth!;* I can't believe my sister lied to me! When I see her again, I'm going to reprimand her severely!
‣ NOTE: The difference between **1.** and **2.** depends on the context.
‣ VARIATION: **to blow someone away** *exp.* • *The robber blew the bank teller away in broad daylight!* The robber shot the bank teller in broad daylight!
‣ SYNONYM: **to waste someone** *exp.* (gangster lingo) • *Let's waste him!;* Let's kill him!

break something to someone (to) *exp.* to disclose information of an emotional nature to someone • *I just don't know how I'm going to be able to break the news to her;* I just don't know how I'm going to be able to disclose this kind of emotional information to her.

check up on someone (to) *exp.* to verify the condition of someone • *I'll be right back. I'm gonna go check up on the baby;* I'll be right back. I'm going to go verify the condition of the baby.

come clean with someone (to) *exp.* to tell someone the entire story • *You're not coming clean with me. What really happened?;* You're not telling me the entire story. What really happened?

come to (to) *exp.* to revive • *Look! She's coming to!;* Look! She's reviving!
‣ SYNONYM: **to snap out of it** *exp.* • *He just fainted but I think he'll snap out of it in just a moment;* He just fainted but I think he'll revive in just a moment.

death warmed over (to look like) *exp.* to look very sick and close to death, pale, exhausted • *I haven't slept in three days because the baby keeps crying. I must look like death warmed over;* I haven't slept in three days because the baby keeps crying. I must look very sick and close to death.
‣ SYNONYM: **to look like something the cat dragged in** *exp.* to look terrible • *What happened to you? You look like something the cat dragged in!;* What happened to you? You look terrible!

doc *n.* abbreviation for "doctor" • *Hey, doc! Good to see you!;* Hey, doctor! Good to see you!
  ‣ NOTE: The usage of *"doc"* is extremely familiar.

double whammy *exp.* one shocking event right after another • *It was a shock to her when she found out that she was pregnant. But it was a double whammy when the doctor told her that she was going to have triplets!;* It was a shock to her when she found out that she was pregnant. But it was a double shock when the doctor told her that she was going to have triplets!

drag on (to) *exp.* to prolong • *This meeting is dragging on!;* This meeting is too prolonged!

dumped (to get) *exp.* to get rejected or abandoned • *I got dumped by my boyfriend;* I got rejected by my boyfriend. • *Your girlfriend isn't very nice to you. Why don't you just dump her?;* Your girlfriend isn't very nice to you. Why don't you just abandon her?
  ‣ ALSO: **to get dumped on** *exp.* to be burdened by someone's problems • *I got dumped on by my best friend;* I was burdened by my best friend's problems.

fling *n.* a love affair • *Didn't he know that his wife would probably find out about his fling sooner or later?;* Didn't he know that his wife would probably find out about his love affair sooner or later?

get over something (not to be able to) *exp.* to be unable to rid oneself of the shock about something • *I just can't get over how he could lie that way;* I just can't stop being astonished about how he could lie that way.

give it to someone straight (to) *exp.* to disclose something to someone in a very direct way • *Give it to me straight. I can take it;* Be frank with me. I can endure it.
  ‣ SYNONYM: **to tell someone something point blank** *exp.* • *He told me point blank that if I didn't start working harder, I'd be fired;* He told me frankly that if I didn't start working harder, I'd be fired.

"Hi there!" *exp.* "Hi!"
  ‣ NOTE: This is a very casual greeting that should only be used in informal situations.

hitched (to get) *exp.* (humorous) to get married • (lit); to get fastened together • *So, when are you two finally gonna get hitched?;* So, when are you two finally going to get married?

in full swing (to be) *exp.* • **1.** to be fully operational • *The airport is back in full swing;* The airport is back to being fully operational. • **2.** to be completely underway • *The party's in full swing;* The party is completely underway.

in no time *adv.* quickly • *He figured out the math problem in no time;* He figured out the math problem quickly.
▸ VARIATION (1): **in no time flat** *adv.*
▸ VARIATION (2): **in no time at all** *adv.*

knock someone up (to) *exp.* to get someone pregnant • *If she doesn't stop sleeping around, she's gonna get herself knocked up;* If she doesn't stop sleeping around, she's going to get herself pregnant.
▸ NOTE: This expression is considered to be extremely casual language and should only be used with friends and family.

lift one's spirits (to) *exp.* to make one feel more cheerful • *I think a nice walk outside will lift your spirits;* I think a nice walk outside will make you feel more cheerful.

O.R. *n.* abbreviation for: operating room • *You're wanted in O.R. immediately!;* You're wanted in the operating room immediately!
▸NOTE: When "operating room" is abbreviated to *"O.R.,"* the definite article "the" is usually dropped as demonstrated in the above example. Oddly enough, this abbreviation is commonly heard on television yet rarely, if ever, used within the medical community.

peek one's head in (to) *exp.* to visit someone without ceremony and briefly • *I don't want to disturb her. Well, I'll just peek my head in and say hello;* I don't want to disturb her. Well, I'll just visit her briefly.

pull the plug (to) *exp.* • **1.** to disconnect the life support of someone who has a critical illness • *Since there was no cure for him, the doctor thought it would be best to pull the plug and not let him suffer any longer;* Since there was no cure for him, the doctor thought it would be best to disconnect the life support and not let him suffer any longer. • **2.** to cancel permanently • *The sponsors pulled the plug on the project;* The sponsors canceled the project permanently.

pull through (to) *exp.* to survive a difficult illness or situation • *College was very difficult but I managed to pull through;* College was very difficult but I managed to survive.
▸ SYNONYM: **to make it** *exp.* • *It was a severe illness, but she's gonna make it;* It was a severe illness, but she's going to survive.

slut *n.* girl with loose morals • (lit); prostitute • *She's had sex with every guy in school. I'm telling you, she's a real slut!;* She's had sex with every guy in school. I'm telling you, she's like a prostitute!
 ♦ NOTE: This term is a crude and derogatory synonym for "prostitute."

soap *n.* daytime serial drama • *My mother loves watching soaps every afternoon;* My mother loves watching daytime serial dramas every afternoon.
 ♦ NOTE: These daytime serial dramas were nicknamed *"soap operas"* or simply *soaps* since their backers were primarily soap sponsors.

stop by (to) *exp.* to visit unceremoniously • *Why don't you just stop by after dinner and we'll watch some television together?;* Why don't you just come over here casually after dinner and we'll watch some television together?
 ♦ SYNONYM: **to pop in** *exp.* • *Pop in any time!;* Come over casually any time!

take it easy (to) *exp.* to relax • *The doctor said you have to take it easy for a week. So, get back to bed!;* The doctor said you have to relax for a week. So, get back to bed!
 ♦ SYNONYM: **to mellow out** *exp.* • *I'm just gonna stay here all day and mellow out;* I'm just going to stay here all day and relax.

"That's a load off my mind" *exp.* "That's a relief!" • *It's a real load off my mind to know that you'll be baby sitting the kids tonight;* It's a real relief to me to know that you'll be baby sitting the kids tonight.

ticker *n.* heart • *He has a strong ticker because he jogs every day;* He has a strong heart because he jogs every day.

touch and go (to be) *exp.* to be unpredictable • *I didn't know if the car would make it up the hill. It was touch and go for a while;* I didn't know if the car would make it up the hill. It was unpredictable for a while.

tough cookie (to be a) *exp.* • **1.** to be strong and robust • *My father pulled through beautifully after the operation. He's one tough cookie;* My father pulled through beautifully after the operation. He's really strong and robust. • **2.** to be uncompromising • *I don't think you'll get the boss to let you go on vacation early. He's one tough cookie;* I don't think you'll get the boss to let you go on vacation early. He's very uncompromising.

upshot *n.* outcome • *What was the upshot of the meeting with the new president?;* What was the outcome of the meeting with the new president?

"Yoo hoo!" *exclam.* an exclamation to get someone's attention • *Yoo hoo! Nancy! I'm over here!*

PRACTICE THE VOCABULARY

[Answers to Lesson Three, p. 212]

A. **Complete the sentences by choosing the appropriate words from the list below.**

break	**clean**	**warmed**
whammy	**there**	**swing**
knocked	**plug**	**through**
soap	**easy**	**cookie**

1. Hi _____ ! How are you?

2. She's very sick. I don't know if she's gonna pull _____ .

3. My car was stolen and I got fired. What a double _____ !

4. I don't want her to suffer any longer on the life support system. I think we should pull the _____ .

5. Why are you so upset? Take it _____ !

6. Did you see her? She looked like death _____ over!

7. Did you hear that Jennifer got _____ up by Scott?

8. I still feel so sick, but the doctor said that I'd be in full _____ by tomorrow.

9. Did you _____ the news to her yet?

10. The doctors said that he may not recover, but he's a real tough _____ and keeps regaining his health.

11. Come _____ with me. I want to know just what happened.

12. My favorite _____ is on T.V. now!

B. Underline the words in parentheses that best completes the sentence.

1. I'm so mad at him, I'm gonna blow him off the (**neck, face, head**) of the earth!

2. I wonder if the baby is still asleep. I'm gonna go check (**up, down, over**) on him.

3. He's been unconscious for five minutes. Wait! He's (**arriving, leaving, coming**) to!

4. The lecture today really dragged (**up, in, on**).

5. Did you hear that Monica is having a (**fling, flair, flame**) with the boss?

6. I couldn't get (**up, in, over**) how nasty he was to you yesterday.

7. Give it to me (**straight, curved, circular**). Did you destroy my car?

8. I heard you just got (**hiked, hurt, hitched**)! So, when's the party?

9. When I heard they were having a fight, I got there in (**no, yes, maybe**) time.

10. I was a little depressed, but you really lifted my (**spirits, ghosts, apparitions**).

11. She's had sex with every guy in my class, the (**slap, sleet, slut**)!

12. Jogging every day gives you a strong (**talker, ticker, taker**).

13. Yoo (**hoo, hay, ha**)! Anyone home?

14. It was touch and (**come, stay, go**) for a while, but everything finally worked out fine.

C. Match the columns.

☐ 1. Hello, doctor!

☐ 2. I'm going to verify her condition.

☐ 3. He's reviving.

☐ 4. Is it true they're having a love affair?

☐ 5. I'm going to reprimand him severely.

☐ 6. Did you know I'm getting married next week?

☐ 7. The party is completely underway.

☐ 8. It was one shocking event right after another.

☐ 9. I'll fix this quickly.

☐ 10. He should be out of the operating room in a few more hours.

☐ 11. Do you think she'll survive?

☐ 12. Why don't you casually visit some time?

A. **I'm gonna blow him off the face of the earth.**

B. **It'll take me no time to fix this.**

C. **He should be out of O.R. in a few hours.**

D. **Do you think she'll pull through?**

E. **It was a double whammy.**

F. **Did you know I'm getting hitched next week?**

G. **Why don't you stop by some time?**

H. **I'm gonna go check up on her.**

I. **He's coming to.**

J. **The party's in full swing.**

K. **Hey, doc!**

L. **Is it true they're having a fling?**

A CLOSER LOOK (1):
Baby Talk Slang

These terms are most likely overlooked in any classroom where English is taught to non-native speakers yet they make up a profuse vocabulary common to any small child. And where do these children learn such words? From their parents!

Parents tend to speak to their babies and toddlers (as well as their pets) utilizing diminutive forms of words, perhaps as a way to make these terms less intimidating and more friendly. For that matter, it seems that almost anyone who is simply in the presence of an infant automatically starts using these terms.

It is important to be aware of these words since you can be sure that if there is a baby and an adult in the same room, you will surely hear some interesting baby talk slang coming primarily from the adults. In fact, some baby talk has actually been adopted for use among adults as well which will be noted in the following list.

In the preceding sample sentences, a parent is talking to an infant or toddler.

binkie *n.* pacifier • *What's the matter? Do you want your binkie?;* What's the matter? Do you want your pacifier?

birdie *n.* bird • *See the little birdie?;* See the little bird?
▶ SYNONYM: SEE - **tweet-tweet** *n.*

blankey *n.* blanket • *I'm just going to wrap you up in this blankey so you don't get cold tonight;* I'm just going to wrap you up in this blanket so you don't get cold tonight.

booboo *n.* • **1.** injury • *Let mommy see your booboo;* Let mother see your injury. • **2.** accident • *Did you have a booboo?;* Did you

have an accident?
▶ SYNONYM: SEE - **owie** *n.*

bow-wow *n.* dog • *Do you want to pet the nice bow-wow?;* Do you want to pet the nice dog?
▶ NOTE: This is an onomatopoeia for the sound that a dog makes.
▶ SYNONYM: SEE - **doggie** *n.*

bye-bye *n.* good-bye • *Wave bye-bye!;* Wave good-bye!
▶ NOTE: Adults commonly repeat one syllable words when talking with children, perhaps as a way to help the child's retention.
▶ NOTE: Interestingly enough, this child term has been adopted by adults with a slight change in

pronunciation: *ba-bye* or occasionally seen as: *b'bye*. It is extremely common to end a conversation by saying, *Talk to you later. Bye-bye (B'bye)!;* Talk to you later. Good-bye!

choo-choo *n.* train • *See the big choo-choo?;* See the big train?
 ♦ NOTE: This is an onomatopoeia for the sound that a train makes.
 ♦ VARIATION: **choo-choo train** *n.*

daddy *n.* dad, father • *Can you make a big smile for daddy!;* Can you make a big smile for your father?
 ♦ NOTE: It is not uncommon to hear the term *daddy* used by adults to refer to own's one father.
 ♦ SYNONYM: **dada** *n.* • *Say hi to dada;* Say hi to father.

didy *n.* diaper • *Let's change your didy;* Let's change your diaper.
 ♦ SYNONYM: **dipy** *n.*

doggie *n.* dog • *Isn't that a pretty doggy?;* Isn't that a pretty dog?
 ♦ SYNONYM: SEE - **bow-wow** *n.*

doo-doo *n.* dog excrement • *Spike made doo-doo on the rug again!;* Spike defecated on the rug again!

fall down, go boom (to) *exp.* to fall down and make a thud • *Did you fall down, go boom?;* Did you fall down and make a thud?

feeties *n.* pajamas with feet • *Do you wanna wear your feeties tonight?;* Do you want to wear

your pajamas with the feet tonight?

horsey *n.* horse • *Look at the big horsey!;* Look at the big horse!
 ♦ SYNONYM: SEE - **neigh-neigh** *n.*

jammies *n.pl.* pajamas • *Time to put on your jammies;* Time to put on your pajamas.

kissie *n.* diminutive for "kiss;" little kiss • *Give grampa a kissie;* Give grandfather a kiss.
 ♦ NOTE: A frequent replacement for "grandfather" is *"grandpa,"* commonly pronounced "grampa."

kitty-cat *n.* cat • *See the pretty kitty-cat?;* See the pretty cat?
 ♦ NOTE: Adults commonly use this term as a diminutive for "cat" even among themselves.
 ♦ SYNONYM: SEE - **meow-meow** *n.*

make a messy (to) *exp.* **1.** • to defecate in one's diapers • *Did we make a messy?;* Did you defecate in your diapers? • **2.** to dirty • *You're making a big messy on the table!;* You're dirtying the table!
 ♦ NOTE: It is extremely common to use the first person plural *"we"* when talking to an enfant. For example: *Did we fall down, go boom? - Do we want something to eat? …etc.*

make all gone (to) *exp.* to finish all one's food • *Make all gone!;* Finish all your food!

make caca (to) *exp.* to defecate •
Did you make caca?; Did you
defecate?
  ♦ NOTE: Occasionally, parents will
  simply say *"to make"* and leave
  out the term *"caca:" Did you
  make?*

make nice (to) *exp.* to behave and
act nice • *You make nice and
share your toys with your little
friend here;* You act nice and
share your toys with your little
friend here.

meow-meow *n.* • *Hold the
meow-meow gently;* Hold the cat
gently.
  ♦ NOTE: This is an onomatopoeia
  for the sound that a cat makes.
  ♦ SYNONYM: SEE - **kitty-cat** *n.*

moo-moo *n.* • *Look at all those
moo-moos!;* Look at all those
cows!
  ♦ NOTE: This is an onomatopoeia
  for the sound that a cow makes.
  ♦ VARIATION: **moo-cow** *n.*

mommy *n.* mother • *Can you give
mommy a kiss?;* Can you give
mother a kiss?
  ♦ NOTE: It is not uncommon to
  hear an adult use this term to
  refer to one's own mother.

**Mr. _____ (blanket, pillow,
bunny rabbit, etc.)** *exp.* • *Do
you want Mr. blanket?*
  ♦ NOTE: It is common, when
  dealing with children, to
  personify their belongings as a
  way to establish an intimate and

affectionate relationship between
them. Oddly enough, *"Mrs."* is
not commonly used in this
expression. In fact, *"Mr."* has
become so popular that to use
"Mrs." would actually sound
jarring.

nap-nap (to go) *n.* to take a nap •
Time for you to go nap-nap;
Time for you to take a nap.

neigh-neigh *n.* horse • *Don't get
too close to the neigh-neigh!;*
Don't get too close to the horse!
  ♦ NOTE: This is an onomatopoeia
  for the sound that a horse makes.
  ♦ SYNONYM: SEE - **horsey** *n.*

night-night (to go) *exp.* to go to bed
  • *It's time for you to go
  night-night;* It's time for you to
  go to bed.
  ♦ SYNONYM: **to say night-night**
  exp. to say good night • *Say
  night-night to daddy;* Say good
  night to daddy.

owie (to have an) *exp.* to have a
minor, yet painful, injury • *Oh,
did you get an owie?;* Oh, did
you get a little injury?
  ♦ NOTE: The term *"owie"* is
  diminutive for *"Ow!"* which is
  the common sound that one
  makes when hurt.
  ♦ SYNONYM: SEE - **booboo** *n.*

PJ's *n.pl.* pajamas • *Go put on your
PJ's;* Go put on your pajamas.
  ♦ NOTE: This term is commonly
  used among adults as well.

pee-pee (to go) *exp.* to urinate • *Do you have to go pee-pee?;* Do you have to urinate?
♦ ALSO: **pee-pee** *n.* penis • *Aim your pee-pee in the toilet;* Aim your penis in the toilet.

poo-poo (to go) *exp.* to defecate • *Do you need to go poo-poo?;* Do you need to defecate?
♦ VARIATION: **to make poo-poo** *exp.*

potty *n.* toilet • *Do you have to go potty?;* Do you have to go to the toilet?
♦ NOTE: The expression *"to go potty"* means both "to urinate" and "to defecate" depending on the context.

sleepy-bye (to go) *exp.* to go to bed • *Time to go sleepy-bye;* Time to go to bed.

Tee-Tee (to go) *exp.* to urinate • *Did you go Tee-Tee before you go to bed?;* Did you urinate before you go to bed?

tinkle (to go) *exp.* to urinate • *Make sure to go tinkle before we leave;* Make sure to urinate before we leave.
♦ SYNONYM: **to tinkle** *v.*

♦ NOTE: The literal translation of *"to tinkle"* is "to make a series of short tinkling sounds" which refers to the sound that one makes when urinating directly into water.

tootsies *n.pl.* feet • *Oh, your tootsies are cold!;* Oh, you're feet are cold!

tummy *n.* stomach • *Do you have a tummy ache?;* Do you have a stomach ache?
♦ NOTE: This term is commonly used among adults as well.
♦ SYNONYM: **tummie-tum-tum** *n.*

tweet-tweet *n.* bird • *Hear the tweet-tweet sing?;* Hear the bird sing?
♦ NOTE: This is an onomatopoeia for the sound that a bird makes.

wawa *n.* water • *Do you want some wawa?;* Do you want some water?

wee-wee (to go) *exp.* to urinate • *Make sure to go wee-wee before you go to bed;* Make sure to go urinate before you go to bed.
♦ VARIATION: **to make wee-wee** *exp.*

A CLOSER LOOK (2):
Common Formulae for Speaking Baby Talk

1. Add "y" or "ie" to a word:

$$\begin{array}{rcl} \text{bird} & = & \textit{birdie} \\ \text{kiss} & = & \textit{kissie} \\ \text{horse} & = & \textit{horsy} \\ \text{hug} & = & \textit{huggy} \\ \text{dog} & = & \textit{doggie, etc.} \end{array}$$

   ◆ NOTE: Sometimes the original word is repeated:

$$\text{dog} \quad = \quad \textit{doggie-dog.}$$

2. Using formula 1, pronounce the new term then repeat it replacing the first letter with "w":

$$\begin{array}{rcl} \text{dog} & = & \textit{doggie-woggie} \\ \text{teensy} & = & \textit{teensy-weensy} \\ \text{tootsie} & = & \textit{tootsie-wootsies, etc.} \end{array}$$

3. Change the letter "l" to "w":

$$\begin{array}{rcl} \text{She's so little!} & = & \textit{She's so widdow!} \\ \text{I just love him so much!} & = & \textit{I just wov him so much!} \end{array}$$

4. Change "you" to "him":

$$\text{You're just so cute!} \quad = \quad \textit{Him's just so cute!}$$

   ◆ NOTE: All of the previous formulae can even be used together in the same sentence:

$$\text{You're just the cutest little dog!} \quad = \quad \textit{Him's just the cutest widdow doggie-woggie!}$$

Slang Used in T.V. News

– The News Broadcast –

"...Some of the city's best **private eyes** are **lying in wait** for these **crooks** to **pull their next bank job.** For the time being, they are still **at large!**"

Lesson Four- SLANG USED IN T.V. NEWS

Dialogue In Slang

The News Broadcast

MONOLOGUE

The news anchor is reporting the events of the day.

Anchor: Our next story **comes on the heels of** yesterday's **heist** which
was **carried out in broad daylight** at the First State Bank. This
morning, the same two thieves **knocked off** a flower shop in the
same area. A **crackdown** is **under way** in order to **nab** these
men as they **face up to** two years in the **State Pen**. Witnesses are
being asked to **come forward** to help authorities put the two men
behind bars. Some of the city's best **private eyes** are **lying in
wait** for these men to **pull their next bank job** at which time
they'll see to it that it **backfires**. For the time being, these **crooks**
are **at large**.

A familiar news story which is causing a great deal of **hoopla** is
back on the front burner again. Since **money is getting tighter**
and the government is still **on shaky ground**, **Capitol Hill** is
planning **deep cuts** in the budget this year in order **to jump start**
the economy. They say there's just no **getting around it** since
our financial picture next year **hinges on** our **cutbacks** this year.
Along the same lines, in Congress today, a bill which would
raise taxes by 20% was briefly put **on the floor** but was **shot
down** quickly by the **powers that be**.

Translation of dialogue in standard English

The News Broadcast

MONOLOGUE

The news anchor is reporting the events of the day.

Anchor: Our next story **follows directly behind** yesterday's **robbery** which was **executed in the middle of the day** at the First State Bank. This morning, the same two thieves **robbed** a flower shop in the same area. A **rigorous attack** has **begun** in order to **apprehend** these men as they **will have to serve a maximum of** two years in the **State Penitentiary**. Witnesses are being asked to **identify themselves** to help authorities put the two men **in jail**. Some of the city's best **private investigators** are **waiting attentively** for these men to **execute their next bank robbery** at which time they'll see to it that it **fails**. **Presently**, these **criminals** are **among society**.

A familiar news story which is causing a great deal of **commotion** is **extremely noteworthy** again. Since money is getting **harder to earn** and the government is still **weak**, **Congress** is planning **extensive reductions** in the budget this year in order **to accelerate** the economy. They say there is just no **avoiding it** since our financial picture next year **depends on** our **reductions** this year. **Pertaining to this subject**, in Congress today, a bill which would raise taxes by 20% was briefly **discussed** but was **rejected** quickly by the **people in charge**.

Lesson Four- SLANG USED IN T.V. NEWS

Dialogue in slang as it would be heard

The News Broadcast

MONOLOGUE

The news anchor is reporting the events of the day.

Anchor: Our nex' story **comes on the heels of** yesterday's **heist** which
was **carried oud in broad daylight** at the Firs' State Bank. This
morning, the same two thieves **knocked off** a flower shop 'n the
same area. A **crack down** is **underway** 'n order ta **nab** these
men as they **face up ta** two years 'n the **State Pen**. Witnesses 're
being asked ta **come forward** ta help authoridies put the two men
b'hin' bars. Some 'a the cidy's best **privad' eyes** 're **lying 'n
wait** fer these men ta **execute their next bank job** at which time
they'll see to it thad it **backfires**. Fer the time being, these **crooks**
're **at large**.

A familiar news story which's causing a great deal of **hoopla**'s
back on the front burner again. Since **money is gedding
tighter** 'n the government's still **on shaky ground**, **Capidol
Hill**'s planning **deep cuts** 'n the budget this year 'n order **ta
jump start** the economy. They say there's just no **gedding
around it** since our financial picture next year **hinges on** our
cutbacks this year. **Along the same lines**, in Congress taday, a
bill which would raise taxes by 20% was briefly pud **on the floor**
but was **shot down** quickly by the **powers that be**.

Vocabulary

along the same lines (to be) *exp.* to pertain to the same subject • *We'll talk about that later. Your subject isn't along the same lines as what we're currently discussing;* We'll talk about that later. Your subject doesn't pertain to what we're currently discussing.

at large (to be) *exp.* (said of a criminal who is being pursued by the police) to be among society • *It's frightening to think that the killer has been at large for five years!;* It's frightening to think that the killer has been among society for five years!
  ♦ NOTE: **to take it on the lam** *exp.* to disappear quickly after committing a crime • *After he robbed the bank, the robber took it on the lam;* After he robbed the bank, the robber disappeared.

back on the front burner (to be) *exp.* said of an old news story that is noteworthy again • *Problems arising from severe rainstorms are back on the front burner again;* Problems arising from severe rainstorms are noteworthy again.
  ♦ ALSO: **to put something on the front burner** *exp.* to expedite something that has high priority • *The boss just told me that we have to finish the other project in two hours! We'd better put it on the front burner;* The boss just told me that we have to finish the other project in two hours! We'd better expedite it since it has high priority.
  ♦ ANTONYM: **to be put on the back burner** *exp.* to take low priority • *Due to the emergency, everything else will have to be put on the back burner for a while;* Due to the emergency, everything else will have to take low priority for a while. • *I'm going to have to put fixing my car on the back burner for now. I have to leave town suddenly;* I'm going to have to postpone fixing my car for now. I have to leave town suddenly.
  ♦ NOTE: The term *"burner"* used in these expressions refers to the "burner of a stove." In the culinary world, elements such as gravies, sauces, etc. that aren't used at once are placed on the back burners of the stove where they are allowed to cook slowly or simmer while the chef tends to the more immediate parts of the meal.

backfire (to) *exp.* to have an opposite outcome or effect of what was expected • *I wanted the teacher to like me, so I brought her a small gift and she got mad at me! She accused me of trying to bribe her. That sure backfired* *on me!;* I wanted the teacher to like me, so I brought her a small gift and she got mad at me! She accused me of trying to bribe her. That sure had the opposite outcome or effect of what I was expecting!

bank job (to pull a) *exp.* to execute a bank robbery • *The last time they tried to pull a bank job, they got arrested;* The last time they tried to execute a bank robbery, they got arrested.

behind bars (to be) *exp.* to be in jail • *You can relax now. He's behind bars;* You can relax now. He's in jail.

⬧ SYNONYM: **to be in the slammer** *n.* • *It's very simple. If you steal, you'll end up in the slammer;* It's very simple. If you steal, you'll end up in jail.

⇨ NOTE: The term *"slammer"* is an onomatopoeia for the slamming sound made by a closing jail door. The term comes from gangster lingo and is used by the toughest of gangsters and detectives. For this reason, when *"slammer"* is used by anyone else, it would usually be in jest only. In fact, this kind of language has been used in countless comedies as a way to get a laugh by having a sweet old grandmother-type unexpectedly use this "tough" gangster lingo.

Capitol Hill *exp.* Congress • *Ever since the war began last week, there has been a lot of activity on Capitol Hill;* Ever since the war began last week, there has been a lot of activity in Congress.

⬧ NOTE: *"Capitol Hill"* also stands for the "hill" where the Capitol stands and is commonly used to refer to Washington, D.C. in general.

carry out something (to) *exp.* to execute something • *He carried out the chief's orders;* He executed the chief's orders.

come forward (to) *exp.* to identify oneself • *He came forward and admitted committing the crime;* He identified himself as having committed the crime.

come on the heels of something (to) *exp.* said of an event that follows directly behind another • *The earthquake comes on the heels of the fire that engulfed the city last week;* The earthquake follows directly behind the fire that engulfed the city last week.

crackdown *n.* a rigorous attack • *The police force has implemented a crackdown on gang violence;* The police force has implemented a rigorous attack on gang violence.

crook *n.* criminal • *Two crooks robbed our house yesterday;* Two criminals robbed our house yesterday.

⬧ NOTE: The term *"crook"* is also commonly used figuratively to mean "one who cheats people of money." For example: *How can you trust him? The guy's a crook!;* How can you trust him? The guy's dishonest!

cutback *n.* reduction in spending • *Since we're over-budget this month, we're going to have to make some cutbacks immediately;* Since we're over-budget this month, we're going to have to make some reductions in spending immediately.

♦ SEE: **deep cuts** *exp.*

deep cuts *exp.* severe reductions in spending • *Deep cuts were made in the school's budget this year;* Severe reductions were made in the school's budget this year.

face up to (to) *exp.* to confront • *You have to face up to what you've done;* You have to confront what you've done.

heist *n.* armed robbery • *That's the guy I saw commit the heist today!;* That's the guy I saw commit the armed robbery today!

♦ SYNONYM: **stickup** *n.* • *Did you hear about the stickup today at the bank?;* Did you hear about the armed robbery today at the bank?

hinge on something (to) *exp.* to depend on something • *Whether or not we get the big contract hinges on your dinner tonight with the client;* Whether or not we get the big contract depends on your dinner tonight with the client.

hoopla *n.* commotion • *Why is there so much hoopla about his visit? Who is he, anyway?;* Why is there so much commotion about his visit? Who is he, anyway?

in broad daylight *exp.* in the middle of the day • *My car was stolen in broad daylight!;* My car was stolen in the middle of the day!

♦ ANTONYM: **in the dead of night** *exp.* in the middle of the night • *Why were you out in the dead of night?;* Why were you out in the middle of the night?

jump-start (to) *exp.* to start something suddenly that was completely lifeless • (lit); to restart a dead car battery • *We have to do something to jump-start the economy before it's too late!;* We have to do something to start the economy quickly before it's too late!

knock off something (to) *exp.* to rob something • *Where did you get all that money? What did you do…knock off a bank?;* Where did you get all that money? What did you do…rob a bank?;

♦ SYNONYM: **to hold up something** *exp.* • *I just overheard that man say he's gonna hold up the bank!;* I just overheard that man say he's going to rob the bank!

lie in wait (to) *exp.* said of an animal who hides and waits patiently and silently for its prey to arrive • *I know you want to catch the robber, but you can't just lie in wait for him. That could take days!;* I know you want to catch the robber, but you can't just wait for him. That could take days!

nab (to) *v.* to apprehend • *The cops nabbed the guy who stole my wallet!;* The police officers apprehended the guy who stole my wallet!
‣ SYNONYM: **to bust** *v.* • *They busted the robber just as he was leaving the bank;* They apprehended the robber just as he was leaving the bank.

on shaky ground (to be) *exp.* to be unsure • *Ever since our fight, we've been on shaky ground;* Ever since our fight, we've been on uncertain terms with each other.

on the floor (to be) *exp.* said of a proposal to be considered by an assembly • *We have a motion on the floor to increase taxes;* We have a motion to be considered for discussion to increase taxes.
‣ ALSO (1): **the floor** *n.* members of an assembly • *The chairman took questions from the floor;* The chairman took questions from the assembly.
‣ ALSO (2): **to have the floor** *exp.* to have one's turn to speak before an assembly • *The senator from California has the floor;* The senator from California may now speak.

powers that be (the) *exp.* the people in charge • *I'd like to allow you to come in but I didn't make up the rules...the powers that be did!;* I'd like to allow you to come in but I didn't make up the rules...the people in charge did!

private eye *n.* private investigator • *My father's training me to be a private eye;* My father is training me to be a private investigator.
‣ NOTE: This is actually a shortened and humorous version of "private investigator" which may be abbreviated to: *"P.I."* or *"private I."* However, since comic books depict private investigators as hunters with one huge eye enlarged by the magnifying glass they use to track foot prints, the letter "I" in *"private I"* was replaced with its homonym: *"eye."*

shoot down (to) *exp.* to reject unanimously • *The committee shot down my proposal;* The committee unanimously rejected my proposal.
‣ SYNONYM: **to steam-roll** *exp.* • *They all steam-rolled my decision;* They all rejected my decision.

State Pen *exp.* a common abbreviation for the "State Penitentiary" • *It's practically impossible to escape from the State Pen;* It's practically impossible to escape from the State Penitentiary.

"There's no getting around it" *exp.* "There is no way to evade the issue."

tight (to get) *adj.* **1.** said of money that is hard to acquire • *Money is getting tighter and tighter these days;* Money is getting harder and harder to acquire these days. • **2.** to get intoxicated • *I think I'd better stop drinking. I'm starting to get tight;* I think I'd better stop drinking. I'm starting to get intoxicated.
  ‣ ALSO: **to be tight with money** *exp.* to be miserly with money • *She's so tight with her money;* She's so miserly with her money.

underway (to be/get) *exp.* to begin the first step of a process • *The plan is underway;* The plan has just begun.

PRACTICE THE VOCABULARY

[Answers to Lesson Four, p. 212]

A. Fill in the blank with the appropriate letter.

1. The criminal is still at _____ .
   a. **big**   b. **large**   c. **huge**

2. The two robbers just _____ another bank job.
   a. **pushed**   b. **yanked**   c. **pulled**

3. The police force is implementing a crack _____ on gang violence.
   a. **down**   b. **up**   c. **under**

4. This news story comes on the _____ of another story that we just reported yesterday.
   a. **toes**   b. **ankles**   c. **heels**

5. You have to _____ up to what you've done.
   a. **face**   b. **head**   c. **back**

6. They committed the crime in _____ daylight!
   a. **wide**   b. **narrow**   c. **broad**

7. The robbers knocked _____ the grocery store.
   a. **up**   b. **off**   c. **in**

8. If something isn't done to _____-start the economy, there are going to be a lot more problems next year.
    a. **jump**   b. **skip**   c. **hop**

9. We have a motion on the _____ to decrease taxes.
    a. **ceiling**   b. **wall**   c. **floor**

10. My father investigates crimes. He's a private _____ .
    a. **head**   b. **eye**   c. **nose**

11. Money sure is _____ these days.
    a. **tight**   b. **loose**   c. **squeezed**

12. The convicts will be in the State _____ for another five years.
    a. **Pencil**   b. **Marker**   c. **Pen**

B. Replace the word(s) in italics with the slang equivalent from the right column.

1. The two robbers are still *among*   A. **heist**

    society _____ .

2. Your subject *doesn't pertain to*

    the same subject that _____   B. **isn't along the**
                                                    same lines as what
    _____

    we're discussing.

3. The plan *had an opposite result of what*   C. **crack down**

    we were expecting _____ .

4. The robber is still *in jail* _____

    _____ .

                                                 D. **behind bars**

5. There was a scandal *in Congress*
   _____ today.

   E. **hoopla**

6. He *executed* _____
   the plan.

   F. **carried out**

7. The witness hasn't *identified himself*
   _____
   yet.

   G. **come forward**

8. The police have implemented a
   rigorous attack _____
   _____ on the illegal use
   of drugs.

   H. **crook**

9. That guy over there is a
   criminal _____ !

   I. **on Capitol Hill**

10. The company is making some
    major *reductions in spending*
    _____ this month.

    J. **backfired**

11. What happened? What's all the
    commotion _____ about?

    K. **at large**

12. She's the one I saw commit the *armed*
    robbery _____ today!

    L. **cutbacks**

C. Underline the correct definition of the slang term(s) in boldface.

1. **to pull off a bank job:**
   a. to execute a bank robbery   b. to make a deposit

2. **to be behind bars:**
   a. to go out drinking often   b. to be in jail

3. **crack down:**
   a. an attack of insanity   b. a rigorous attack

4. **cutback:**
   a. a reduction in spending   b. an increase in spending

5. **to face up to:**
   a. to deny   b. to confront

6. **heist:**
   a. armed robbery   b. commotion

7. **hoopla:**
   a. armed robbery   b. commotion

8. **in broad daylight:**
   a. in the middle of the day   b. at the end of day

9. **to knock off a store:**
   a. to rob a store   b. to destroy a store

10. **to nab:**
    a. to run   b. to apprehend

11. **the powers that be:**
    a. godly powers   b. the people in charge

12. **private eye:**
    a. private investigator   b. cyclops

A CLOSER LOOK:

Foreign Words that Have Been Accepted into the English Language

The *odyssey* you're about to embark on through the *potpourri* of foreign words that have been adopted into the English language will surely help you to become a *bona fide aficionado* of Americanese. You may experience some *malaise* and feel a little like a *klutz* if you try to learn all their definitions *verbatim*. Just don't worry about any *faux pas* that you may accidentally make. And remember…the most important part in learning is that you're *gung-ho!*

Chinese

gung-ho *adj.* enthusiastic • *He's very gung-ho about selling his book overseas;* He's very enthusiastic about selling his book overseas.

kowtow to someone (to) *v.* to grovel before someone • *I'm tired of having to kowtow to everyone at work;* I'm tired of having to grovel before everyone at work.

kung fu *n.* Chinese art of self-defense much like karate • *He's a kung fu fighter;* He knows self-defense.

French

♦ NOTE: In the following examples, the colloquial pronunciation will be given only in cases where Americans have excessively changed the original French pronunciation.

adieu *exclam.* (pronounced "a-doo" by Americans) good-bye (usually forever) • (lit); to God (go with God) • *I bid you adieu!;* I say good-bye to you forever.
♦ NOTE: In French, the correct spelling is: *à Dieu.* The use of *"adieu,"* is considered extremely formal language.

à la carte *exp.* each item priced separately • (lit); according to the menu • *Let's order à la carte and then share;* Let's order each item separately and then share.
♦ NOTE: The French accent marks are used in the English spelling as well.

ambiance *n.* mood of the surroundings • *I like the ambiance in this restaurant;* I like the mood in this restaurant.
♦ NOTE: In English, this term may be spelled *"ambiance"* or *"ambience."*

aperitif *n.* an alcoholic beverage (served before dinner) • *Would you like an aperitif before dinner?;* Would you like an alcoholic beverage before dinner?
♦ NOTE: In French, the correct spelling is: *apéritif.*

apropos *adj.* appropriate • *How apropos that his son give the speech;* How appropriate that his son give the speech.
♦ NOTE: In French, the correct spelling is: *à propos.*

"A tout à l'heure!" *exp.* "See you later!"
♦ NOTE: In an attempt to pronounce *"à tout à l'heure,"* Americans began saying *"Toodaloo!"* which has become the accepted pronunciation. *"Toodaloo!"* and *"Toodles!"* is occasionally used to mean "See you later!"

attaché *n.* diplomat • *He's the French attaché;* He's the French diplomat.

avant garde *adj.* ahead of one's time • *Her style is very avant garde;* Her style is ahead of its time.

blasé *adj.* indifferent • *When I asked her to give an opinion about the scandal, she seemed very blasé;* When I asked her to give an opinion about the scandal, she seemed very indifferent.
♦ NOTE: The French accent marks are used in the English spelling as well.

"Bon appétit!" *exclam.* "Enjoy your meal!"
♦ NOTE: The French accent marks are used in the English spelling as well.

bon vivant *n.* one who enjoys life to the fullest • *He's a real bon vivant!;* He really enjoys life to the fullest.

"Bon voyage!" *exclam.* "Have a good trip!"

bourgeois *adj.* middle class • *She's so bourgeois!;* She's so middle class!
♦ NOTE: In English, the adjective *"bourgeois"* does not change when referring to a woman, unlike French where the adjective *"bourgeois"* would take on the feminine form *"bourgeoise."*

boutique *n.* a small specialty shop • *They have lots of gift ideas in this boutique;* They have lots of gift ideas in this small shop.

bric-a-brac *n.* a collection of small objects with sentimental value • *Did you see all the bric-a-brac she has all over her house?;* Did you see all the small objects she has all over her house?
♦ NOTE: In French, the correct spelling is: *bric-à-brac.*

brouhaha *n.* commotion • *What's that brouhaha outside?;* What's the commotion outside?

camaraderie *n.* friendship • *I love the camaraderie we have with each other;* I love the friendship we have with each other.

carte blanche *n.* complete discretionary freedom • (lit); white card (which refers to a blank slate that one may fill in at one's discretion) • *He gave me carte blanche to redecorate the house any way I want;* He gave me complete discretionary freedom to redecorate the house any way I want.

"C'est la vie!" *exp.* That's life! • *I can't believe I lost the contest again. Well, c'est la vie!;* I can't believe I lost the contest again. Well, that's life!

chateau *n.* castle • *Next week, we're visiting the chateaus of Austria;* Next week, we're visiting the castles of Austria.
♦ NOTE: In France, the correct spelling is: *château* (singular) and *châteaux* (plural).

collage *n.* an artistic design made of various pieces of material glued to a surface • *I remember making my first collage when I was 8 years old;* I remember making my first art piece made of various pieces of material glued to a surface when I was 8 years old.

concierge *n.* janitor; doorkeeper; hotel manager (definition depends on context) • *What a beautiful hotel. Let's find the concierge;* What a beautiful hotel! Let's find the manager.

connoisseur *n.* one who enjoys the qualities of life with great appreciation and discrimination • *He's a wine connoisseur;* He's an authority of wine.
♦ NOTE: The common pronunciation is *connaisseur.*

coup *n.* a sudden stroke of good luck • *That was a real coup!;* That was a real sudden stroke of good luck!
♦ NOTE (1): Pronounced: *koo.*

coup d'état *n.* violent overthrow or transformation of the government • *There was a coup d'état yesterday in the Philippines;* There was a violent overthrow of the government yesterday in the Philippines.
♦ NOTE: Pronounced: *koo d'ay-tah.*

crème de la crème *exp.* the cream of the crop, the very best • *This class of students represents the crème de la crème;* This class of students represents the very best.
♦ NOTE: The French accent marks are used in the English spelling as well.

cul-de-sac *n.* street closed at one end • (lit); bottom of the bag • *They live on a cul-de-sac;* they live at the closed end of the street.

debacle *n.* a complete failure or disaster • *The entire project was a debacle;* The entire project was a complete failure.
▶ NOTE: In French, the correct spelling is: *débâcle.*

debut *n.* (pronounced "day-bew" by Americans) first appearance • *She made her singing debut in California;* She made her first singing appearance in California.
▶ NOTE: In French, the correct spelling is: *début.*

debutante *n.* (pronounced "day-bew-tant" by Americans) one who is making a first appearance • *Although she's a debutante, she's one of the best performers in the play;* Although she's making her first appearance, she's one of the best performers in the play.
▶ NOTE: In French, the correct spelling is: *débutante.*

déclassé *adj.* said of something lacking in style and class • *Can you believe she's serving hamburgers to her guests? How déclassé!;* Can you believe she's serving hamburgers to her guests? How lacking in style and class!
▶ NOTE: The French accent marks are used in the English spelling as well.

déjà vu *exp.* a psychic feeling of having already seen a particular place or event • (lit); already seen • *I know I've never been here*

before, but I recognize everything. Talk about déjà vu!; I know I've never been here before, but I recognize everything. Talk about a psychic feeling of having already seen a particular place!
▶ NOTE: The French accent marks are used in the English spelling as well.

double entendre *exp.* that which has two meanings, one of which is oftentimes sexually suggestive. For example: *Wanna play with me?* means **1.** Do you want to play games with me? [or] **2.** Do you want to play with me sexually? The difference between **1.** and **2.** depends on the context.
▶ NOTE: Interestingly enough, the expression *double entendre,* literally meaning "double hear," does **not** exist in the French language. In France, a *double entendre* is referred to as *double sens.*

echelon *n.* (pronounced "e-che-lawn" by Americans) hierarchy, rank • *She's part of the upper echelon;* She's part of the upper class.
▶ NOTE: In French, the correct spelling is: *échelon.*

éclair *n.* (pronounced "ee-klair" by Americans) an oblong pastry filled with custard • *We had éclairs for dessert at my mother's house;* We had pastries filled with custard at my mother's house.

◆ NOTE: The French accent marks are used in the English spelling as well.

elite *n.* (pronounced "a-leet" by Americans) aristocracy • *He's part of the elite;* He's part of the aristocracy.
◆ NOTE: In French, the correct spelling is: *élite.*

emigre *n.* (pronounced "e-mee-gray" by Americans) immigrant • *She's a foreign emigre;* She a foreign immigrant.
◆ NOTE: In French, the correct spelling is: *émigré.*

ennui *n.* boredom • *I don't think I can stand another day of ennui;* I don't think I can tolerate another day of boredom.

en route *exp.* on the road • *We've been en route for an hour now;* We've been on the road for an hour now.

ensemble *n.* (pronounced "on-sombl" by Americans) performing group • (lit); together • *This is one of the best musical ensembles in town;* This is one of the best musical performing groups in town.

entree *n.* (pronounced "on-tray" by Americans) main course • *What did they serve for the entree?;* What did they serve for the main course?
◆ NOTE: In French, the correct spelling is: *entrée.*

fait accompli *exp.* said of something which is already under way • (lit); accomplished fact • *You can't stop them now. It's a fait accompli;* You can't stop them now. The terms have already been put into motion.

faux pas *exp.* social error • *You made a real faux pas when you started talking about his mistress in front of his wife!;* You made a real social error when you started talking about his mistress in front of his wife!

finale *n.* (pronounced "fi-nalee" by Americans) end of a performance • (lit); end • *This is the finale;.* This is the end of the performance.
◆ ALSO: **grand finale** *exp.* the big ending.

finesse *n.* diplomacy • *Let her handle the problem. She has a lot of finesse;* Let her handle the problem. She's very diplomatic.

gourmand *n.* (pronounced "gour-mand" by Americans) glutton • *He's such a gourmand!;* He's such a glutton!

gourmet • **1.** *n.* one who has discriminating taste in the art of fine cooking • *People are nervous about inviting him over for dinner because he's such a gourmet;* People are nervous about inviting him over for dinner because he has such discriminating taste in the art of fine cooking. • **2.** *adj.* exquisitely prepared • *I love gourmet food!;* I love exquisitely prepared food!

haute couture *exp.* • (lit); high fashion • *This boutique specializes in haute couture;* This shop specializes in high fashion.
♦ NOTE: In French, as well as in English, *"haute couture"* is pronounced: "oat koo-tur."

haute cuisine *exp.* fine and elaborate cooking • (lit); high cooking • *Forgive my son for not eating. He's not used to haute cuisine;* Forgive my son for not eating. He's not used to fine and elaborate cooking.
♦ NOTE: In French, as well as in English, *"haute cuisine"* is pronounced: "oat kui-zeen."

hors d'oeuvre *exp.* (pronounced "or derve" by Americans) appetizer • *Would you care for an hors d'oeuvre?;* Would you care for an appetizer?
♦ NOTE: In French, the correct spelling is: *hors d'œuvre.*

je ne sais quoi *exp.* an undefinable quality in a person • *I really like him. He has a certain je ne sais quoi;* I really like him. He has a certain undefinable quality.

laissez faire *exp.* an attitude of noninvolvement • *His attitude is very laissez faire;* His attitude is one of noninvolvement.

maître d'hôtel *exp.* headwaiter • (lit); master of the establishment

• *Ask the maître d'hôtel for a table by the window;* Ask the headwaiter for a table by the window.
♦ NOTE: The French accent marks are used in the English spelling as well.

malaise *n.* uneasiness • *Did you notice the malaise he was experiencing with us last night?;* Did you notice the uneasiness he was experiencing with us last night?

Mardi Gras *exp.* a carnival in New Orleans culminating on Shrove Tuesday • (lit); Fat Tuesday • *Wanna go to mardi gras with us?;* Do you want to go to the carnival with us?

mélange *n.* mixture • *What's this mélange you're making?;* What's this mixture you're making?
♦ NOTE: The French accent marks are used in the English spelling as well.

melee *n.* a fist fight involving many people • (lit); mix • *Look at the melee outside!;* Look at the fight outside!
♦ NOTE: In French, the correct spelling is: *mêlée.*

ménage à trois *exp.* arrangement in which three people who live in the same home share sexual relations • (lit); household of three • *I think they're having a ménage à trois;* I think all three of them are living together and

having sex.
‣ NOTE: The French accent marks are used in the English spelling as well.

milieu *n.* (pronounced "miliew" by Americans) environment • *How can you live in this milieu?;* How can you live in this environment?

monsieur *n.* **1.** Mr. (a polite form of address referring to someone from France) • *Do you know Monsieur Dubois?;* Do you know Mr. Dubois? • **2.** sir • *Good evening, monsieur;* Good evening, sir.

nom de plume *exp.* pseudonym for a writer • (lit); pen name • *What is his nom de plume?;* What is his pen name?

nouveau riche *exp.* newly rich • (lit); new rich • *This is where all the nouveau riche live;* This is where the newly rich live.

nouvelle cuisine *exp.* refers to the newest form of cooking which consists of little fat, elaborate presentation, and generally meager portions • *I love the taste of nouvelle cuisine but I'm always hungry after I eat!;* I love the taste of the new form of cooking but I'm always hungry after I eat!

passé *adj.* outdated • (lit); passed • *That style of clothing is passé;* That style of clothing is outdated.
‣ NOTE: The French accent marks

are used in the English spelling as well.

pièce de résistance *exp.* climax in a presentation (theater, cuisine, etc.) • (lit); piece of resistance • *And now for the pièce de résistance!;* And now for the climax in our presentation!
‣ NOTE: The French accent marks are used in the English spelling as well.

pied-à-terre *n.* temporary or secondary dwelling • (lit); foot to ground • *We have a pied-à-terre in London;* We have a secondary dwelling in London.
‣ NOTE: The French accent marks are used in the English spelling as well.

poignant *adj.* powerful and emotionally moving • *This part of the movie is very poignant;* This part of the movie is very powerful and moving.

potpourri *exp.* an assortment • (lit); rotten pot • *My sister is now going to perform a potpourri of songs for you;* My sister is now going to perform an assortment of songs for you.
‣ NOTE: In French, the correct spelling is: *pot pourri.*

répondez s'il vous plaît *exp.* always seen as *R.S.V.P.* • (lit); respond if you please.
‣ NOTE (1): The initials *R.S.V.P.* are commonly added to the bottom of an invitation where a response is requested by the host

or hostess.

◆ NOTE (2): The French accent marks are used in the English spelling as well.

risqué *adj.* sexually suggestive • *That photo is awfully risqué!;* That photo is awfully sexually suggestive!

◆ NOTE: The French accent marks are used in the English spelling as well.

salon *n.* an elegant business establishment • (lit); living room • *Did you see the new hair salon on the corner?;* Did you see the new hair establishment on the corner?

savoir faire *exp.* a keen understanding of proper conduct in a given situation • (lit); to know how to do • *He has a great deal of savoir faire;* He has a great understanding of proper conduct in a given situation.

◆ NOTE: A common variation of *"savoir faire"* is the adjective *"savvy"* meaning "knowledgeable of proper conduct in a given situation."

soupe du jour *exp.* • (lit); soup of the day • *Excuse me, waiter. What is your soupe du jour?;* Excuse me, waiter. What is your soup of the day?

tête-à-tête *exp.* a private meeting between two people • *Alicia and Susan are having a tête-à-tête in the conference room;* Alicia and Susan are having a private

meeting together in the conference room.

◆ NOTE: The French accent marks are used in the English spelling as well.

"Touché!" • **1.** exclamation by a fencer when he/she touches the opponent with the sword • *Touché!;* I touched you with my sword! • **2.** exclamation used to indicate the successful conclusion of an argument • *That was a very good point you made. Touché!;* That was a very good point you made. That successfully concludes our argument.

◆ NOTE: The French accent marks are used in the English spelling as well.

tour de force *exp.* a demonstration of strength or ability • *Your idea was a real tour de force;* Your idea was a real demonstration of ability.

trompe l'oeil *exp.* that which deceives the eye (said in art) • *That painting looks like a photograph. What a trompe l'oeil!;* That painting looks like a photograph. What a deception to the eye!

◆ NOTE: In French, the correct spelling is: *trompe l'œil.*

vis-à-vis *exp.* in relationship to • (lit); face to face • *How does this problem compare vis-à-vis our situation of yesterday?;* How does this problem compare in relationship to our situation of yesterday?

♦ NOTE: The French accent marks are used in the English spelling as well.

"Voilà!" *exclam.* "There!"

♦ NOTE (1): This exclamation is used to call attention to an act. Magicians commonly used this term upon completion of a magician feat.

♦ NOTE (2): The French accent marks are used in the English spelling as well.

German

angst *n.* a feeling of great anxiety • *Why is your face so full of angst?;* Why do you look so anxious?

ersatz *n.* imitation • *This isn't real butter. It's ersatz;* This isn't real butter. It's imitation.

gesundheit *n.* a common response to a sneeze • (lit); restored to health • *Gesundheit! I hope you're not getting sick;* May you be restored back to health! I hope you're not getting sick.

kaput *n.* broken • *My car went kaput again;* My car broke down again.

kindergarten *n.* first year of primary school directly after nursery school • (lit); garden of children • *My niece just started her first day at kindergarten;* My niece just started her first day of primary school.

verboten *adj.* (pronounced "ferboten" in German and English) forbidden • *It's strictly verboten to enter that room;* It's strictly forbidden to enter that room.

wunderkind *n.* (pronounced "vunderkint" in German, and "wonderkint" in English) prodigy • (lit); wonder child • *Your son is a real wunderkind;* Your child is a real prodigy.

Greek

Achilles' heel *exp.* one's vulnerable area • *If we want to beat him, we'll have to find his Achilles' heel;* If we want to beat him, we'll have to find his vulnerable area.

♦ NOTE: Achilles is a character from Greek mythology known for being vulnerable only in his heel.

Adonis *n.* handsome and muscular man • *What an Adonis!;* What a handsome and muscular man!

ambrosia *n.* any delicious drink • *This wine is pure ambrosia!;* This wine is delicious!

aphrodisiac *n.* that which excites sexually • *They say that chocolate is an aphrodisiac;* They say that chocolate excites people sexually.

♦ NOTE: This term comes from the Greek goddess of love, Aphrodite.

charisma *n.* magnetism and charm
• *Your father has so much charisma;* Your father has so much magnetism and charm.

colossal *adj.* enormous • *I have to make a colossal decision about my career;* I have to make an enormous decision about my career.

cosmos *n.* galaxy • *Some day, I want to be an astronaut and travel through the cosmos;* Some day, I want to be an astronaut and travel through the galaxy.

erotic *n.* sexually stimulating • *This book is very erotic;* This book is very sexually stimulating.
❯ ALSO: **erotica** *n.* books which are sexually stimulating • *This bookstore specializes in erotica;* This bookstore specializes in sexually stimulating books.

"Eureka!" used as an exclamation of excitement and triumph • *Eureka! I found the answer!*

marathon *n.* a long distance race • *I heard your father is participating in the marathon;* I heard your father is participating in the long distance race.

mentor *n.* teacher and guide • *I'm learning so much from her. She's a fantastic mentor;* I'm learning so much from her. She's a fantastic teacher.

narcissism *n.* excessive self-love • *The way he stares at himself in the mirror, I think he's into narcissism;* The way he stares at himself in the mirror, I think he loves himself too much.
❯ ALSO: **narcissistic** *adj.* excessively vain • *Stop looking at yourself in the mirror all the time! You're so narcissistic!;* Stop looking at yourself in the mirror all the time! You're so vain!
❯ NOTE: These terms come from Greek mythology where the character Narcissus was known for falling in love with his own reflection.

nectar *n.* any delicious drink • (lit); the drink of the Gods • *This champagne is nectar;* This champagne is delicious.

nemesis *n.* enemy, rival • *That man is my nemesis;* That man is my enemy.
❯ NOTE: This comes from the Greek goddess of retributive justice, Nemesis.

odyssey *n.* a long journey (physical or mental) • *He's very tired after his odyssey;* He's very tired after his long journey.
❯ NOTE: This comes from the Greek leader of the Trojan War, Odysseus, who wandered for several years before finding his home.

platonic *adj.* nonphysical relationship with someone • *They have a platonic relationship;* They have a friendship which does not involve sex.

‣ NOTE: This term comes from the teachings of the Greek philosopher Plato.

stoic *adj.* emotionally detached • *He never cries about anything. I don't know why he's always so stoic;* He never cries about anything. I don't know why he's always so emotionally detached.

thespian *n.* devoted actor • *Are you a thespian?;* Are you an actor?
‣ NOTE: This term comes from Thespis who was known for being the originator of the actor's role.

typhoon *n.* hurricane • *Did you hear about the typhoon in the Philippines?;* Did you hear about the hurricane in the Philippines?

Italian

a capella *exp.* (in music) without accompaniment • (lit); in the style of the chapel • *Now let's sing the song a capella;* Now let's sing the song without accompaniment.

accelerando *adv.* (in music) steadily gathering speed • (lit); accelerated • *This musical piece should be played accelerando;* This musical piece should be played so that it steadily gathers speed.

agitato *adv.* (in music) very fast tempo • (lit); agitated • *The third movement is played agitato;* The third movement is played in a very fast tempo.

al dente *adj.* not overcooked • (lit); to the tooth • *It's best to serve broccoli al dente;* It's best to serve broccoli a little on the crunchy side.

allegretto *adv.* (in music) rather slowly • *Make sure to play the fugue allegretto;* Make sure to play the fugue rather slowly.

allegro *adv.* (in music) lively • *This musical piece should be played allegro;* This musical piece should be played lively.

andante *adv.* (in music) slowly • *All his preludes are played andante;* All his preludes are played slowly.

aria *n.* (in music) an operatic melody • *She sang the most beautiful aria;* She sang the most beautiful operatic melody.

arpeggio *n.* (in music) rolled chord starting at one end of the keyboard and finishing at the other end • *I'll play an arpeggio, then you begin singing;* I'll play a rolled chord from one end of the keyboard to the other, then you begin singing.

a tempo *exp.* (in music) back to the original tempo • (lit); to tempo • *The music slows down here, then goes back to a tempo (pronounced "ah tempo");* The music slows down here, then goes back to the original tempo.

cantata *n.* (in music) choral composition • *My sister is performing a cantata with her singing group tonight;* My sister is performing a choral composition with her singing group tonight.

♦ NOTE: This comes from the verb *"cantare"* meaning "to sing."

cappuccino *n.* coffee with steamed milk • *Wanna go get a cappuccino after the movie?;* Do you want to go get some coffee with steamed milk after the movie?

coloratura *n.* (in music) highest female voice in a choir • (lit); coloring • *Your sister is a coloratura? When she speaks her voice is so low!;* Your sister has the highest voice in the choir? When she speaks her voice is so low!

con spirito *exp.* (in music) lively • (lit); with spirit • *This musical piece should be played con spirito;* This musical piece should be played lively.

contralto *n.* (in music) lowest female voice in a choir • *My voice is getting lower. I used to be a coloratura, now I'm a contralto!* My voice is getting lower. I used to have the highest voice in the choir, now I have the lowest!

crescendo *n.* (in music) becoming louder and louder • (lit); growing • *Whenever you're watching a movie and there's a crescendo in the music, you can be sure that something is about to happen!;* Whenever you're watching a movie and the music gets louder and louder, you can be sure that something is about to happen!

diminuendo *adv.* (in music) becoming softer and softer • (lit); diminishing • *After a crescendo in the music, there's usually a diminuendo;* After there's an increase in the volume in the music, there's usually a decrease.

falsetto *n.* (in music) a voice that goes above one's normal register • (lit); false • *My sister can sing so high because she goes into falsetto;* My sister can sing so high because she goes into a voice that's above her normal register.

forte *adv.* **1.** (in music) loudly • (lit); strong • *This part of the music should be played forte;* This part of the music should be played loudly. • **2.** one's specialty or talent • *Oil painting is my forte, but I also work a little with water color;* Oil painting is my specialty, but I also work a little with water color.

fortissimo *adv.* (in music) very loudly • (lit); very strong • *Make sure to play the ending fortissimo;* Make sure to play the ending very loudly.

glissando *adv.* (in music) a fast up and down gliding of the musical scale • (lit); gliding • *In this piece, the harp does a beautiful glissando toward the end;* In this piece, the harp does a beautiful fast up and down gliding of the musical scale toward the end.

grave *adv.* • **1.** extremely serious • *This matter is extremely grave;* This matter is extremely serious. • **2.** (in music) slow and somber • *This funeral piece should be played grave;* This funeral piece should be played slow and somber.

incognito *adj.* disguised • (lit); unknown • *I didn't recognize him because he was incognito;* I didn't recognize him because he was disguised.

larghetto *adv.* (in music) somewhat slowly • *Make sure to play the first movement of the sonata larghetto;* Make sure to play the first movement of the sonata somewhat slowly.

largo *adv.* (in music) very slowly • *You're playing the piece too fast! You're playing it larghetto when you should be playing it largo!;* You're playing the piece too fast! You're playing it somewhat slowly when you should be playing it very slowly!

lento *adv.* (in music) slowly and sluggishly • *I wonder why they're playing this piece lento when it's supposed to be a happy tune?;* I wonder why they're playing this piece slowly and sluggishly when it's supposed to be a happy tune!

maestro *n.* (in music) conductor • (lit); master • *I'd like to present our maestro;* I'd like to present our conductor.

mezzo soprano *exp.* (in music) female voice that is lower than that of the soprano • (lit); half soprano • *The older I get, the lower my voice gets. I'm now a mezzo soprano;* The older I get, the lower my voice gets. I now sing lower than a soprano.

mezzo voce *exp.* (in music) quietly • (lit); half voice • *This part should be sung mezzo voce;* This part should be sung at half the volume.

partita *n.* (in music) a musical suite or section • *I love all of Bach's partitas;* I love all of Bach's suites.
‣ NOTE: This comes from the verb *"partire"* meaning "to divide."

pianissimo *adv.* (in music) very softly • *The end of the movement should be played pianissimo;* The end of the movement should be played very softly.

piano *adv.* (in music) softly • *You don't need to play this part so pianissimo, just piano;* You don't need to play this part so softly, just somewhat softly.

pizzicato *adv.* (in music) notes played on the violin by plucking the strings • (lit); plucked • *In the Nutcracker Suite, the violins commonly play pizzicato;* In the Nutcracker Suite, the violins commonly pluck the strings.

presto *adv.* (in music) extremely fast • *Don't expect me to be able to play this piece presto the first time!;* Don't expect me to be able to play this piece exremely fast the first time!

prima donna *exp.* • (lit); first lady • **1.** lead female singer in an opera • *I'd like to introduce you to our prima donna;* I'd like to introduce you to our lead singer. • **2.** pretentious woman • *She's such a prima donna!;* She's such a pretentious woman!

rubato *adv.* (in music) expressively played through one's own interpretation and not adhering to a steady rhythm • *This beautiful romantic piece should be played rubato;* This beautiful romantic piece should be played through the performer's own interpretation.

sforzando *adv.* (in music) suddenly loudly • *The last chord of this piece should be played sforzando to indicate the climax;* The last chord of this piece should be played suddenly loudly to indicate the climax.

soprano *n.* singer with the highest voice in a choir • *When my brother was nine years old, he was a soprano;* When my brother was nine years old, he had the highest voice in the choir.

staccato *adv.* quickly and disjointed • **1.** *He speaks in a staccato manner;* He speaks quickly and disjointedly. • **2.** (in music) • *Make sure not to sustain these chords. They should be played staccato;* Make sure not to sustain these chords. They should be played quickly and disjointedly.

vibrato *adv.* (in music) the quivery execution of a musical note • (lit); vibrated • *Violinists commonly add a little vibrato to the end of each note;* Violinists commonly add a little quiver to the end of each note.

virtuoso *n.* (in music) highly skilled musician • *Your son is a virtuoso!;* Your son is a highly skilled musician!

Latin

ad hoc *adj.* formed in order to tend to specific needs • (lit); for this • *We're forming an ad hoc committee to take care of the problems that occurred during the big storm;* We're forming a special committee to take care of the problems that occurred during the big storm.

ad infinitum *exp.* endless • (lit); to infinity • *The sky is so clear* tonight. *You can see stars ad infinitum;* The sky is so clear tonight. You can see an endless number of stars.

ad lib (to) *v.* to improvise • *Let's ad lib this part of the song;* Let's improvise this part of the song.

ad nauseam *exp.* to a nauseating extent • (lit); to nausea • *She always gives lengthy speeches ad nauseam;* She always gives lengthy speeches to a nauseating extent.

alma mater *exp.* one's former school • (lit); fostering mother • *I hope my son goes to Hollywood High School. That's my alma mater!;* I hope my son goes to Hollywood High School. That's my former school!

alter ego *exp.* other side of one's personality • (lit); second self • *He's always so nice, I just can't believe he would be so nasty to you. Maybe it was his alter ego speaking;* He's always so nice, I just can't believe he would be so nasty to you. Maybe it was the other side of his personality speaking.

alumnus *n.* a graduate • *I'm finally an alumnus!;* I'm finally a graduate!
♦ NOTE: **alumni** *pl.* • *Tomorrow there's going to be a huge party for all of the alumni of my school;* Tomorrow there's going to be a huge party for all the graduates of my school.

ante meridiem *n.* before noon • *I'll come and pick you up at 9:00 A.M.;* I'll pick you up at 9:00 in the morning.
♦ NOTE: This is always seen as "A.M."

bona fide *n.* legitimate • *He's a bona fide lawyer;* He's a legitimate lawyer.

caveat *n.* warning • *There are certain caveats that you need to be aware of;* There are warnings that you need to be aware of.

ego *n.* conceit • *She has an ego problem!;* She's really conceited!

et cetera *exp.* and so forth • *My mother is wonderful, generous, funny, etc.;* My mother is wonderful, generous, funny, and so forth.
♦ NOTE: This expression is commonly seen in its shortened form: *etc.*

fetus *n.* a developing baby in the mother's womb • *We could actually see pictures of the fetus!;* We could actually see pictures of the developing baby!

gratis *adj.* free • *The dinner tonight was gratis;* The dinner tonight was free.

hypothesis *n.* theory • *What is your hypothesis about this condition?;* What is your theory about this condition?

id est *exp.* for example • *This shirt comes in many different types of* *fabric, i.e. wool, cotton, silk, etc.;* This shirt comes in many different types of fabric; for example, wool, cotton, silk, etc. ◆ NOTE: The expression *"id est"* is commonly used as *"i.e."*

in absentia *exp.* in absence • *The Film Academy gave her the award in absentia;* The Film Academy gave her the award in her absence.

libido *n.* sex drive • *I hear he has a powerful libido;* I hear he has a powerful sex drive.

magna cum laude *exp.* with high honors • *She graduated magna cum laude;* She graduated with high honors.

per capita *exp.* per segment of population • *They have the highest crime rate per capita of any other state;* They have the highest crime rate per segment of population of any other state.

per se *exp.* as such • *I don't mind houseguests per se, but lately we've been having so many that our home looks like a boarding house!;* I don't mind houseguests as such, but lately we've been having so many that our home looks like a boarding house!

persona *n.* personality • *He has a very nice persona;* He has a very nice personality.

post meridiem *n.* afternoon through midnight • *It's 2:00 P.M.;* It's 2:00 in the afternoon.

◆ NOTE: This is always seen as *"P.M."*

postmortem *adv.* after death • *The coroner did a postmortem examination on the body;* the coroner did an after death examination on the body.

post scriptum *n.* after the writing. ◆ NOTE: The abbreviated form of this term, *"P.S."* is commonly used to add additional information after the closing salutation of a letter. For example: *P.S. I'll write to you again next week.*

pro forma *exp.* rough draft (as in contracts) • *He sent us a pro forma contract;* He sent us a rough draft of the contract.

pro/con(tra) *n.* for/against • *He is pro/con equal rights for women;* He is for/against equal rights for women.

quantum *adj.* momentous • *He made a quantum leap in his grades at school;* He made a momentous leap in his grades at school.

rectum *n.* the area of the intestine just beyond the anus • *He's getting a hemorrhoid removed from his rectum;* He's getting a hemorrhoid removed from the area of the intestine just beyond the anus.

scrotum *n.* the sack containing the testes • *In bull fights, it's common to offer the bull's* *scrotum to the winning matador;* In bull fights, it's common to offer the sack containing the bull's testes to the winning matador.

sputum *n.* mucus • *The baby is getting sputum all over his bib;* The baby is getting mucus all over his bib.

status *n.* condition • *What is the status of your father's car after the accident?;* What is the condition of your father's car after the accident?

status quo *n.* the existing situation or status • *The president decided not to make any changes in government right now in order to preserve the status quo;* The president decided not to make any changes in government right now in order to preserve the existing situation.

verbatim *adv.* quoted exactly • *Let me tell you what he said verbatim;* Let me tell you exactly what he said.

vice versa *exp.* conversely • *You have to share your belongings with him and vice versa;* You have to share your belongings with him and he has to share his belongings with you.

Spanish

aficionado *n.* devotee • *He's always been an aficionado of country*
music; He's always been a devotee of country music.

caballero *n.* horseman • *You're a real caballero!;* You're a real horseman!

cabana *n.* a small structure with an open wall facing a waterfront or swimming pool • *My parents have a cabana in their backyard;* My parents have a small structure with an open wall facing the pool in the backyard.
▶ NOTE: In Spanish, the correct spelling is: *cabaña.*

cantina *n.* a small barroom or saloon • *Let's go get something to drink at the cantina;* Let's go get something to drink at the saloon.

chaparral *n.* a very dry area with shrubby plants • *There are parts of southern California that are considered chaparral country;* There are parts of southern California that are considered very dry with lots of shrubby plants.

Chicano *n.* an American of Mexican ancestry • *There are a lot of Chicanos living in the city of Los Angeles;* There are a lot of Americans of Mexican ancestry living in the city of Los Angeles.

gringo *n.* term for any foreigner to Mexico (often used derogatorily) • *Gringo, go home!;* Non-native to Mexico, go home!

"Hasta la vista!" *exp.* "See you later!"

"Hasta mañana!" *exp.* "See you tomorrow!"
▶ NOTE: The Spanish accent marks are used in the English spelling as well.

incommunicado *adj.* unable to be contacted • *I'm afraid the boss can't speak to you right now. He's incommunicado;* I'm afraid the boss can't speak to you right now. He's unable to be contacted.

macho *adj.* extremely masculine • *Your brother is so macho!;* Your brother is so masculine!
▶ SYNONYM: **machismo** *adj.*

matador *n.* bullfighter • *Wouldn't you be scared to be a matador?;* Wouldn't you be scared to be a bullfighter?

mucho *exp.* extremely • *What's wrong? You look mucho scared;* What's wrong? You look extremely scared.

padre *n.* priest, father • *I have a confession to make, Padre;* I have a confession to make, Father.

poncho *n.* article of clothing resembling a blanket with a hole in the middle which fits over the head • *Did you see the poncho Nancy wore to school today? It looked so warm!;* Did you see the blanket-like cloak Nancy wore to school today? It looked so warm!

pronto *adv.* immediately • *Get in here pronto!;* Get in here immediately!

pueblo *n.* village • *Her family lives in a little pueblo just outside the city;* Her family lives in a little village just outside the city.

que será será *exp.* what will be will be • *I hope you win the contest but que será será!;* I hope you win the contest but what will be will be!
▶ NOTE: The Spanish accent marks are used in the English spelling as well.

señor *n.* • **1.** Mr. (a polite form of address referring to someone from a Spanish speaking country) • *Do you know señor Baldez?;* Do you know Mr. Baldez? • **2.** sir • *Good evening, señor;* Good evening, sir.
▶ NOTE: The Spanish accent marks are used in the English spelling as well.

señora *n.* • **1.** Mrs. (a polite form of address referring to someone from a spanish speaking country) • *Do you know señora Baldez?;* Do you know Mrs. Baldez? • **2.** ma'am • *Good evening, señora;* Good evening, ma'am.
▶ NOTE: The Spanish accent marks are used in the English spelling as well.

señorita *n.* • **1.** Miss (a polite form of address referring to someone from a spanish speaking country)

• *Do you know señorita Baldez?;*
Do you know Miss Baldez? •
2. miss • *Good evening, señorita;*
Good evening, miss.
‣ NOTE: The Spanish accent
marks are used in the English
spelling as well.

sombrero *n.* a large hat usually
made of straw • *My sombrero
helps protect me from the sun;*
My large hat helps protect me
from the sun.

toro *n.* bull • *When matadors are in
the ring, it's common to hear
them yell, "Toro! Toro!;"* When
bullfighters are in the ring, it's
common to hear them yell, "Bull!
Bull!"

Yiddish

bagel *n.* ring-shaped bread roll •
*Would you like toast or a bagel
with your breakfast?;* Would you
like toast or a ring-shaped bread
roll with your breakfast?

kosher *adj.* acceptable • *What he
did was not kosher;* What he did
was not unacceptable.
‣ NOTE: The literal translation of
kosher is "acceptable by Jewish
law."

klutz *n.* clumsy person • *I can't
believe you spilled your drink for
the second time! You're such a
klutz!;* I can't believe you spilled
your drink for the second time!
You're such a clumsy person!

matzoh *n.* flat and crispy
unleavened bread • *I love eating
matzoh with my dinner;* I love
eating flat and crispy unleavened
bread with my dinner.

nosh *n.* snack • *I'm going to have a
little nosh before dinner;* I'm
going to have a little snack before
dinner.

"Oy!" *exclam.* exclamation of
displeasure • *Oy! I can't believe I
locked my keys in the car!*
‣ VARIATION: **"Oy, vay!"**

putz *n.* jerk • (lit); penis • *You
acted like a real putz tonight!;*
You acted like a real jerk tonight!

schlemiel *n.* clumsy person • *He fell
down again? What a schlemiel!;*
He fell down again? What a
clumsy person!

schlimazl *n.* unlucky person • *His
car is always breaking down on
him. He's such a schlimazl;* His
car is always breaking down on
him. He's such an unlucky
person.
‣ NOTE: A common explanation
of the difference between
"schlemiel" and *"schlimazl"* told
by Jews is that a *"schlemiel"* will
undoubtedly spill a bowl of soup
and the *"schlimazl"* is the one
that the soup is spilled on.

schlepp (to) *v.* **1.** to dawdle • *Hurry
up and quit schlepping!;* Hurry
up and quit dawdling! • **2.** to
carry something with a great deal
of effort • *I had to schlepp that*

huge box all the way down here!; I had to drag that huge box all the way down here!

schlock *n.* inferior merchandise • *You're actually gonna buy that schlock?;* You're actually going to buy that inferior merchandise?

schmaltz *n.* excessive melodrama • (lit); chicken fat • *That movie is so full of schmaltz!;* That movie is so full of melodrama!
‣ ALSO: **schmaltzy** *adj.* excessively melodramatic • *The movie is so schmaltzy!;* That movie is so melodramatic!

schmear *v.* related articles • *It doesn't sound like you're going to have time to do your laundry before you leave on your trip. Just bring the whole schmear over here and I'll do it for you;* It doesn't sound like you're going to have time to do your laundry before you leave on your trip. Just bring all your laundry over here and I'll do it for you.

schmo *n.* jerk, fool • *You actually like that schmo?;* You actually like that jerk?

schmooze (to) *v.* to converse with someone without genuine interest as a way to gain that person's

esteem • *Bob's schmoozing with the boss again;* Bob's conversing with the boss again to gain his esteem (in the hopes of a promotion).

schmuck *n.* jerk • (lit); penis • *That guy's such a schmuck!;* That guy's such a jerk!

schnook *n.* a gullible person • *He believes everything you tell him. What a schnook!;* He believes everything you tell him. What a gullible person!

schtick *n.* **1.** an actor's overdone performing routine • *I don't like that actor's schtick;* I don't like that actor's overdone performing routine. • **2.** an actor's performing routine in general • *That was such a funny schtick!;* That was such a funny routine!
‣ ALSO: **schticky** *adj.* said of a theatrical routine that is excessively physical in order to get laughs • *Charlie Chaplin was very schticky but it was always funny;* Charlie Chaplin was very physical in his theatrical routines but it was always funny.

tchotchke *n.* object in general • *Did you see all the tchotchkes she has in her house?;* Did you see all the objects she has in her house?

Slang Used in T.V. Sports News

– *The Sports Broadcast* –

"...After two **running plays** that got **stuffed**,
Burke threw a **bullet** to his **wide receiver**
on a **crossing pattern** for the touchdown!"

Dialogue In Slang

The Sports Broadcast

The sports anchor is reporting the news.

In the **top of the seventh** with the score **knotted** at zero, the Tigers' **ace hurler**, Smith, **walked** two batters and yielded an **infield hit to load the bases**. The next batter **worked Smith to a full count** and **drove a three-two fastball** into the **cheap seats** in **deep left center** for a **grand slam**. This led to a 4 to **zip** Dragon lead.

In football, after **hitting** his **wide receiver** on a neat **sideline route** for 35 yards, Burke **faked a handoff** for a **draw play**. This resulted in a 15 yard gain. After two **running plays** that got **stuffed**, he threw a **bullet** to his wide receiver on a **crossing pattern** for the touchdown. The **PAT** made the score 13 to 6.

What a **barnburner** today in basketball! At first, the game looked like a **wash,** but Jones created a **turnover** after a **steal** in the far court. He was **fouled** on the **lay-up** and made the **freethrow** to **cut the lead** to 11. After a missed shot, Smith **pulled down the rebound**, **dribbled** past **half court** and threw the **alley-oop** to Taylor for the **jam**. These guys can really **shoot hoop**!

Lesson Five - SLANG USED IN T.V. SPORTS NEWS

Translation of dialogue in standard English

The Sports Broadcast

The sports anchor is reporting the news.

In the **first part of the seventh inning** with the score **tied** at zero, the Tigers' **best pitcher**, Smith, allowed two players **to advance to first base** and yielded **a ball that was hit inside the diamond-shaped playing area** which put one **player on each base**. The next batter made Smith **pitch the ball in such a way that the next throw would result in the batter either advancing or forfeiting his turn**. (He then) **propelled the ball** toward the **cheaper seats where the view is minimal** for **the perfect hit which allowed each man on base to score a point** for the touchdown. This led to a 4 to **zero** lead by the Dragon team.

In football, after throwing the ball to **the player who receives passes and getting 35 yards closer to the goal**, Burke **pretended to give the ball to another player** in order **to dupe the others into thinking that someone else had it**. This resulted in **the team getting closer to the goal by 15 yards**. After two **attempts were made to advance the football toward the goal** that got **prevented by the other team**, he threw a **very fast pass** to the **receiving player** while he was **running diagonally from one side of the field to the other**. The **additional point after touchdown made by kicking the ball over the goal** made the score 13 to 6.

What an **exciting and close game** today in basketball! At first, the game looked like a **one-sided game**, but Jones **took the ball away from the other team** after an **act of illegally knocking the ball away from the opponent**. He was **charged with an illegal play** while trying **to score a point** and **successfully threw the ball in the basket** to **change the direction of the game** and **reduced the lead** by 11 points. After a **missed try for the goal**, Smith **seized the ball that bounced off the backboard**, **bounced the ball with successive taps of one hand** past the **half-way point of the court** and threw the **ball high in the air** to Taylor who **successfully and forcefully put the ball through the basketball hoop**. These guys can really **play basketball!**

Lesson Five - SLANG USED IN T.V. SPORTS NEWS

Dialogue in slang as it would be heard

The Sports Broadcast

The sports anchor is reporting the news.

In the **top 'a the seventh** with the score **knodded** at zero, the Tigers' **ace hurler**, Smith, **wakt** two badders n' yielded 'n **infield hit ta load the bases**. The next badder **workt Smith to a full count** 'n **drove a three-two fastball** inta the **cheap seats** 'n **deep left cenner** fer a **gran' slam**. This led to a 4 da **zip** Dragon lead.

In football, after **hidding** his **wide receiver** on a neat **sideline route** fer 35 yards, Burke **fakt a handoff** fer a **draw play**. This resulted in a 15 yard gain. After two **running plays** that got **stuft**, he threw a **bullet** to 'is wide receiver on a **crossing paddern** fer the touchdown. The **PAT** made the score 13 ta 6.

Whad a **barnburner** t'day in basketball! At first, the game lookt like a **wash**, but Jones creaded a **turnover** after a **steal** in the far court. He was **fouled** on the **lay-up** 'n made the **freethrow** ta **cut the lead** ta 11. After a misst shot, Smith **pulled down the rebound, dribbled** past **half court** and threw the **alley-oop** ta Taylor fer the **jam**. These guys c'n really **shoot hoop**!

Vocabulary

ace hurler *n.* (baseball) the best pitcher • *Jones is our ace hurler;* Jones is our best pitcher.
> ⯈ ALSO: **ace** *n.* an outstanding player (used by all sports) • *Have you ever seen her play tennis? She's a real ace!;* Have you ever seen her play tennis? She's an outstanding player!

alley-oop *n.* (basketball) a shot made whereby a player jumps up next to the basket, catches a pass from another player at the height of the jump, and then stuffs the ball in the basket before hitting the ground • *Magic Johnson was famous for his alley-oop shots;* Magic Johnson was famous for catching passes while in mid air and stuffing the ball in the basket.

barnburner *n.* (used by all sports) an exciting game • *What a barnburner! That was the best soccer game I've ever seen!;* What an exciting game! That was the best soccer game I've ever seen!

bullet *n.* (football) an extremely fast pass • *Did you see the bullet he threw? I could hardly follow it!;* Did you see the fast pass he threw? I could hardly follow it!

cheap seats *exp.* (baseball) the least desirable seats in the ball park located at the other end of the ball park where the view is poor • *I couldn't believe how far the batter hit the ball. It went all the way into the cheap seats!;* I couldn't believe how far the batter hit the ball. It went all the way into the seats at the other end of the ball park!

crossing pattern *exp.* (football) a strategy whereby the receiver of the ball runs diagonally from one side of the field to the other in an effort to evade the other team's defenders while trying to approach the goal • *The only way he's gonna be able to avoid getting stopped by the other team is to perform a crossing pattern;* The only way he's going to be able to avoid getting stopped by the other team is to run diagonally from one side of the field to the other.

cut the lead (to) *exp.* (used in all sports) to reduce the difference in scores late in the game • *With moments left in the game, the losing team suddenly* *cut the lead;* With moments left in the game, the losing team suddenly reduced the lead.

deep left center *n.* (baseball) the portion of the ball park between left and center field. This part of the playing field is often called *"the power alleys"* since a ball hit in these poorly guarded areas is not likely to be retrieved quickly • *Look who's coming up to bat! We'd better cover deep left center since he always aims for the power alleys!;* Look who's coming up to bat! We'd better cover the area between left and center field since he always aims for this part of the playing field!

draw play *exp.* (football) a strategy whereby a player pretends to hand off the ball to another player in order to divert the other team. This *"draws"* the defenders toward the wrong player while the player who actually has the ball runs freely toward the goal • *That draw play was executed perfectly!;* That fake handoff was executed perfectly!

drive a three-two fastball (to) *exp.* (baseball) to hit a fast pitch thrown to the batter when he has three balls and two strikes against him.
  ▶ NOTE (1): **drive (to)** *v.* to project a ball with great force.
  ▶ NOTE (2): Once the batter has missed three balls that were legally thrown from the pitcher (*"strikes"*), the batter loses his turn. If the batter misses four balls that were illegally or incorrectly thrown from the pitcher (*"balls"*), the batter is allowed to advance freely to first base. When the batter has three balls and two strikes against him, this is called a *"full count."* This is a crucial moment in the game since the next pitch is especially important; one more ball, the batter advances — one more strike, the batter is *"out."*

fake a handoff (to) *exp.* (football) to pretend to pass the ball in order to dupe the other players into thinking that another player has the ball. This technique enables the player with the ball to run freely toward the goal • *Did you see how he just faked a handoff to the other player?;* Did you see how he just pretended to give the ball to the other player?
  ▶ SEE: **draw play** *exp.*

foul (to) *v.* (used in all sports) to commit a violation against another player • *Thompson fouled his opponent by pushing him;* Thompson committed a violation against his opponent by pushing him.

freethrow *n.* (basketball) an unobstructed toss at the basket, made from a specific line, awarded a team due to a foul being committed by the opposing side • *Our team won because we were awarded two freethrows;* Our team won because we were awarded two unobstructed tosses at the basket because the other side committed fouls against us.

grand slam *exp.* (baseball) a home run with three runners on base, resulting in four home runs • *He hit a grand slam!;* He hit a home run with a player on each base!
▶ SEE: **load the bases (to)** *exp.*
▶ ALSO: **grand slam home run** *exp.*
▶ VARIATION: **grand slammer** *exp.*

half court *n.* (basketball) the halfway point on a basketball court • *He made a shot into the basket all the way from half court!;* He threw the ball into the basket all the way from the halfway point on the basketball court!

hit (to) *v.* (football) to complete a pass to a receiver • *Although he got tackled in the process, Hirsch managed to hit his receiver;* Although he got tackled in the process, Hirsch managed to complete a pass to his receiver.

infield hit *exp.* (baseball) a hit made by a batter where the ball does not leave the part of the field enclosed by the three bases and home plate, also referred to as the *"diamond"* • *He made a clean infield hit and got to first base;* He made a perfect hit inside the diamond-shaped playing field and got to first base.

jam *n.* (basketball) the act of pushing or *"dunking"* the ball through the hoop • *With seconds to spare, Olson made the jam!;* With seconds to spare, Olson pushed the ball through the hoop!
▶ ALSO: **to jam** *v.* to push or *"dunk"* the ball through the hoop.

knotted (to be) *v.* (used in all sports) to be tied (said of the score) • *The score's been knotted for the past half hour!;* The score has been tied for the past half hour!

lay-up *n.* (basketball) the act of dribbling the ball toward the goal, bringing the ball up with one hand and gently placing the ball either directly in the basket or off the backboard into the basket.
▶ VARIATION: **lay-in** *n.*

load the bases (to) *exp.* (baseball) to successfully get a player on each base • *The bases are loaded. If he hits a home run now, they'll get four runs and win!;* Each base has a player on it. If he hits a home run now, they'll get four points and win!

♦ NOTE: **run** *n.* a point made by a player who has successfully run around the entire diamond, hitting all three bases and home plate.

PAT *exp.* (football) an abbreviation for *"point after touchdown"* which refers to a team's chance to get another point by kicking the ball over the goalpost • *The PAT brought the score up to 15 to 13;* The extra point made by kicking the ball over the goalpost brought the score up to 15 to 13.

pull down the rebound (to) *exp.* (basketball) to seize a missed ball that has bounced off the backboard or the basket • *Robinson pulled down the rebound and ended up scoring two points for his side!;* Robinson seized the ball from the other team as it bounced off the backboard and ended up scoring two points for his side!

running play *exp.* (football) a play where an attempt is made to advance the football toward the goal by running with it as opposed to passing it through the air • *He tried twice to make a running play but he kept getting tackled;* He tried twice to run with the ball but he kept getting tackled.

shoot [some] hoop (to) *exp.* (basketball) to play basketball (since the goal of the game is to shoot the ball through the hoop) • *Wanna come over and shoot [some] hoop today?;* Do you want to come over and play some basketball today?

♦ VARIATION: **to shoot some hoops** *exp.*

sideline route *n.* (football) a common route taken by a receiver as he runs with the football along the edge of the field as opposed to running down the middle of the field.

steal *n.* (basketball) the act of snatching the ball away from another player.

♦ ALSO: **to steal** *v.* to snatch the ball away from another player • *Just as Adams was about to shoot, Beaver stole the ball;* Just as Adams was about to throw the ball into the basket, Beaver snatched the ball away.

stuffed (to get) *exp.* (football) to halt a play by the opposing team preventing the ball from advancing • *The receiver tried running with the ball but kept getting stuffed;* The receiver tried running with the ball but kept getting halted.

top of the seventh *exp.* (baseball) the first part of the seventh inning.

♦ ANTONYM: **bottom of the seventh** *exp.* the second part of the seventh inning.

♦ NOTE: Baseball games are divided into nine innings. Each inning is then separated into two parts; the first part or *"top"* where one team is allowed to bat and the second part or *"bottom"* where the opposing team gets a chance at bat. Both expressions *"top of the..."* and *"bottom of the..."* can be used with any inning.

turnover *n.* (basketball) the act of a team losing possession of the ball • *Just as the team was going to score, there was an unexpected turnover;* Just as the team was going to score, they unexpectedly lost possession of the ball.

♦ ALSO: **to turnover** *v.* to lose possession of the ball.

walk (to) *v.* (baseball) to be allowed to walk freely to the next base due to four unsatisfactory balls being thrown by the pitcher • *Since the bases are loaded, if the next batter gets to walk, the team will score one more run;* Since there is a player on each base, if the next batter gets to walk freely to the next base due to four unsatisfactory balls being thrown by the pitcher, the team will score one more point.

wash *n.* (used in all sports) a one-sided game • *Let's leave. This game looks like it's gonna be a wash;* Let's leave. This game looks like it's going to be one-sided.

♦ VARIATION: **washout** *n.* • **1.** a boring game • **2.** rained out • *We got washed out today;* We were unable to play today due to rain.

wide receiver *n.* (football) a player who generally runs down the field with the intention of receiving passes • *In order to be a wide receiver, you have to be fast!;* In order to be the player who receives passes while running down the field, you have to be fast!

work a pitcher to a full count (to) *exp.* (baseball) said of a batter who has received three balls and two strikes from the pitcher. The next throw from the pitcher is now critical in determining whether or not the batter will be allowed to walk to the next base or be eliminated.

zip *n.* (used in all sports) zero • *The score is 3 to zip;* The score is 3 to zero.

PRACTICE THE VOCABULARY

[Answers to Lesson Five, p. 213]

A. Choose the slang equivalent of the italicized word(s) in the left column by filling in the box with the corresponding letter.

☐ 1. What *an exciting game* yesterday!

☐ 2. Did you see the *fast pass* he threw?

☐ 3. That guy over there is their *best pitcher.*

☐ 4. The score is *tied.*

☐ 5. That basketball player *snatched* the ball from the other player.

☐ 6. Wanna *play basketball?*

☐ 7. This game is *one-sided.*

☐ 8. The score is three to *zero.*

☐ 9. The batter hit a *home run with a runner on each base.*

☐ 10. The football player *pretended to pass the ball to another player.*

☐ 11. We're in the *first part* of the third inning.

☐ 12. Johnson *seized the ball as it bounced off the backboard.*

A. **shoot some hoop**

B. **knotted**

C. **stole**

D. **a barnburner**

E. **a wash**

F. **zip**

G. **grand slam**

H. **bullet**

I. **pulled down the rebound**

J. **top**

K. **faked a handoff**

L. **ace hurler**

B. **Fill in the blanks by choosing the appropriate word(s) from the list below.**

hit	jam	load
draw	fouled	freethrow
alley-oop	barnburner	cut
stuffed	turnover	count

1. **work a pitcher to a full** _____**(to)** *exp.* (baseball) said of a batter who has received three balls and two strikes from the pitcher.

2. _____ **(to)** *v.* (football) to complete a pass to a receiver.

3. _____ *n.* (basketball) the act of a team losing possession of the ball.

4. _____ *n.* (basketball) the act of pushing or "*dunking*" the ball through the hoop.

5. _____ **(to get)** *exp.* (football) to halt a play by the opposing team preventing the ball from advancing.

6. _____ **the bases (to)** *exp.* (baseball) to successfully get a player on each base.

7. _____ **play** *exp.* (football) a strategy whereby a player pretends to handoff the ball to another player in order to divert the other team.

8. _____ *n.* (basketball) an unobstructed toss at the basket made from a specific line awarded a team due to a foul being committed by the opposing side.

9. _____ **(to be)** *v.* (used in all sports) to have a violation committed against oneself.

10. _____ *n.* (used by all sports) an exciting game.

11. _____ *n.* (basketball) a shot made whereby a player jumps in the air next to the basket, catches a pass from another player at the height of the jump, and then stuffs the ball in the basket before hitting the ground.

12. _____ **the lead (to)** *exp.* (used in all sports) to reduce the difference in score late in the game.

C. Find and circle the word from exercise B in the scoreboard below.

hit	jam	load
draw	fouled	freethrow
alley-oop	barnburner	cut
stuffed	turnover	count

F	R	E	E	T	H	R	O	W	W
J	D	R	A	W	C	U	T	F	H
A	F	O	U	L	E	D	F	F	I
M	L	O	A	D	C	O	U	N	T
F	Y	S	T	U	F	F	E	D	F
A	L	L	E	Y	O	O	P	F	F
B	A	R	N	B	U	R	N	E	R
F	F	T	U	R	N	O	V	E	R

A CLOSER LOOK:
Popular Words and Expressions Taken from Sports

Since sports are such a large part of the American culture, it's no wonder they have generated an array of colorful expressions. Interestingly enough, although the following list comes from baseball, football, basketball, and more, these expressions are commonly used outside of sports as well.

ball park figure *exp.* estimate • *"How much do you think they'll charge me for this car?" "I can only give you a ball park figure;"* "How much do you think they'll charge me for this car?" "I can only give you an estimate."

batting a thousand (to be) *exp.* to be extremely successful • *Every client you approach wants to sign a contract with you! You're really batting a thousand!;* Every client you approach wants to sign a contract with you! You're really successful!
◆ ORIGIN: Said of a baseball player with an excellent batting average.

call foul (to) *exp.* to expose someone's questionable methods • *His methods are highly questionable. I'm calling foul!;* His methods are highly questionable. I'm exposing them!
◆ ORIGIN: The exclamation *"Foul!"* is used by a team when

illegal methods are detected by the opposing team.

call time out (to) *exp.* to stop all action • *I really enjoy exercising with you right now, but time out! I need to catch my breath!;* I really enjoy exercising with you right now, but stop everything! I need to catch my breath!
◆ ORIGIN: When the exclamation *"Time out!"* is called by a coach, the clock stops in order that a quick consultation with the team may be held. Upon its completion, *"Time in!"* is called.

come out of left field (to) *exp.* •(lit); said of a player whose position is to cover the far left field of the baseball diamond • **1.** said of a statement which has nothing to do with the subject at hand • *"Now, let's continue with this math problem." "By the way. What do you think of Janet?" "Well, that came out of left field!";* "Now, let's continue with this math problem." "By the way. What do you think of Janet?" "Well, that certainly has nothing to do with the subject at hand!" • **2.** said of a negative statement which suddenly changes the mood of a conversation and consequently causes great surprise • *"I really had a great time with you and Mark yesterday." "I can't stand Mark!" "Well, that came out of left field!"*; "I really had a great time with you and Mark yesterday." "I dislike Mark intensely!" "Well, I'm sure surprised to hear you say that!" • **3.** to be far from being correct • *Did you hear the answer she gave the teacher? She was really out in left field!*; Did you hear the answer she gave the teacher? She was really far from being correct! ▶ ORIGIN: Said of baseball which uses a playing ground divided into fields.

dirty pool *exp.* corrupt methods (used to obtain a goal) • *He said he'd lie to my boss about me in order to get me fired if I don't give him what he wants. That's really dirty pool;* He said he'd lie to my boss about me in order to get me fired if I don't give him what he wants. Those are corrupt methods to get what he wants. ▶ ORIGIN: Said of the game of pool where one of the contestants is a swindler.

even up the score (to) *exp.* to counter someone's advance with

an equal advance of one's own • *When my little brother hit me, I evened up the score by hitting him back;* When my little brother hit me, I countered by hitting him back.

field a call (to) *exp.* to intercept a telephone call • *Want me to field that call for you?;* Do you want me to intercept that telephone call for you? ▶ NOTE: This is a play on words of the expression *"to field a ball"* meaning "to intercept the ball."

get to first base (to) *exp.* to get to the first step in having sex which is kissing • *I got to first base with her last night;* I kissed her last night. ▶ NOTE (1): **to get to second base** *exp.* to be sexually physical while clothed. ▶ NOTE (2): **to get to third base** *exp.* to be sexually physical while unclothed. ▶ NOTE (3): **to get to home base** *exp.* to have sexual intercourse. ▶ ORIGIN: baseball.

go to bat for someone (to) *exp.* to support someone • (lit); to substitute an average batter with a superior batter in order to help the winning effort • *No one believed that I was telling the truth so Cecily went to bat for me;* No one believed that I was telling the truth so Cecily supported me (by trying to convince everyone that I wasn't

lying).
♦ ORIGIN: baseball.

good sport (to be a) *exp.* to be an agreeable person who is lighthearted about potentially negative situations • (lit); said of a sportsman who always plays by the rules and is congenial even about losing • *You were a good sport about driving my friend home even though he lives an hour away;* You were very nice about driving my friend home even though he lives an hour away.

heavyweight (to be a) *exp.* • **1.** to be an important and powerful person • (lit); to be a boxer whose weight puts him in the heavyweight category • *When he tells the employees to do something, they listen. He's a real heavyweight;* When he tells the employees to do something, they listen. He's a very important and powerful person. • **2.** said of a person with an extremely high tolerance for alcohol • *Did you see how much she drank? She's a real heavyweight!;* Did you see how much she drank? She's got a really high tolerance for alcohol!
♦ ANTONYM: **to be a lightweight** *exp.* • **1.** to be least important on the job hierarchy • (lit); to be a boxer whose weight puts him in the lightweight category • *Don't let him tell you what to do. He's just a lightweight around here;*

Don't let him tell you what to do. He has a lower position around here. • **2.** said of a person with an extremely low tolerance for alcohol • *He drank half a glass of wine and fainted. He's such a lightweight!;* He drank half a glass of wine and fainted. He's got such a low tolerance for alcohol!
♦ ORIGIN: boxing.

hit a home run (to) *exp.* to succeed at achieving a goal • (lit); to achieve the ultimate goal in baseball by hitting the ball so far the player is able to run around the baseball diamond and score a point • *Welcome to the sales meeting. I'm proud to announce that this year, we really hit a home run!;* Welcome to the sales meeting. I'm proud to announce that this year, we really achieved our goal!
♦ NOTE: The term *"homer"* is a popular abbreviation for "home run." For example: *We really hit a homer!*
♦ ORIGIN: baseball.

"It's back to the ol' ball game" *exp.* " "It's back to the original plan" • (lit); said by a baseball player who returns back to the game after a short break • *We've tried every possible plan but none of them works as well as the first one. I guess it's back to the ol' ball game;* We've tried every possible plan but none of them

works as well as the first one. I
guess we'd better go back to the
original plan.

jockey for position (to) *exp.* to
maneuver for an advantage •
*We'll have to jockey for position
if we want to get a good contract;*
We'll have to maneuver for an
advantage if we want to get a
good contract.
  ORIGIN: horse-racing.

kick off something (to) *exp.* to start
an event • (lit); to start a soccer
or football game • *We're going to
kick off the show with a few
songs;* We're going to start the
show with a few songs.
  ORIGIN: soccer/football.

make a pit stop (to) *exp.* to deviate
from one's routine in order to go
to the bathroom • (lit); said of a
race car driver who leaves the
competition momentarily by
driving into the pit where repairs
are rapidly done to the car • *I'll
be right back. I have to go make a
pit stop;* I'll be right back. I have
to go to the bathroom.
  ORIGIN: car racing.

neck and neck (to be) *exp.* to be
even in a contest • (lit); said of
horses in a race who are even
with one another • *The two
candidates are neck and neck.
This election is going to be
close!;* The two candidates are
running totally even. This

election is going to be close!
  ORIGIN: horse races.

off base (to be) *exp.* to be wrong •
(lit); said of a baseball player
who is not on a base and is
therefore vulnerable to being
tagged • *Your answer isn't
correct. You're way off base;*
Your answer isn't correct. You're
completely wrong.
  ORIGIN: baseball.

pinch hit (to) *exp.* to take
someone's place • (lit); said of a
baseball player who takes over
for another player at bat (usually
because he is a superior batter
and it is at a crucial point in the
game) • *Can you pinch hit at the
meeting for me? I have to leave
town suddenly;* Can you
substitute for me at the meeting?
I have to leave town suddenly.
  NOTE: **pinch hitter** *n.* one who
takes over for another person •
(lit); a baseball player who takes
over for another player at bat.
  ORIGIN: baseball.

pitch one's ideas (to) *exp.* to
present one's concepts about
something one after the other
(like a baseball pitcher who
throws one ball after the other) •
*Tomorrow I'm going to pitch my
movie ideas to some big
Hollywood producers!;*
Tomorrow I'm going to present
my concepts to some big
Hollywood producers!
  VARIATION: **to make a pitch**

exp.
‣ ORIGIN: baseball.

right off the bat (to be) *exp.* from the very beginning • (lit); said of a baseball that is hit with full force after the first pitch • *I liked him right off the bat;* I liked him immediately.
‣ ORIGIN: baseball.

right out of the chute (to be) *exp.* brand new • (lit); said of a horse who dashes out of the starting chute at a race • *Don't give him too many responsibilities right away. He's right out of the chute and may need to get some more experience first;* Don't give him too many responsibilities right away. He's brand new and may need to get some more experience first.
‣ ORIGIN: horse racing.

score big (to) *exp.* to earn one's high esteem • *You sure scored big with the boss today!;* You sure earned the boss's esteem today!
‣ ORIGIN: sports in general.

settle a score with someone (to) *exp.* to resolve a problem with someone • *I'm going to settle the score with him right now!;* I'm going to resolve this problem with him right now!
‣ VARIATION: **to have a score to settle with someone** *exp.* • *I have a score to settle with him;* I

have a problem to resolve with him.

strike out (to) *exp.* to be defeated • (lit); said of a baseball player at bat who misses the ball three times *(three "strikes")* and loses his turn • *I tried to go up and talk to her but she wasn't interested in me. I really struck out;* I tried to go up and talk to her but she wasn't interested in me. I really got defeated.
‣ ORIGIN: baseball.

tackle a problem (to) *exp.* to attack a problem with full force (as a football player "tackles" another player) • *I know we can tackle this problem together;* I know we can attack this problem with full force together.
‣ ORIGIN: football.

take the wind out of one's sails (to) *exp.* to lose one's momentum due to discouragement • (lit); said of a sailboat that loses momentum due to lack of wind in its sails • *I was so excited about my new job until I found out that I was only going to be paid half my normal salary. That took the wind out of my sails;* I was so excited about my new job until I found out that I was only going to be paid half my normal salary. That made me lose my momentum because I got so discouraged.
‣ ORIGIN: sailing.

"The ball's in your court" *exp.*
"It's up to you to make the next move" • (lit); said to a tennis player whose ball landed on his/her side of the court and must therefore make the next move • *I know you're angry and don't want to talk to me, but I'm willing to reconcile. The ball's in your court;* I know you're angry and don't want to talk to me, but I'm willing to reconcile. It's up to you to make the next move.
♦ ORIGIN: tennis.

throw someone a curve [ball] (to)
exp. to deceive someone unexpectedly • (lit); said of a baseball pitcher who throws a ball whose direction is curved • *I can't believe I trusted him. He really threw me a curve;* I can't believe I trusted him. He really deceived me unexpectedly.

whole new ball game (to be a)
exp. to be an entirely different situation • *"I'm glad we've finally agreed on which movie we're going to go see. Now suppose we invite Bob?" "Wait! That's a whole new ball game!";* "I'm glad we've finally agreed on which movie we're going to go see. Now suppose we invite Bob?" "Wait! That's an entirely different matter!"

Slang Used in T.V. Weather News

– The Weather Report –

Dialogue In Slang

The Weather Report

MONOLOGUE

The weather anchor is reporting the news.

Anchor: The **ridge** that **moved in** gave us a real **scorcher** today with the **mercury** soaring to record highs but the **heat wave** is just about over. Many people forget to take precautions when **soaking up the rays** and end up getting **burnt to a crisp**, so do be careful. **On the flip side**, that **high** will be followed closely by a **trough** and we should have some colder weather **on tap** in just a few days. It could be pretty **nasty** out there for about a week. In fact, we're **calling for** a big storm which should be a real **doozie**, so make sure to **batten down the hatches** as this system **rolls in**. The danger of any **twisters** has completely passed although winds should **kick up** slightly around noon. Earlier, we thought it was going to **rain buckets** in the mountains but now we're predicting some snow flurries which should change that **hard pack** to **powder** ideal for skiing.

Translation of dialogue in standard English

The Weather Report

MONOLOGUE

The weather anchor is reporting the news.

Anchor: The **high pressure area** that **arrived** gave us a very **hot day** today with the **temperature** soaring to record highs but the **continuous hot weather** is just about over. Many people forget to take precautions when **sunbathing** and end up getting **sunburned**, so do be careful. **Conversely**, that **high pressure area** will be followed closely by a **low pressure area** and we should have some colder weather **here** in just a few days. It could be pretty **severe** out there for about a week. In fact, we're **predicting** a large storm which should be extremely **forceful** so make sure to **secure your homes** as this system **approaches**. The danger of any **tornados** has completely passed although winds should **become slightly active** around noon. Earlier, we thought it was going to **rain heavily** in the mountains but now we're predicting some snow flurries which should change that **packed snow** to **powdered snow** ideal for skiing.

Dialogue in slang as it would be heard

The Weather Report

MONOLOGUE

The weather anchor is reporting the news.

Anchor: The **ridge** that **moved in** gave us a real **scorcher** t'day with the **mercury** soaring ta record highs but the **heat wave** is just aboud over. Many people ferget ta take precautions when **soaking up the rays** 'n end up getting **burnt to a crisp**, so do be careful. **On the flip side**, that **high**'ll be followed closely by a **trough** and we should have s'm colder weather **on tap** 'n just a few days. It could be preddy **nasty** out there fer about a week. In fact, we're **calling for** a big storm which should be a real **doozie**, so make sher da **batten down the hatches** as this system **rolls in**. The danger of any **twisters** has completely passed although wins should **kick up** slightly aroun' noon. Earlier, we thawd it was gonna **rain buckets** 'n the mountains but now we're predicting s'm snow flurries which should change that **hard pack** ta **powder** ideal fer skiing.

Vocabulary

batten down the hatches (to) *exp.* to secure one's home by making it watertight • (lit); (nautical expression) to make the hatch of a ship watertight by sealing it with a wooden plank or batten • *Batten down the hatches! We have rough seas ahead!;* Make the hatch watertight! We have rough seas ahead!

burnt/burned to a crisp (to get) *exp.* to get extremely sunburned • *Make sure to cover yourself or you're gonna get burnt/burned to a crisp;* Make sure to cover yourself or you're going to get extremely burnt/burned by the sun's rays.
▸ NOTE: The past tense of the verb *"to burn"* is "burnt" and "burned."
▸ SYNONYM: **to get fried** *exp.*

call for (to) *exp.* to predict • *The weather report is calling for rain today;* The weather report is predicting rain today.
▸ NOTE: This expression is used primarily in reference to the weather.

doozie (to be a) *adj.* to be impressive • *Did you see the black eye he got? What a doozie!;* Did you see the black eye he got? It's impressive!
▸ NOTE: This adjective comes from one of the most admired cars of the mid 1920's; the *"Deusenberg."*
▸ SYNONYM: **humdinger** *n.*

hard pack *n.* snow that has been packed down due to traffic • *I don't like skiing on hard pack because I have trouble stopping!;* I don't like skiing on snow that's packed down because I have trouble stopping!

heat wave *n.* continuous high temperatures • *We're having a heat wave in the middle of the winter!;* We're having continuous high temperatures in the middle of the winter!

high *exp.* • high pressure area in the atmosphere which results in clear skies • *There's been a high sitting over the city for the past week which is why the weather's been so beautiful;* There's been a high pressure area in the atmosphere sitting over the city for the past week which is why the weather has been so beautiful.

kick up (to) *exp.* (said of wind, dust, pollen, etc.) to begin to blow around in the air • *The dust is really kicking up all of a sudden;* The dust is really blowing around suddenly.

mercury *n.* temperature • (lit); the metallic liquid in thermometers which rises in hot temperatures and drops in cold temperatures • *Where's the mercury today?;* What's the temperature today? • *The mercury's rising;* The temperature's rising.

move in (to) *exp.* **1.** to approach • We better get home. The clouds are really moving in fast!; We had better get home. The clouds are really approaching fast! • **2.** to relocate to a new home • *When are you planning on moving in?;* When are you planning on relocating to your new home?
   ▸ NOTE: In the first sentence, *We better get home,* the verb "to have" is purposely missing: *We **had** better get home.* Although incorrect in standard English, it is extremely common in colloquial speech to omit "had" before "better."

nasty (to be) *adj.* said of severe weather • (lit); to be extremely unpleasant • *Have you ever seen such nasty weather?;* Have you ever seen such unpleasant weather?

on tap (to be) *exp.* to be pending • (lit); (bar slang) said of various beverages (beer, sodas, etc.) which are discharged through spigots on the bar • *We have good weather on tap for tomorrow;* We have good weather pending for tomorrow.

on the flip side *exp.* conversely • (lit); on the reverse side of the record • *If our plan succeeds, we could earn thousands of dollars. On the flip side, if we fail, we could lose everything;* If our plan succeeds, we could earn thousands of dollars. Conversely, if we fail, we could lose everything.

powder *n.* fresh light powdery snow • *Skiing on powder requires a different technique than skiing on hard pack;* Skiing on fresh light powdery snow requires a different technique than skiing on hard packed snow.

rain buckets (to) *exp.* to rain heavily • *It's really raining buckets outside today!;* It's really raining heavily outside today!
   ▸ SYNONYM: **to rain cats and dogs** *exp.*

ridge *n.* (meteorology term) a high pressure area characterized by clear skies • *We have clear skies today due to a ridge that's sitting above the city;* We have clear skies today due to a high pressure area that's sitting above the city.

roll in (to) *exp.* • **1.** to approach in a rolling motion • *Look at those clouds roll in;* Look at those clouds approach. • **2.** to arrive casually • *She rolled into work an hour late!;* She casually arrived at work an hour late!

scorcher *n.* an extremely hot day (which leaves everything scorched by the heat) • *It's a real scorcher today! I'm going swimming;* It's an extremely hot day today! I'm going swimming.

soak up the rays (to) *exp.* to sunbathe • (lit); to absorb the rays of the sun • *I'm gonna go lie by the pool and soak up the rays;* I'm going to go lie by the pool and absorb the rays of the sun.
  ‣ NOTE: As seen in lesson one, teens have modified this expression to: *"to bag some rays."*
  ‣ VARIATION (1): **to soak up some rays** *exp.*
  ‣ VARIATION (2): **to catch some rays** *exp.*

trough *n.* (meteorology term) a low pressure area characterized by cloudy skies or even rain • *We're going to have cloudy skies tomorrow due to a trough that's moving in from the west;* We're going to have cloudy skies tomorrow due to a low pressure area that's moving in from the west.

twister *n.* tornado • *The twister picked up our house and dropped it two blocks away!;* The tornado picked up our house and dropped it two blocks away!

PRACTICE THE VOCABULARY

[Answers to Lesson Six, p. 214]

A. Complete the sentences by choosing the appropriate word from the list below.

crisp	wave	kick
flip	buckets	tap
scorcher	rays	twister
nasty	roll	doozie

1. I got burnt to a _____ at the beach yesterday.

2. That _____ just picked that car up in the air! It's amazing how destructive wind can be.

3. It's been raining _____ all week.

4. I can't believe how hot it is today. What a _____ !

5. It's strange that we're having a heat _____ in the middle of the winter!

6. The wind is really starting to _____ up.

7. If I report the accident to my insurance company, they'll pay for the repairs. On the _____ side, my insurance rate will go up!

8. I'm gonna go lie outside and soak up some _____ .

9. The storm last night was a real _____ !

10. It's been rainy and cold here for over two weeks. We sure are experiencing some _____ weather here.

11. We have good weather on _____ for tomorrow.

12. Look at those rain clouds starting to _____ in.

B. Match the columns.

☐ 1. We're having continuous high temperatures today.

☐ 2. The weatherman is predicting rain this afternoon.

☐ 3. There's lots of good packed-down snow in the mountains ideal for skiing.

☐ 4. I got extremely sunburned at the beach today.

☐ 5. Seal the house tightly! This storm is going to be huge!

☐ 6. The storm is going to arrive around 3:00.

☐ 7. What severe weather!

A. **The weatherman is calling for rain this afternoon.**

B. **I wonder what kind of weather we have on tap for tomorrow.**

C. **I got burnt to a crisp at the beach today.**

D. **What nasty weather!**

E. **Did you see that twister?**

F. **A trough is going to pass over the city tomorrow.**

G. **The storm is gonna roll in around 3:00.**

☐ 8. It's still getting hotter today.

☐ 9. I wonder what kind of weather we have pending for tomorrow.

☐ 10. Did you see that tornado?

☐ 11. It's a real hot day!

☐ 12. A low pressure area is going to pass over the city tomorrow.

H. **Batten down the hatches! This storm is gonna be a doozie!**

I. **The mercury's still rising.**

J. **We're having a heat wave today.**

K. **It's a real scorcher!**

L. **There's lots of good hard pack in the mountains ideal for skiing.**

C. Underline the correct definition of the word(s) in boldface.

1. **to be on tap:**
   a. to be pending   b. to be in rhythm

2. **powder:**
   a. heavy rain   b. fresh light powdery snow

3. **to roll in:**
   a. to approach   b. to laugh loudly

4. **scorcher:**
   a. an extremely cold day   b. an extremely hot day

5. **twister:**
   a. snow storm   b. tornado

6. **trough:**
   a. high presure area   b. low pressure area

7. **to kick up:**
   a. to subside   b. to blow around

8. **to get burnt to a crisp:**
   a. to get extremely sunburned   b. to get reprimanded

9. **to call for:**
   a. to predict
   b. to deny

10. **to be a doozie:**
    a. to be extreme
    b. to be mild

11. **heat wave:**
    a. a warm greeting
    b. continuous high temperatures

12. **on the flip side:**
    a. conversely
    b. on one's back

D. FIND-THE-WORD-CUBE

Step 1:　Fill in the blanks with the correct word using the list below.

Step 2:　Find and circle the word in the grid on the opposite page. The first one has been done for you.

crisp	**call**	**tap**
ridge	**doozie**	**scorcher**
twister	**nasty**	**kick**
buckets	**wave**	**hatches**

1. I can't believe how hot it is outside! What a _____ !

2. It's been raining for an entire week. The weather sure has been _____ this season!

3. Yesterday at the beach, I got burnt to a _____ .

4. Wasn't that storm a _____ last night?

5. The wind from the _____ actually picked up his house!

6. Batten down the _____ ! We're going to have a huge storm tonight!

7. A _____ is passing over the city today which is why we have such nice weather.

8. The weatherman will probably _____ for rain again tomorrow.

9. I wonder if the winds are going to _____ up again tonight like they did last night.

10. We have good weather on _____ for tomorrow.

11. It's going to rain _____ today.

12. It's been so hot for three weeks! When is this heat _____ ever going to end?

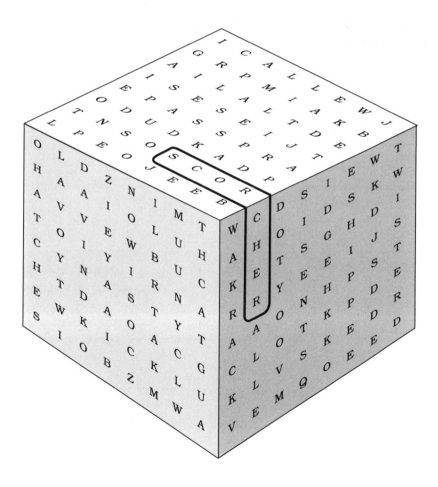

A CLOSER LOOK
Weather Terms Used in Slang Idioms

As demonstrated in the previous dialogue, there are many slang terms used when reporting the weather. In addition, there are many terms having to do with the weather that have given birth to a broad array of common slang expressions.

The following list includes idioms that have to do with the weather, as well as elements that have to do with the planet such as the earth, the moon, heaven, and hell.

You'll also notice that liberty was taken under the heading of *"Blow."* Since this verb is used to describe the wind *and* one's breath, the list contains expressions using *blow* in both senses.

Blow

blowhard *exp.* one who is quick to boast • *He's such a blowhard!;* He's always boasting!

blow hot and cold (to) *exp.* to be approachable one moment and unfriendly the next • *I can't understand him. He blows hot and cold;* I can't understand him. He's approachable one moment and unfriendly the next.

blow in *exp.* to arrive unexpectedly or nonchalantly • *When did you blow into town?;* When did you arrive in town?

blow off steam (to) *exp.* to vent one's frustration or anger • *Don't pay attention to what he says. He's just blowing off steam;* Don't pay attention to what he says. He's just venting his frustration.

blow one's brains out (to) *exp.* **1.** to commit suicide by shooting oneself in the head • *If I don't pass the test, I'm gonna blow my brains out!;* If I don't pass the test, I'm going to commit suicide! • **2.** to murder • *He blew his wife's brains out;* He murdered his wife.

blow one's cool (to) *exp.* to lose one's temper • *Don't blow your cool!;* Don't lose your temper!

blow one's cover (to) *exp.* to reveal one's true identity • *If I don't do what she wants, she threatened to blow my cover to the cops;* If I don't do what she wants, she threatened to reveal my true identity to the police.

blow one's mind (to) *exp.* • **1.** to become wildly ecstatic • *It blew my mind when I found out I won all that money!;* I became wildly ecstatic when I found out I won all that money! • **2.** to be overcome with emotion • *The news of her death blew my mind;* The news of her death overwhelmed me.

blow one's own horn (to) *exp.* to brag • *Every time I see him, he blows his own horn;* Every time I see him, he brags about himself. ‣ VARIATION: **to toot one's own horn** *exp.*

blow one's stack (to) *exp.* to lose one's temper • *She blew her stack when I told her the news;* She lost her temper when I told her the news.

blow one's top (to) *exp.* to lose one's temper • *You should have seen how my sister blew her top at me!;* You should have seen how my sister lost her temper with me!

blow over (to) *exp.* to subside (like a storm) • *I know she's mad at you now, but it'll blow over soon;* I know she's mad at you now but it'll subside soon.

blow someone away (to) *exp.* **1.** to kill someone • *He got himself blown away by the cops yesterday;* He got himself killed by the police yesterday. • **2.** to flabbergast • *The news of her* death just blew me away!; The news of her death shocked me!

blow something (to) *exp.* • **1.** to fail • *I blew the test;* I failed the test. • **2.** to make a huge mistake • *I forgot to pick her up at the airport today! I blew it;* I forgot to pick her up at the airport today! I made a huge mistake.

blow the lid off something (to) *exp.* to expose the truth about something • *The authorities just blew the lid off the scandal;* The authorities just exposed the truth about the scandal.

blow the whistle on someone (to) *exp.* to inform on someone • *I blew the whistle on her when I found out she was stealing from the company;* I informed on her when I found out she was stealing from the company.

blow up at someone (to) *exp.* to become suddenly furious at someone • *She blew up at me for no reason;* She became suddenly furious at me for no reason.

come to blows (to) *exp.* to fight physically or verbally • *They got so mad at each other that they came to blows!;* They go so mad at each other that they got into a fight!

Breeze

breeze (to be a) *adj.* to be easy •
This work is a breeze; This work
is easy.

breeze into a room (to) *exp.* to
enter a room (nonchalantly) • *She
breezed into the room unaware
that everyone was angry with
her;* She entered the room
nonchalantly, unaware that
everyone was angry with her.

shoot the breeze (to) *exp.* to chat •
*We stood in front of the house
shooting the breeze for an hour;*
We stood in front of the house
chatting for an hour.

Cloud

**"Behind every cloud is a silver
lining"** *exp.* "Behind every bad
situation is a good situation."

on cloud nine (to be) *exp.* to be
euphorically happy • *She's on
cloud nine now that she has a
boyfriend;* She's euphorically
happy now that she has a
boyfriend.

**walk around with a black cloud
over one's head (to)** *exp.* to live
every day in a state of gloom •
*Why do you always walk around
with a black cloud over your
head?;* Why do you live each day
in a state of gloom?

Earth

down-to-earth (to be) *exp.* to be
unpretentious and sincere • *I like
her 'cause she's so
down-to-earth;* I like her because
she's so unpretentious.

"What on earth!" *exclam.*
exclamation of great surprise •
*What on earth! That can't be
possible!*
➧ NOTE: This exclamation is not
as popular with the younger
generation. For a list of
exclamations and expletives used
by teens, refer to **Bleep! - *A
Guide to Popular American
Obscenities*** by David Burke.

Fog

foggiest (not to have the) *exp.* not
to have the slightest idea • *I don't
have the foggiest why he's in
such a bad mood;* I don't have
the slightest idea why he's in
such a bad mood.
➧ NOTE: This is a shortened
version of *"not to have the
foggiest idea."*

in a fog about something (to be)
exp. to be in a daze about
something • *I can't answer your
question. I'm in a fog;* I can't
answer your question. I'm in a
daze.

Heaven

"Good heavens!" *exclam.*
exclamation of surprise • *Good heavens! What happened to your car?*
◆ NOTE: This exclamation is not as popular with the younger generation.

heavenly (to be) *adj.* to be blissful • *Come in for a swim! The water in this river is heavenly!;* Come in for a swim! The water in this river is blissful.
◆ NOTE: This exclamation is not as popular with the younger generation.

"Heavens!" *exclam.* exclamation of surprise • *Heavens! Why are you so late?*
◆ NOTE: This exclamation is not as popular with the younger generation.

"Heavens to Betsy!" *exclam.*
exclamation of surprise •
Heavens to Betsy! Where are we?
◆ NOTE: This exclamation is not as popular with the younger generation.

in seventh heaven (to be) *exp.* to be in ecstasy • *She's been in seventh heaven ever since she met her new boyfriend;* She's been in ecstasy ever since she met her new boyfriend.

move heaven and earth (to) *exp.* to do everything in one's power in order to accomplish something •
I'll move heaven and earth in
order to attend her wedding; I'll do everything in my power in order to attend her wedding.

"My heavens!" *exclam.*
exclamation of surprise • *My heavens! Why are you all wet?*
◆ NOTE: This exclamation is not as popular with the younger generation.

Hell

◆ NOTE: The following expressions containing the noun *"hell"* should be used cautiously since this term is considered somewhat coarse, though not vulgar, when used in expressions.

as hell *exp.* to extreme • *I'm mad as hell!;* I'm extremely mad!

"Come hell or high water!" *exp.*
"No matter what happens!" • *I'm going to get a raise come hell or high water!;* I'm going to get a raise no matter what happens!

"Go to hell!" *exp.* a strong command aimed at a contemptuous person.

"Hell if I know!" *exp.* "I certainly don't know!"

"Hell, yes!" / **"Hell, no!"** *exclam.*
"Absolutely!" / "Absolutely not!"

"Like hell!" *exclam.* "That's absolutely incorrect! • *He thinks I actually like doing all this work? Like hell!;* He thinks I actually like doing all this work? That's absolutely incorrect!

through hell (to go) *exp.* to have great difficulty • *I went through hell finding just the car I wanted;* I had great difficulty finding just the car I wanted.

"What the hell" *exp.* **1.** (as a question) denotes annoyance and surprise • *What the hell?!;* What is that?! • **2.** (as a statement) denotes resignation • *I'm not going to let you use my car tonight! ...Oh, what the hell. You can use it but only for an hour!;* I'm not going to let you use my car tonight! ...Oh, all right. You can use it but only for an hour!

"When hell freezes over!" *exclam.* "Never!"

Moon

moon someone (to) *exp.* to expose one's buttocks to someone • *He mooned us as we drove by!;* He exposed his buttocks to us as we drove by!
  ♦ NOTE: This is a common college prank performed primarily by men to evoke a response from women.

once in a blue moon *exp.* very rarely • *Events like this happen only once in a blue moon;* Events like this happen rarely.

promise someone the moon (to) *exp.* to make someone all sorts of

unrealistic promises • *He'll promise you the moon in order to get what he wants;* He'll promise you anything in order to get what he wants.

Rain

know enough to come in out of the rain (not to) *exp.* to be hopelessly dumb • *He doesn't know enough to come in out of the rain;* He's hopelessly dumb.

rain cats and dogs (to) *exp.* to rain heavily • *It's raining cats and dogs outside!;* It's raining heavily outside!

rain on someone's parade (to) *exp.* to stifle someone's fun or moment of glory • *I was having so much fun before he arrived. Why does he always have to rain on my parade?;* I was having so much fun before he arrived. Why does he always have to stifle my fun?

save something for a rainy day (to) *exp.* to safeguard something until it is needed • *I know you don't need this money right now, but save it for a rainy day;* I know you don't need this money right now, but safeguard it until it is needed.

take a rain check (to) *exp.* to postpone • *Thank you for your invitation for dinner but I already have plans tonight. May I have a rain check?;* Thank you for your invitation for dinner but I already have plans tonight. May we do it another time?

"When it rains, it pours!" *exp.* "When significant events start to happen, they all occur at once!"

Snow

give someone a snow job (to) *exp.* to mislead someone • *I bought the car because I believed what the salesman said. Now I realize that he gave me a snow job!;* I bought the car because I believed what the salesman said. Now I realize that he misled me!
‣ ALSO: **to snow someone** *exp.* • *He really snowed you!;* He really misled you!

Storm

brainstorm *n.* fantastic idea • *I just got a brainstorm!;* I just got a fantastic idea!

eat up a storm (to) *exp.* to eat abundantly • *We ate up a storm at my mother's house;* We ate abundantly at my mother's house.

storm into a room (to) *exp.* to enter a room quickly and angrily • *You should have seen the way she stormed into the room!;* You should have seen the way she entered the room so quickly and angrily!

take something by storm (to) *exp.* to do something boldly with the

intent of attaining a goal quickly • *He took the entertainment industry by storm;* He succeeded quickly at penetrating the entertainment industry.

Thunder

thunder into a room (to) *exp.* to enter a room angrily and noisily • *He scared me the way he thundered into the room;* He scared me the way he entered the room so angrily and noisily.

thunder thighs *exp.* humorous expression for "fat thighs" • *I've gotta go to the gym. I'm getting thunder thighs;* I've got to go to the gym. I'm getting fat thighs.

Weather

fair-weather friend (to be a) *exp.* a friend who is faithful only when things are going well • *When I needed him the most, he turned out to be a fair-weather friend;* When I needed him the most, he turned out to be a friend who is only there when things are going well.

feel under the weather (to) *exp.* to feel sick • *I'm feeling under the weather;* I'm feeling sick.

Wind

break wind (to) *exp.* to have flatulence • *Who broke wind?;* Who had flatulence?

get a second wind (to) *exp.* to get a sudden burst of energy • *The runner got a second wind and won the race;* The runner got a sudden burst of energy and won the race.

get wind of something (to) *exp.* to discover some news • *I got wind that you're planning on leaving the company;* I discovered the news that you're planning on leaving the company.

get winded (to) *exp.* to get out of breath due to over exertion • *I got winded climbing up the stairs;* I got out of breath from climbing up the stairs.

knock the wind out of someone (to) *exp.* to engage in an activity that makes one unable to catch one's breath • *When he hit me, it knocked the wind right out of me;* When he hit me, I couldn't catch my breath. • *The long walk we took really knocked the wind out of me;* The long walk we took really made me lose my breath.

make a lot of wind (to) *exp.* to make a lot of fuss about nothing • *Don't mind him. He's just making a lot of wind;* Don't mind him. He's just making a lot of fuss about nothing.

whirlwind tour *exp.* quick trip to many locations in a short period of time • *We're doing a whirlwind tour of Europe;* We're taking a quick trip throughout Europe.

Slang Used in Traffic Reports

– The Traffic Report –

Dialogue In Slang

The Traffic Report

MONOLOGUE

The traffic anchor is reporting the news.

Anchor: It's a **tough row to hoe** out there today so let me **clue you in on** what's happening on the highways. Due to **rush hour**, traffic is **heavy** right now with a lot of **slow-and-go**. You may even find yourself at a **dead stop** as you **work your way down to** the commercial district. The **bunch-up** is due to the numerous **rubberneckers** gawking at the **tangle** between a **pickup** and a **big rig** on **I-5**. Both vehicles **spun out** and got into a **fender bender** but are now off on the right **shoulder**. Police will be arriving on the **scene** shortly so **heads up**. You should find yourselves moving at a quick **clip** once you leave the city as traffic starts **to break up**. You'll have a **clear shot** for a few miles then traffic will **pick up** again due to a **bottleneck** on the highway. We'll keep **tabs on** the traffic conditions for you every 20 minutes.

Translation of dialogue in standard English

A Traffic Report

MONOLOGUE

The traffic anchor is reporting the news.

Anchor: It's a **difficult job driving** out there today so let me **inform you about** what's happening on the highways. Due to **everyone leaving work at the same time**, traffic is **congested** right now with a lot of **braking and accelerating**. You may even find yourself at a **complete stop** as you **slowly approach** the commercial district. The **congestion** is due to the numerous **spectators** gawking at the **accident** between a **pickup truck** and a **big commercial truck** on **Interstate 5**. Both vehicles **lost control** and got into a **small accident** but are now off on the right **edge of the highway**. Police will soon be arriving **where the accident occurred** so **be alert**. You should find yourselves moving at a quick **pace** once you leave the city as traffic starts **to diminish**. You'll have an **unobstructed passage** for a few miles then traffic will **increase** again due to **merging lanes** on the highway. We'll keep **a close surveillance on** the traffic conditions for you every 20 minutes.

Dialogue in slang as it would be heard

A Traffic Report

MONOLOGUE

The traffic anchor is reporting the news.

Anchor: It's a **tough row da hoe** out there t'day so lemme **clue you in on** what's happ'ning on the highways. Du da **rush hour**, Traffic's **heavy** right now with a lot 'a **slow -'n-go**. You may even fin' djerself ad a **dead stop** as you **work yer way down ta** the commercial district. The **bunch-up** is due da the numerous **rubberneckers** gawking at the **tangle** b'tween a **pickup** 'n a **big rig** on **I-5**. Both vehicles **spun out** 'n god into a **fender bender** but 'r now off on the right **shoulder**. Police'll be arriving on the **scene** shortly so **heads up**. You should fin' djerselves moving ad a quick **clip** once you leave the cidy as traffic starts **ta break up**. You'll have a **clear shot** fer a few miles then traffic'll **pick up** again due do a **boddleneck** on the highway. We'll keep **tabs on** the traffic conditions for you every 20 minutes.

Vocabulary

big rig *n.* a large commercial multi-wheeled truck that carries a trailer • *Your mother drives a big rig?;* Your mother drives a large commercial truck?

bottleneck *n.* traffic congestion due to a sudden decrease in lanes • *There's always a bottleneck on this part of the highway because it decreases from four lanes to two;* There's always congestion on this part of the highway because it decreases from four lanes to two.
  ♦ NOTE: The shape of a bottle is similar to the shape of a roadway that decreases in the number of lanes, becoming increasingly narrow at one end.

break up (to) *exp.* (of traffic) to decrease in congestion • *I can't believe all this congestion. Hopefully, it'll break up after the construction work on the highway;* I can't believe all this congestion. Hopefully, it'll decrease after the construction work on the highway.

bunch-up *n.* sudden traffic congestion • *Slow down! There's a bunch-up ahead!;* Slow down! There's some sudden traffic congestion ahead!
  ♦ NOTE: It is very common to say either *"Slow down!"* or *"Slow up!"* to advise someone to decrease his/her speed. Both expressions are identical and may be used interchangeably.

clear shot *n.* an unobstructed passage • *After all that traffic, it's finally nice to have a clear shot the rest of the way;* After all that traffic, it's finally nice to have an unobstructed passage the rest of the way.

clip *n.* speed • *Your boat is really powerful. We're moving at quite a fast clip!;* Your boat is really powerful. We're moving at quite a fast speed!

clue someone in on something (to) *exp.* to inform someone of something • *Let me clue you in on what's been going on while you've been on vacation;* Let me inform you of what's been going on while you've been on vacation.

dead stop *n.* complete stop • *We were at a dead stop for an entire hour on the highway!;* We were at a complete stop for an entire hour on the highway!
  ♦ ALSO: **to stop dead** *exp.* to stop completely and suddenly • *When I saw the snake, I stopped dead in my tracks;* When I saw the snake, I stopped completely and suddenly.

fender-bender *exp.* a minor traffic accident without any casualties • *I got into a little fender-bender on the way to work today;* I got into a minor traffic accident on the way to work today.
  ♦ NOTE (1): This expression is part of the extensive world of *Rhyming Slang.*
  ♦ NOTE (2): For additional rhyming slang, see page 131.

"Heads up!" *exp.* "Be alert and look up!"
  ♦ NOTE: This is a common cry to warn people that something is flying through the air and could potentially cause harm on its way down.

heavy *adj.* (of traffic) dense • *Traffic was heavy all the way home;* Traffic was dense all the way home.

I *n.* an extremely common abbreviation for "interstate" • *I-10 is one of the few interstate highways that stretches all the way across the United States;* Interstate 10 is one of the few interstate highways that stretches all the way across the United States.

keep tabs on something for someone (to) *exp.* to keep a close surveillance on something for someone • *While I'm on vacation, will you keep tabs on any new developments at work for me?;* While I'm on vacation, will you keep a close surveillance on any new developments at work for me?

pick up speed (to) *exp.* to increase in speed • *Our sled started picking up speed as we went down the hill;* Our sled started increasing in speed as we went down the hill.

pickup *n.* a popular abbreviation of "pickup truck" • *I've always wanted to buy a pickup because I like driving high off the ground;* I've always wanted to buy a pickup truck because I like driving high off the ground.

rubbernecker *n.* gawker, one who cranes his/her neck (as if it were made of rubber) in order to observe a traffic accident or unusual occurrence on the road • *On my way home, I was behind a rubbernecker who kept slowing down every time we passed a traffic accident;* On my way home, I was behind a gawker who kept slowing down every time we passed a traffic accident.
  ♦ NOTE: **to rubberneck** *v.* to gawk • *Stop rubbernecking and drive!;* Stop gawking and drive!

rush hour *exp.* period of heavy traffic due to the close of business at the end of the day • *If we go to the movies now, we're going to hit rush hour;* If we go to the movies now, we're going to be on the roads when traffic is heaviest.

scene *n.* (of police) the exact place where an incident took place • *The police arrived at the scene of the crime;* The police arrived at the exact place where the crime took place.

shoulder *n.* the edge of the roadway where a car may park without obstructing traffic • *I had to pull off onto the right shoulder to change my tire;* I had to drive my car off to the side of the road to change my tire.

slow-and-go *exp.* braking and accelerating • *There's a lot of slow-and-go on the road right now due to rush hour;* There's a lot of braking and accelerating on the road right now due to everyone leaving work at the same time.
  ‣ ALSO: **stop-and-go** *exp.* stopping and accelerating.

spin out (to) *exp.* said of a car that is out of control and begins to spin due to slippery roads, applying the brakes suddenly, a flat tire, etc. • *I was driving on the highway and I suddenly got a flat tire which made the car spin out. Luckily, there was no one else on the road at the time;* I was driving on the highway and I suddenly got a flat tire which made the car spin from the loss of control. Luckily, there was no one else on the road at the time.

tangle *n.* a traffic accident where two or more cars have collided • *Did you see the tangle on the highway today?;* Did you see the traffic accident on the highway today?

tough row to hoe (to be a) *exp.* to be a difficult job to accomplish • (lit); to be a difficult row of crop to hoe • *If he doesn't learn how to be independent, he's going to have a tough row to hoe;* If he doesn't learn how to be independent, he's going to have difficulty in life.

work one's way down/through/over/etc. (to) *exp.* to approach a destination laboriously • *As you work your way down the mountain, be sure to take the time to rest;* As you slowly descend the mountain, be sure to take the time to rest.

PRACTICE THE VOCABULARY

[Answers to Lesson Seven, p. 216]

A. Circle the word in parentheses that best completes the sentence.

1. It took me an entire hour to get home because of a (**turtleneck, crookneck, bottleneck**) on the highway.

2. Let me (**glue, clue, slue**) you in on what happened yesterday!

3. All the cars were at a (**live, living, dead**) stop on the road.

4. We were moving at a real fast (**clip, flip, slip**)!

5. I was involved in a little fender (**blender, bender, gender**) today.

6. If we leave now, we're going to hit rush (**hour, minute, second**).

7. Traffic is really (**heavy, slim, slender**) this afternoon.

8. There's a lot of slow-and-(**mow, blow, go**) on the roads tonight.

9. Did you see the (**tangle, tango, tangelo**) on the highway?

10. The police just arrived on the (**scene, spleen, screen**).

11. (**Feet, Heads, Hands**) up! Something's flying toward us!

12. Every time there's an accident on the road, you can be sure there will be lots of (**turtlenecks, rubberneckers, crooknecks**).

B. Match the columns.

☐ 1. There's a lot of braking and accelerating on the road right now.

☐ 2. He laboriously arrived at the top of the mountain.

☐ 3. The accident has been moved to the edge of the roadway.

☐ 4. I had trouble getting home because of the traffic accident on the highway.

☐ 5. The police just arrived where the accident took place.

☐ 6. They just closed Interstate 5 for repairs.

☐ 7. It was only a minor traffic accident without any casualties.

☐ 8. How fast was the pickup truck moving?

☐ 9. Traffic was so dense that we came to a complete stop.

☐10. I've always wanted to drive a large commercial multi-wheeled truck.

☐11. We should have an unobstructed passage the rest of the way.

☐12. Heads up!

A. **I had trouble getting home because of the tangle on the highway.**

B. **I've always wanted to drive a big rig.**

C. **It was only a fender bender.**

D. **There's a lot of slow-and-go on the road right now.**

E. **They just closed I-5 for repairs.**

F. **How fast was the pickup moving?**

G. **We should have a clear shot the rest of the way.**

H. **The police just arrived on the scene.**

I. **Traffic was so heavy that we came to a dead stop.**

J. **The accident has been moved to the shoulder.**

K. **He worked his way to the top of the mountain.**

L. **Be alert and look up!**

C. Complete the following sentences by using the word list below.

bottleneck	**rubbernecker**	**break**
clue	**dead**	**heavy**
tabs	**scene**	**rush**
go	**spin**	**row**

1. We came to a _____ stop on the highway because of all the traffic congestion.

2. _____ hour seems to be starting earlier and earlier.

3. Get ready to slow down. There's always a _____ in the highway around here.

4. The ambulance arrived on the _____ one minute after the accident took place.

5. I'll keep _____ on the situation for you while you're gone.

6. Finally! There's a _____ in the traffic!

7. There's a lot of slow-and- _____ on the roads today.

8. Don't ever apply the brakes hard when driving over icy roads or you may _____ out.

9. I can't wait to pass that _____ ! He's more interested in watching the accident than watching the road!

10. I'm afraid that traffic is going to be _____ all the way home.

11. _____ me in. What happened at work today?

12. It's a tough _____ to hoe on the roads this afternoon.

A CLOSER LOOK:
Rhyming Slang

Hidden away in the depths of the English language is a type of whimsical rhyming slang as seen demonstrated in the dialogue with the expression *fender bender*. Rhyming slang is extremely common, yet most native speakers aren't even aware that they use it. It isn't until you rattle off a few popular examples that a surprised native born American will say, *"Geez Louise! You're right! Holy moley! We do use a hodge-podge of rhyming terms!*

(one's last name)'s the name, (one's profession)'s my game *exp.* • *Burke's the name, writing's my game;* Burke is my name, writing is my profession.

as snug as a bug in a rug (to be) *exp.* to be extremely cozy and warm • *I'm as snug as a bug in a rug in this bed;* I'm cozy and warm in this bed.

Boo hoo! *exclam.* used to indicate sadness • *We can't go to the park today because it's raining. Boo hoo!*
♦ NOTE: This is an onomatopoeia for the sound one makes when crying.

bummer in the summer (to be a) *exp.* to be a shame • *What a bummer in the summer!;* What a shame!
♦ NOTE: This expression is considered outdated and is only used in jest.

by hook or by crook *exp.* by any means • *I'm gonna attend her*

wedding by hook or by crook!; I'm going to attend her wedding by any means!

cruising for a bruising (to be) *exp.* to be asking for a fight • *You're cruisin' for a bruisin', pal;* You're asking for a fight, pal.
♦ NOTE: Common pronunciation: *cruisin' fer a bruisin'.*

Different strokes for different folks *exp.* Different people like different things.

double trouble *exp.* twice as many problems • *If my boss finds out that I called in sick and went to the beach in the company car, I'll be in double trouble!;* If my boss finds out that I called in sick and went to the beach in the company car, I'll be in twice as much trouble!

drunk as a skunk (to be) *exp.* to be extremely intoxicated • *He's drunk as a skunk;* He's extremely intoxicated.

fair and square *exp.* in a fair manner • *I won fair and square;* I won in a fair manner.

fender-bender *exp.* a small car accident • *My brother got into a fender-bender with our dad's car;* My brother got into a small car accident with our dad's car.

fuddy-duddy *n.* one who is old-fashioned and conventional • *He never likes to try new things. He's such a fuddy-duddy;* He never likes to try new things. He's so old-fashioned and conventional.

fun in the sun *exp.* fun at the beach • *We're going to Hawaii for some fun in the sun;* We're going to Hawaii for some fun at the beach.

Geez, Louise! *exp.* • **1.** said in surprise • *Geez, Louise! Look how tall she is!* • **2.** said in disappointment • *Geez, Louise. I can't believe I failed the final!* ♦ NOTE: The difference in connotation between **1.** and **2.** depends on the context and delivery of the speaker.

go with the flow (to) *exp.* to comply with the natural progression • *I know you don't like what's happening in your life right now, but instead of resisting all the time, just go with the flow;* I know you don't like what's happening in your life right now, but instead of resisting all the time, just comply with the natural progression.

hanky-panky *exp.* secretive sexual activity • *I think there's some hanky-panky going on between them;* I think there's some secretive sexual activity going on between them.

heebie-geebies *exp.* anxiety • *I get the heebie-geebies in the dark;* I get anxious and nervous in the dark.

Hell's bells! *exp.* said in surprise and disappointment • *She got chosen for the job instead of me? Hell's bells!*

helter-skelter *adj.* chaotic • *Everything was helter-skelter at my house today;* Everything was chaotic at my house today.

hocus-pocus *exp.* magic tricks • *She's into all sorts of hocus-pocus;* She enjoys all sorts of magic tricks. ♦ NOTE: This is also a common incantation used by magicians to manifest a magical feat.

hodge-podge *exp.* conglomeration • *The stew I made for dinner is just a hodge-podge of leftovers;* The stew I made for dinner is just a conglomeration of leftovers.

hoity-toity *exp.* pretentious • *Her parents are so hoity-toity!;* Her parents are so pretentious!

hokey-dokey *exp.* all right • *"Wanna go to the movies*

tonight?" "Hokey-dokey;" "Do you want to go to the movies tonight?" "All right."
♦ VARIATION: **okey-dokey** *exp.*

Holy Moley! *exp.* • **1.** said in surprise • *Holy Moley! How much money did you win?* • **2.** said in disappointment • *Holy Moley. I broke my favorite vase.*

hot to trot (to be) *exp.* to be extremely sexy • *She's hot to trot!;* She's extremely sexy!

hotshot *n.* a flamboyantly skillful person • *He thinks he such a hotshot!;* He thinks he's so superior at everything he does!
♦ NOTE: The term *hotshot* is also used in fun to indicate that the speaker is impressed: *Hey, hotshot! That was quite a performance!*

humdrum *adj.* boring • *It's so humdrum around here;* It's so boring around here.

hustle and bustle *n.* commotion and chaos • *We're moving to the country to get away from the hustle and bustle of the city;* We're moving to the country to get away from the commotion and chaos of the city.
♦ NOTE: Common pronunciation: *hustle 'n bustle.*

If you snooze, you lose! *exp.* If you're not alert, you'll never succeed.

In a while, Crocodile! *exp.* See you later!

itsy-bitsy (to be) *adj.* to be extremely small • *It's so itsy-bitsy, I can hardly see it!;* It's so small, I can hardly see it!

Jeepers creepers! *exclam.* exclamation of surprise or disappointment.
♦ NOTE: This expression, although outdated, was very common in the late 1920s and is only used today in jest or in old movies of the era. *"Jeepers creepers!"* is actually a euphemism for the exclamation "Jesus Christ!"

jet set *n.* group of wealthy individuals who regularly travel by air • *You're traveling to Europe again? What are you...part of the jet set?;* You're traveling to Europe again? What are you...part of the group of wealthy individuals who travel regularly by air?
♦ ALSO: **jet setter** *n.* wealthy individual who travels regularly by air.

Joe Shmoe *Prn.* name given as a variable for any individual • *I don't share my secrets with just any Joe Shmoe;* I don't share my secrets with just anyone.
♦ NOTE: In rhyming slang, it is common to repeat a word but replace the first letter with *shm* as a way to show contempt for the subject matter: *fancy-shmancy;* excessively flamboyant •

nice-shmice; unimpressively nice; *etc.*

local yokel *exp.* inhabitant of a particular region • *She's a local yokel;* She's an inhabitant of this region.

Loose lips sink ships! *exp.* If you divulge secrets, trouble is going to develop.

lovey-dovey *exp.* extremely affectionate • *They're very lovey-dovey with each other;* They're extremely affectionate with each other.

made in the shade (to be) *exp.* to have an easy time of something • *Once I answer this one question on the test, I'll have it made in the shade;* Once I answer this one question on the test, the remainder will be easy.

make or break someone (to) *exp.* to cause someone to be extremely prosperous or terribly unsuccessful • *The reviews that the producers get on their movie will either make or break them;* The reviews that the producers get on their movie will either make them extremely prosperous or terribly unsuccessful.

mean and lean (to be) *exp.* to have a very athletic body • *He is mean and lean!;* He has a very athletic body!
♦ NOTE: Oftentimes when emphasis is being made on an adjective, the subject and verb are

not contracted: *He is mean and lean!;* rather than *He's mean and lean!* The contraction would actually tend to soften the statement.

mumbo-jumbo *n.* gibberish, nonsense • *Did you understand all that mumbo-jumbo he was using?;* Did you understand all that gibberish he was using?

namby-pamby *adj.* spineless and weak • *He's so namby-pamby;* He's so spineless and weak.
♦ NOTE: The "a" in *namby* and *pamby* is pronounced like the "a" in *at.*

nitty-gritty (to get down to the) *exp.* to discuss the most important elements • *Now that we've discussed what we want to do, let's get down to the nitty-gritty. How are we going to get the work done?;* Now that we've discussed what we want to do, let's discuss the most important elements. How are we going to get the work done?

nitwit *adj.* fool • *What a nitwit!;* What a fool!

No fuss, no muss! *exp.* No trouble, no disorder!
♦ NOTE: This is a common sales line heard in commercials as a way to attract buyers to purchase a product.

No pain, no gain *exp.* If you don't push yourself beyond your limits, you're never going to improve.

No way, José! *exp.* Absolutely not!

out and about (to be) *exp.* to be wandering about or doing errands • *She's out and about today;* She's out doing errands today.

palsy-walsy (to be) *adj.* to be extremely friendly with one another • *We've very palsy-walsy;* We've very friendly with each other.
  ◆ NOTE: The "a" in *palsy* and *walsy* is pronounced like the "a" in *at*.

party hearty (to) *exp.* to have a good time at a party • *Let's go party hearty!;* Let's go party a lot!

payday *n.* the day that paychecks are received by employees • *Today is payday!;* Today I'm receiving my paycheck!

plain Jane (to be a) *exp.* to be an ordinary-looking woman • *She's such a plain Jane;* She's such an ordinary-looking woman.

pooper-scooper *n.* shovel for picking up dog excrement • *If you're going to take the dog for a walk, make sure to take the pooper-scooper;* If you're going to take the dog for a walk, make sure to take the shovel for picking up dog excrement.

roly-poly (to be) *adj.* to be rather plump • *He's not really fat, just roly-poly;* He's not fat, just rather plump.

rootin' tootin' (highfalutin) *exp.* remarkable • *He's the meanest rootin' tootin' (highfalutin) cowboy in the West!;* He's the meanest and most remarkable cowboy in the West.
  ◆ NOTE: The expression *rootin' tootin'* comes from Western slang and is still heard in old movies of the pioneer days and cartoons focusing on the old West. The adjective *highfalutin,* meaning "pompous," is commonly attached to *rootin' tootin'* to add emphasis as well as continue the rhyming pattern.

Say it, don't spray it! *exp.* a common barb given to someone who inadvertently spits when speaking • *Hey! Say it, don't spray it!;* Hey! Speak what you want to say, don't spit it!

scarf and barf (to) *exp.* to gorge oneself and then vomit • *She's gonna go scarf and barf again;* She's going to go gorge herself and vomit again.
  ◆ NOTE: Common pronunciation: *scarf 'n barf.* This is also a humorous term for the condition of bulimia.

See ya later, Alligator! *exp.* a well-known, yet dated, way to say "good-bye."
  ◆ VARIATION: **"Later, Gator!"** *exp.*

shop till one drops (to) *exp.* to shop until exhaustion • *Let's shop till* *we drop!;* Let's shop until we're exhausted!

silly Billy *exp.* name given to one who is nonsensical and humorous • *You're such a silly Billy!;* You're such a nonsensical and humorous person!

super-duper *exp.* gigantic • *I'm gonna treat myself to a super-duper ice cream cone!;* I'm going to treat myself to a gigantic ice cream cone!
♦ NOTE: Common pronunciation: *sooper-dooper.*

Tee-hee! *exclam.* used to indicate amusement • *Tee-hee! I tricked you!*
♦ NOTE: This is an onomatopoeia for the sound one makes when laughing hard yet quietly.

Up your nose with a rubber hose! *exp.* euphemistic statement of contempt for an annoying person.

warm for one's form (to be) *exp.* to be sexually excited by someone's body • *I think she's warm for my form!;* I think she's sexually excited by my body.

wear and tear *exp.* deterioration due to excessive use • *There's a lot of wear and tear on my car*

driving it to work every day; There's a lot of deterioration happening to my car driving it to work every day.
♦ NOTE: Common pronunciation: *wear 'n tear.*

Wham-bam, thank you ma'am! *exp.* to have quick sex and say good-bye • *I'm afraid he's not very romantic. With him it's just "Wham-bam, thank you ma'am!;* I'm afraid he's not very romantic. With him it's just quick sex and good-bye!

What's the plan, Sam? *exp.* What are we going to do now?
♦ VARIATION: **"What's the plan, Stan?"**

wheel and deal (to) *exp.* to negotiate • *A lot of wheeling and dealing goes on in his office;* A lot of negotiating goes on in his office.
♦ NOTE: Common pronunciation: *wheel 'n deal.*

Yo, bro! *exp.* Hi, friend!
♦ NOTE: This is a greeting primarily among black men since they commonly refer to each other as brothers or *"bro"* for short.

TEEN/COLLEGE SLANG
– At the Record Store –

I'm **way stoked**! My favorite group just **cut** a new **C.D.**! The lead singer is such **the stud**!

And he's so gorgeous... **not**! I can't believe you're **scamming** on that **goob**! Make me **spew**!

Dialogue In Slang

At the Record Store

DIALOGUE

Debbie and Alicia are looking for some albums.

Debbie: I'm **way stoked**! My favorite group just **cut** a new **C.D.**! Have you heard their **latest hit**, "**Baggin' Some Rays** on the Beach with My **Homey**?" It's **deadly**!

Alicia: I know. It's got the best **hook**. My mom always **bags on** me 'cause I **blast** the stereo every time that song comes on.

Debbie: A few of us **shined bio** yesterday, which is a total **mick class** anyway, **to hit** one of their **jam sessions**. The lead singer did the **meanest** guitar **licks** at their last **gig**! That guy is such the **stud**!

Alicia: And he's so gorgeous… **not**! I can't believe you're **scamming** on that **goob**! **Hello**! He's so **lame**. Make me **spew**. I dunno **what his deal is** but he dresses like a **dode** and his hair is always **majorly tweaked out**. I'm starting to wonder about the kind of people you **hang with**.

Lesson Eight - TEEN/COLLEGE SLANG

Translation of dialogue in standard English

At the Record Store

DIALOGUE

Debbie and Alicia are looking for some albums.

Debbie: I'm **really excited**! My favorite group just **recorded** a new **compact disc**! Have you heard their **newest successful song**, "**Sunbathing** on the Beach with My **Friend**?" It's **fantastic**!

Alicia: I know. It's got the most **memorable section**. My mother always **criticizes** me because I **turn up the volume** on the stereo every time that song comes on.

Debbie: A few of us **didn't go** to **biology class** yesterday, which is a **real easy class** anyway, in order **to listen** to one of their **music sessions**. The lead singer played the **best** guitar **melodies** at their last **performance**. That guy is so **masculine**!

Alicia: And he's so gorgeous… **not really**! I can't believe you're **hoping for a sexual encounter** with that **fool**! **Are you serious**? He's so **stupid**. That makes me **vomit**. I don't know **what his problem is** but he dresses like an **idiot** and his hair is always **extremely messy**. I'm starting to wonder about the kind of people you **socialize with**.

Lesson Eight - TEEN/COLLEGE SLANG

Dialogue in slang as it would be heard

At the Record Store

DIALOGUE

Debbie 'n Alicia 'r lookin' fer s'm albums.

Debbie: I'm **way stoked**! My fav'rit group jus' **cud** a new **C.D.**! Have ya heard their **ladest hit**, "**Baggin' S'm Rays** on the Beach with My **Homey**?" It's **deadly**!

Alicia: I know. It's got the best **hook**. My mom always **bags on** me 'cause I **blast** the stereo every time that song comes on.

Debbie: A few of us **shined bio** yesterday, which is a todal **mick class** anyway, **ta hit** one 'a their **jam sessions**. The lead singer did the **meanest** guitar **licks** at their last **gig**. That guy's such the **stud**!

Alicia: And 'e's so gorgeous… **not**! I can't believe yer **scammin'** on that **goob**! **Hello**! He's so **lame**. Make me **spew**. I dunno **what 'is deal is** but 'e dresses like a **dode** 'n 'is hair's always **majorly tweaked out**. I'm starding ta wonder about the kind 'a people you **hang with**.

Vocabulary

bag on someone (to) *exp.* **1.** to reprimand someone • *My mom bagged on me for coming home late last night;* My mother reprimanded me for coming home late last night. • **2.** to criticize • *My dad keeps baggin' on me about my clothes;* My dad keeps criticizing me about my clothes.
  ▶ SYNONYM: **to rag on someone** *exp.* • *My girlfriend ragged on me for an hour 'cause I forgot our date;* My girlfriend reprimanded me for an hour because I forgot our date. • *My mom always bags on me about my taste in music;* My mother always criticizes me about my taste in music.

goob *n.* fool • *What a goob!;* What a fool!
  ▶ NOTE: This term comes from the old television series "The Andy Griffith Show" which featured a foolish character named "Goober."

bio *n.* common abbreviation for "biology" • *She's the best student in bio class;* She's the best student in biology class.
  ▶ NOTE: For additional common abbreviations used in school, refer to page 163.

blast the stereo (to) *exp.* to turn the volume up loudly on the stereo • *I can't believe she blasts the stereo at midnight!;* I can't believe she turns the volume up loudly on the stereo at midnight!
  ▶ SYNONYM (1): **to crank up the stereo** *exp.* • *Let's crank up the stereo and party!;* Let's turn up the volume on the stereo and have a party!

C.D. *n.* (used by all ages) common abbreviation for "compact disc" • *My parents bought me a new C.D. player for my birthday;* My parents bought me a new compact disc player for my birthday.

cut [a record, a C.D., an album, etc.] (to) *exp.* to record • *Did you hear that Nancy was just hired to cut an album?;* Did you hear that Nancy was just hired to record an album?
  ▶ ALSO (1): **cut** *n.* **1.** song from a recording • *I like the first cut on that album;* I like the first song on that album. • **2.** share of profits • *My cut is 70%, yours is 30%;* My share of the profits is 70%, yours is 30%. • **3.** elimination round in a contest • *Congratulations! You made the first cut!;* Congratulations! You avoided being eliminated in the first round!
  ▶ ALSO (2): **to lay down tracks** *exp.* • This is a common expression in the music industry referring to recording on multi-track tape. Each track contains a different musical line either instrumental or vocal. When all tracks are played at the same time, a complete song is produced.

deadly *adj.* **1.** excellent • *That group plays the most deadly music;* That group plays the best music. • **2.** extremely difficult • *The math final was deadly;* The math final was extremely difficult.

  ▶ NOTE: For additional popular adjectives with opposite meanings, refer to page 167.

dode *n.* fool • *Our new teacher is the biggest dode!;* Our new teacher is the biggest fool!

  ▶ SYNONYM: **dork** *n.* • *What a dork!;* What a fool!

  ▶ NOTE: **dode** = *dork* + *dude*

gig *n.* musical performance • *I was asked to perform tomorrow but the gig doesn't pay enough!;* I was asked to perform tomorrow but the performance doesn't pay enough!

hang with someone (to) *exp.* to spend time with someone (and do nothing in particular), to socialize with someone • *She likes hanging with her friends in the park;* She likes socializing with her friends in the park.

  ▶ SYNONYM: **to kick it with someone** *exp.* • *I'm going to Bob's house to kick it for a while;* I'm going to Bob's house to socialize for a while.

  ▶ NOTE: The expression *"to hang with someone"* is a shortened version of *"to hang **out** with someone."* It is extremely popular among teens to drop the preposition *"out"* from commonly used expressions. For example:

    to freak out (to lose control of one's emotions) = ***to freak;***

    to chill out (to relax) = ***to chill;***

    to space out (to become forgetful) = ***to space;*** *etc.*

"Hello!" *exclam.* "Become realistic!" • *You just got a job as a Spanish translator? Hello! You don't speak Spanish!;* You just got a job as a Spanish translator? Get realistic! You don't speak Spanish!

  ▶ NOTE: *"Hello!"* is a humorous exclamation commonly used in response to a ridiculous comment.

  ▶ SYNONYM: **"Have you lost it?"** *exp.* • *You're going skydiving? Have you lost it?;* You're going skydiving? Have you lost touch with reality?

hit *n.* (used by all ages) popular song, movie, play, person, etc. • *My brother just wrote a song that I know is going to be a hit;* My brother just wrote a song that I know is going to be popular. • *You're going to be a big hit at the party;* You're going to be very popular at the party.

  ▶ ALSO: **smash hit** *exp.* very popular song, movie, play, person, etc.

  ▶ ANTONYM: **bomb** *n.* unsuccessful song, movie, play, person, etc. • *That movie is going to be a big bomb;* That movie is going to be a big failure.

hit (to) *v.* (used by all ages) to go to • *Wanna hit the stores with me?;* Do you want to go to the stores with me? • *Did you hit the concert last night?;* Did you go to the concert last night?

homey *n.* close friend, pal • *Have you met Jeff? He's been my homey for the past 10 years;* Have you met Jeff? He's been my close friend for the past 10 years.
▶ SYNONYM: **goomba** *n.* • *Hey, my goomba! Can I borrow five dollars?;* Hey, good friend! Can I borrow five dollars?

hook *n.* the part of the song which is the most memorable, whether it be the lyrics or melody • *This song has the greatest hook. I keep singing it all day!;* This song has the most memorable section. I keep singing it all day!

jam session *exp.* a meeting of musicians who come together to do musical improvisations • *I couldn't sleep 'cause my brother's group had a jam session in his bedroom all night!;* I couldn't sleep because my brother's group got together and did musical improvisations in his bedroom all night!

lame *adj.* **1.** stupid, moronic • *He's so lame;* He's so moronic. • **2.** mediocre • *I can't believe how lame the new teacher is;* I can't believe how mediocre the new teacher is.
▶ ANTONYM: **dope** *adj.* excellent • *You look dope, today!;* You look great today!

latest *adj.* (used by all ages) newest, most recent • *Her dress is the latest fashion from Paris;* Her dress is the newest fashion from Paris.

lick *n.* musical phrase • *That lick is too complicated for me to play on the guitar;* That musical phrase is too complicated for me to play on the guitar.

majorly *adv.* extremely • *He's majorly weird!;* He's extremely weird!
▶ SYNONYM: **mega** *adv.* • *He's mega hot!;* He's extremely sexy!

meanest *adv.* **1.** best • *That's the meanest car I've ever driven!;* That's the best car I've ever driven! • **2.** most difficult • *This is the meanest homework assignment we've ever had!;* This is the hardest homework assignment we've ever had!
▶ ALSO: **mean** *adj.* (used by all ages) **1.** menacing • *The weather looks mean today;* The weather looks menacing today. • **2.** great • *She's a mean cook!;* She's a great cook!
▶ NOTE: For additional popular adjectives with opposite meanings, refer to page 167.

mick class *exp.* easy class • *What a mick class!;* What an easy class!
▶ NOTE: This is a shortened version of the expression: **Mickey Mouse class.**
▶ ALSO: *This class is really mick!* [or] *This class is really Mickey Mouse!;* This class is really easy!

not *exclam.* not really, just kidding • *That's such a beautiful jacket you're wearing! Not!;* That's such a beautiful jacket you're wearing! Not really!
‣ NOTE: This exclamation has become extremely popular among teenagers. It is used humorously to turn a positive statement or compliment into an insult.

scam (to) *v.* to scrutinize people in the hopes of a possible sexual encounter • *He always goes to bars to scam on chicks;* He always goes to bars to scrutinize girls for possible sexual encounters.
‣ SYNONYM: **to cruise** *v.* • *I think that guy is cruising me;* I think that guy is scrutinizing me for a possible sexual encounter.

shine something (to) *exp.* to exclude something from one's plans • *He didn't feel like going to work today, so he just shined it;* He didn't feel like going to work today, so he just excluded it from his plans.
‣ SYNONYM: **to blow something off** *exp.* • **1.** to exclude something from one's plans • *I'm blowing off my classes today;* I'm not going to my classes today. • **2.** to ignore something or someone • *Just blow it off!;* Just ignore it!

spew (to) *v.* to vomit • (lit); to spout or gush • *If I eat that, I'll spew!;* If I eat that, I'll vomit!
‣ SYNONYM (1): **to blow chow** *exp.* • *Her brother got sick at the dinner table and blew chow;* Her brother got sick at the dinner table and vomited.
‣ SYNONYM (2): **to blow chunks** *exp.*
‣ SYNONYM (3): **to hurl** *v.* • *Make me hurl!;* That makes me sick!

stoked (to be) *adj.* to be excited • (lit); to be fueled (as in a furnace) • *I passed the final! I'm stoked!;* I passed the final! I'm excited!
‣ SYNONYM: **to be jazzed** *exp.* • *Tomorrow's a holiday! I'm jazzed!;* Tomorrow's a holiday! I'm excited!

stud *n.* a muscular and virile man • (lit); a male animal • *That's your brother? What a stud!;* That's your brother? What a muscular and virile man!
‣ ALSO: **studmuffin** *n. What a studmuffin!;* What a muscular and virile man!
‣ SYNONYM: **babe** *n.* any sexually attractive person • *He/She is a major babe!;* He/She is a real sexy person!
‣ NOTE: In the opening dialogue, the definite article "the" was used in front of *stud* instead of the usual indefinite article "a": *That guy is such **the** stud!* This construction is extremely popular with the younger generation.

tweaked [out] (to be) *exp.* **1.** to be in a state of disarray • *My hair is all tweaked [out] today;* My hair is in a state of disarray today. • **2.** to be unresponsive and lethargic • *After seeing the car accident, I feel sort of tweaked [out];* After seeing the car accident, I feel sort of unresponsive. • **3.** to be defective • *This computer is all tweaked [out]. I can't get it to work right;* This computer is completely defective. I can't get it to work right.

way *adv.* very • *He's way handsome!;* He's very handsome!
‣SYNONYM: **fully** *adv.* • *"Do you like him?" "Fully!";* "Do you like him?" "Very much!"

"What is your/his/her/their deal?" *exp.* "What is your/his/her/their problem?" • *I don't know what her deal is but she's always angry;* I don't know what her problem is but she's always angry.
‣ ALSO: **"What's the deal?"** *exp.* "What's the problem?"

PRACTICE THE VOCABULARY

[Answers to Lesson Eight, p. 216]

A. Underline the appropriate word that best completes the phrase.

1. I heard your music group is going to (**cut, slice, chop**) a new album!

2. Their song is a big (**punch, smack, hit**).

3. Bring your guitar to my house for a (**marmalade, jam, butter**) session.

4. Her dress is the (**earliest, latest, longest**) fashion from Paris.

5. I passed every math test. It's such a (**mick, sick, lick**) class.

6. Stop (**scorning, skipping, scamming**) on her. That's my girlfriend.

7. I don't feel like going to the gym today. I'm (**glowing, shining, brightening**) it.

8. I feel sick. I think I'm gonna (**spout, spew, scam**).

9. This is great news! I'm (**stoked, stacked, sloshed**)!

10. I can't go to the party like this. My hair's all (**tweeded, thrashed, tweaked**)!

11. He is (**way, wicked, wasted**) handsome!

12. She's upset again? What's her (**studmuffin, dode, deal**)?

B. Replace the word(s) in parentheses with the slang synonym from the right column.

1. That song was *(fantastic)* _____ !

    A. **goob**

2. Here comes the *(most memorable section of the song)* _____ .

    B. **hang**

3. Do you know my *(close friend)* _____ ?

    C. **hook**

4. I'm gonna go *(spend time)* _____ at the park with Alicia.

    D. **shining**

5. Why do you always *(criticize)* _____ him all the time?

    E. **meanest**

6. You actually like that *(fool)* _____ ? You can't be serious!

    F. **bag on**

7. What a *(muscular and virile man)* _____ ?

    G. stud

8. My favorite music group is doing a *(performance)* _____ at my school!

    H. **deadly**

9. I'm *(extremely)* _____ tired!

    I. **gig**

10. He plays the *(best)* _____ saxophone!

    J. **stoked**

11. I'm *(passing on)* _____ work today.

    K. **homey**

12. I'm starting to feel sick. I think I'm gonna *(throw up)* _____ .

    L. **spew**

13. I'm so *(excited)* _____ that I passed the final!

    M. **majorly**

14. That guy's so *(stupid)* _____ ! How can you possibly go out with him?

    N. **lame**

C. WORD SEARCH: Circle the words in the grid below that fit the following expressions. Words may be spelled up/down, left/right, or diagonally. The first one has been done for you.

1. fool

2. extremely

3. **1.** to be in a state of disarray • **2.** to be unresponsive and lethargic • **3.** to be defective

4. musical phrase

5. an assembly of musicians who get together and do musical improvisations

6. ugly or foolish man

7. popular song, movie, play, person, etc.

8. to _____ . To scrutinize people in the hopes of a sexual encounter

9. to _____ . To vomit

10. to _____ something. To exclude something from one's plans

11. newest, most recent

J	A	M	S	E	S	S	I	O	N	L	A
D	M	I	C	O	H	S	T	I	S	A	E
L	M	G	A	G	I	O	D	A	J	T	I
E	C	O	M	E	N	W	A	J	T	E	O
I	L	O	O	E	E	W	J	K	K	S	M
G	A	B	W	P	S	K	B	H	I	T	A
A	V	E	S	K	H	D	E	E	R	H	J
I	O	Y	X	X	I	J	H	O	S	A	O
E	Y	W	H	I	P	S	O	P	E	R	R
O	T	X	R	K	P	D	O	D	E	L	L
T	W	E	A	K	E	D	J	E	E	E	Y
L	I	C	K	O	E	E	B	X	D	N	A

A CLOSER LOOK (1):

Popular Teen and College Slang

Slang is used by individuals as a way to integrate into groups and as a means for groups to identify themselves. The younger generation has certainly proven this by creating their own complex lingo which tends to keep parents in a constant state of confusion. A common complaint from parents is that they can't understand what their teenagers are saying. There is a simple reason for this. They don't want them to!

The following is a medley of slang terms and expressions popular among the teen and college groups.

a ___ and a half *exp.* an extreme (noun) • *He's a stud and a half!;* He's an extreme stud! • *She's a jerk and a half!;* She's a complete jerk!

ace a test (to) *exp.* to achieve a high grade on a test • *I aced my bio exam!;* I achieved a high grade on my biology test!

baby *n.* thing • *You bought this computer? This baby must have really been expensive!;* You bought this computer? This thing must have really been expensive!

bail (to) *v.* **1.** to leave • *I'm late! I gotta bail!;* I'm late! I have to leave! • **2.** to leave a relationship • *After being together for three months, she suddenly decided to bail;* After being together for three months, she suddenly decided to leave the relationship.

ballistic (to go) *adj.* to become uncontrollably upset • *Don't go ballistic on me!;* Don't become uncontrollably upset with me!
♦ NOTE: "Ballistics" refers to the study of the processes within a firearm when it is fired.

Betty *n.* pretty girl • *What a Betty!;* What a pretty girl!

bitchin' (to be) *adj.* to be terrific • *That shirt's bitchin'!;* That shirt's terrific!
♦ NOTE (1): The adjective *bitchin'* originated in the 1960s but has gained new popularity.
♦ NOTE (2): This adjective is always pronounced in its contracted form *bitchin';* never *bitching.*
♦ NOTE (3): Occasionally seen as *"bitchen."*

blasted (to be) *adj.* to be drunk • *They got blasted last night;* They got drunk last night.

blitzed (to be) *adj.* to be extremely drunk • *Don't let the boss see you so blitzed!;* Don't let the boss see you so drunk!

blow chow (to) *exp.* to vomit • *I feel sick. I think I'm gonna blow chow;* I feel sick. I think I'm going to throw up.
 ♦ NOTE: **chow** *n.* food • *Great chow!;* Great food!
 ♦ ALSO: **to blow chunks** *exp.* to vomit.

blow off (to) *exp.* **1.** to ignore • *I know he says mean things but just blow it off;* I know he says mean things but just ignore it. • **2.** not to attend (a class, meeting, function, etc.) • *I'm blowing off math today;* I'm not attending mathematics class today.
 ♦ ALSO: **a blow-off class** *exp.* an easy class.

bolt (to) *v.* to leave • *My class starts in five minutes! I gotta bolt!;* My class starts in five minutes! I have to leave!
 ♦ NOTE: As seen in the above example, it is very common among teens to contract "have/has got to" to *"gotta."*

bombed (to be) *adj.* to be extremely drunk • *I got bombed off the spiked punch!;* I got extremely drunk from the alcoholic punch!
 ♦ NOTE: The adjective *spiked* is a popular slang term used to refer to anything into which alcohol or drugs have been added.

boogie (to) *v.* to leave • *Let's boogie!;* Let's leave!

book (to) *v.* to leave • *I'm bored. Let's book;* I'm bored. Let's leave.

brain-dead (to be) *adj.* to be stupid • (lit); medical term referring to the discontinuation of brain waves which occurs before death • *I can't believe I got lost driving home. I must have gone brain-dead!;* I can't believe I got lost driving home. The brain waves in my head must have stopped!

brewsky *n.* beer • *I think I'll have another brewsky;* I think I'll have another beer.
 ♦ NOTE: The noun *brewsky* is a variation of *brew* which literally translates as "mixture" or "concoction."
 ♦ ALSO: **brewski.**

buffed [out] (to be) *exp.* to be muscular • *Your younger brother really is buffed [out]!;* Your younger brother really is muscular!
 ♦ VARIATION: **to be buff** *adj.*

bum around (to) *exp.* to idle • *I'm just gonna bum around the house today;* I'm just going to idle around the house today.

bum something off someone (to) *exp.* to borrow something from someone • *Can I bum a pen off you?;* Can I borrow a pen from you?
♦ NOTE: In the above sentence, *"can"* is actually used incorrectly since its meaning is "to be able." For example:
Can I borrow a pen from you? = *Am I able* to borrow a pen from you?
The correct term should be *"may"* which means "to be permitted." For example:
May I borrow a pen from you? = *Would you permit me to* borrow a pen from you?
However, to the chagrin of English teachers, *"can"* is commonly used, although incorrectly, by all age groups to mean "may."

bummed (to be) *adj.* to be disappointed • *We were planning on going horseback riding tomorrow for my birthday but now they say it's going to rain! I'm bummed;* We were planning on going horseback riding tomorrow for my birthday but now they say it's going to rain! I'm disappointed.
♦ NOTE: This is a shortened

version of the popular expression *"to be bummed out."* It is extremely popular among teens to drop the final prepositions such as *"out"* and *"off"* in just about every expression.

bummer *n.* a disappointment • *I can't go with you to the movies tonight 'cause I have to babysit my little sister. What a bummer!;* I can't go with you to the movies tonight because I have to babysit my little sister. What an unfortunate situation!
♦ NOTE (1): From time to time, you may even hear the rhyming expression *"Bummer in the summer!"* meaning "What a huge disappointment." This expression was popularized in a song from the 1960s and is still occasionally used in jest.
♦ NOTE (2): For additional rhyming slang, see 131.

burn out on someone or something (to) *exp.* to tire of someone or something • *I'm burned out on this homework;* I'm tired of doing all this homework.

burned/burnt out (to be) *exp.* **1.** to be exhausted (physically or mentally) • *I'm gonna go to bed. I'm burned out;* I'm going to go to bed. I'm exhausted. • **2.** to be incoherent (due to excessive drug or alcohol use) • *That guy's* *really burned out!;* That guy's really incoherent!

♦ NOTE (1): **burn out** *n.* one who is incoherent (due to excessive drug or alcohol use) • *What a burn out!;* What an incoherent individual!

♦ NOTE (2): **to get burned/burnt** *exp.* to get taken advantage of • *He really burned/burnt me by selling me a car he knew was junk;* He really took advantage of me by selling me a car he knew was defective.

butt ugly (to be) *exp.* to be extremely ugly • *He's butt ugly!;* He's extremely ugly!

♦ VARIATION: **buttly** *adj.* • *She's buttly!;* She's really ugly!

♦ CAUTION: Both *butt ugly* and *buttly,* although somewhat humorous, are considered moderately vulgar.

cake (to be) *adj.* to be extremely easy • *This class is cake;* This class is extremely easy.

♦ NOTE: Teens are notorious for taking common slang and shortening it as a way to claim it as their own. The expression *to be cake* is actually a shortened version of the popular expression *to be a piece of cake* meaning "to be extremely easy."

♦ SEE: For additional common abbreviations, see page 163.

cap on someone (to) *exp.* to criticize someone • *Every time I go to her house, her mother starts capping on me!;* Every time I go to her house, he mother starts criticizing me!

catch a buzz (to) *exp.* to become slightly inebriated • *I'm catching a buzz off/from this wine;* I'm getting slightly inebriated from this wine.

♦ VARIATION: **buzzed** *adj.* **1.** slightly inebriated • *I'm getting buzzed off/from all the alcohol in this drink!;* I'm getting slightly inebriated from all the alcohol in this drink! • **2.** wide awake • *I can't sleep. I'm too buzzed after my exciting day;* I can't sleep. I'm too wide awake after my exciting day.

catch flack (to) *exp.* to get reprimanded • *I caught flack from my parents for coming home late;* I got reprimanded by my parents for coming home late.

♦ VARIATION: **to get flack** *exp.*

catch some Zs (to) *exp.* to go to sleep, to take a nap • *I'm gonna catch some Zs before dinner;* I'm going to take a nap before dinner.

♦ NOTE: This humorous expression was adopted from comic strips where characters are drawn with several Zs over their heads portraying sound sleeping.

choke (to) *v.* to do poorly at something • *I choked on the final;* I did poorly on the final.

chug (to) *v.* to drink quickly (usually beer) • *He can really chug it!;* He can really drink beer quickly!
‣ NOTE: **chugging contest** *exp.* a contest to see who can drink the most beer the fastest.

clueless (to be) *adj.* **1.** to be confused • *I was clueless why she was so mad at me;* I was confused as to why she was so mad at me. • **2.** to be ignorant • *How can you be so clueless? She's mad because you forgot her birthday!;* How can you be so ignorant? She's mad because you forgot her birthday!
‣ ALSO: **"Get a clue!"** *exp.* "Stop being so ignorant!"

crash (to) *v.* to sleep • *Can I crash on your floor for the night?;* Can I sleep on your floor for the night?

cruise (to) *v.* to look for a date for a possible sexual encounter • *He goes to bars every night to cruise chicks;* He goes to bars every night to look for women for possible sexual encounters.

cut class (to) *exp.* not to attend class • *I'm cutting class tomorrow 'cause it's my birthday;* I'm not

attending class tomorrow because it's my birthday.

cut up (to) *exp.* to misbehave through joking and raucous conduct • *She always cuts up in class;* She always misbehaves in class.
‣ NOTE: **cut up** *n.* one who misbehaves through joking and raucous conduct • *He's such a cut up!;* He's such a clown!

ditz *n.* unreliable and foolish individual • *She washed her car with oven cleaner? What a ditz!;* She washed her car with oven cleaner? What a fool!
‣ VARIATION: **ditzy** *adj.* foolish • *He's sort of ditzy;* He's sort of foolish.

dope *adj.* terrific • *That's dope!;* That's terrific! • *You look dope!;* You look terrific!

dork *n.* fool • *Don't be such a dork!;* Don't be such a fool!

down (to) *v.* to drink • *He downed a six pack in an hour!;* He drank a six pack of beer in an hour!
‣ NOTE: *Six pack* is a common shortened version of "six pack of beer."

dragging (to be) *adj.* to be tired and sluggish • *I'm draggin' today since I stayed up all night;* I'm sluggish today since I stayed up all night.

drive the porcelain bus (to) *exp.* (humorous) to vomit • *I drove the porcelain bus all night;* I vomited all night.
♦ NOTE: This humorous expression was originated because the vomiting individual oftentimes places hands on each side of the round porcelain toilet bowl in the same position that one would when maneuvering the large steering wheel of a bus.

dude *n.* **1.** man in general • *Do you know that dude?;* Do you know that man? • **2.** girl • *What's goin' on, dudes?;* What's happening girls (or guys, depending on the audience). • **3.** *exclam. Dude! Look at that!;* Wow! Look at that!

dust (to be) *n.* **1.** to be in trouble • *If you forget his birthday again, you're dust!;* If you forget his birthday again, you're in trouble! • **2.** to leave • *I'm dust;* I'm leaving.

dweeb *n.* fool • *You like him? He's such a dweeb!;* You like him? He's such a fool.

faced (to be) *adj.* to be drunk • *You're already faced after one drink?;* Are you already drunk after one drink?
♦ NOTE: This adjective is a euphemism for the vulgar yet popular expression *"to be shitfaced."*

flag a class (to) *exp.* not to attend class • *She's gonna fail if she keeps flagging class all the time;* She's going to fail if she continues to be absent from class all the time.

flail a test (to) *exp.* to fail a test due to being flustered; fluster + fail = *flail* • *I totally flailed my test;* I totally failed my test (because I was flustered).

flake *n.* an unreliable and irresponsible person • *What a flake!;* What an unreliable person!
♦ ALSO (1): **flaky** *adj.* unreliable • *That guy's flaky!;* That guy's unreliable!
♦ ALSO (2): **to flake** *v.* to be unreliable • *He was supposed to pick me up at the airport but he flaked;* He was supposed to pick me up at the airport but he was irresponsible.

fly *adj.* terrific • *That's a fly stereo system!;* That's a terrific stereo system!

freak *n.* extremely attractive and sexy person • *Look at all the freaks at this party?;*
♦ VARIATION (1): **freakazoid** *n.*
♦ VARIATION (2): **super freak** *n.*

freak [out] (to) *exp.* to lose control of one's emotions • *Don't freak [out]...just relax;* Don't lose control of your emotions…just relax.

fresh *adj.* terrific, excellent • *That car is fresh!;* That car is terrific!

fried (to be) *adj.* to be extremely drunk • *She got fried during lunch today!;* She got extremely drunk during lunch today!

fully *adv.* absolutely • *"Do you think she likes me?" "Fully!;"* "Do you think she likes me?" "Absolutely!"

funky *adj.* fashionably unconventional • *What a funky shirt!;* What a fashionably unconventional shirt!

G.Q. *adj.* stylish and good-looking (from Gentleman's Quarterly magazine) • *Your hair is very G.Q.;* Your hair is very stylish.

geek *n.* fool • *She's a real geek!;* She's a real fool!

"Get a life!" *exp.* **1.** "Find something useful to do with yourself!" • **2.** "Stop talking nonsense!"
♦ VARIATION: **"Get a job!"**

get down (to) *exp.* to abandon all inhibitions • *She can really get down when she dances;* She can really abandon all inhibitions when she dances.
♦ SYNONYM: **to cut loose** *exp.*

get moded (to) *exp.* to get caught or humiliated • *Since I bragged about being a great tennis player, I got moded when I lost the match;* Since I bragged about being a great tennis player, I was humiliated when I lost the match. • *I thought you were a good tennis player! Moded!;* I thought you were a good tennis player! I caught you (in an exaggeration)!

give someone a melvin (to) *exp.* a prank launched toward an unsuspecting target whereby the attacker yanks up the victim's underwear from behind in order to get caught between the buttocks.
♦ SYNONYM: **to give someone a skid mark** *exp.*

go for it (to) *exp.* to take a chance • *Don't be scared. Just go for it!;* Don't be scared. Just take a chance!
♦ NOTE: This expression is used by all age groups.

go off on someone (to) *exp.* to lose one's temper and reprimand someone • *He went off on me for no reason;* He lost his temper and reprimanded me for no reason.

go on a _____ run (to) *exp.* to go on an errand to purchase (beer run, milk run, etc.) • *Who wants to go on a beer run with me?;*

Who wants to go on an errand to purchase beer with me?

goober *n.* fool • *Don't be such a goober!;* Don't be such a fool!
▸ NOTE: This term comes from the old television series called "The Andy Griffith Show" where a character named Goober was known for being eccentric and moronic.
▸ VARIATION: **goob** *n.* a common abbreviation for *goober*.

hairy *adv.* scary, difficult • *That was a hairy car trip!;* That was a scary car trip!

hammered (to be) *adj.* to be extremely drunk • *Don't let him drive. He's hammered!;* Don't let him drive. He's extremely drunk!

hang a B.A. (to) *exp.* a popular expression in colleges meaning to expose one's buttocks to a group of people • *He hung a B.A. in front of the crowd!;* He exposed his buttocks in front of the crowd!
▸ NOTE: The term *B.A.* is a common abbreviation and euphemism for *bare ass*.

have the munchies (to) *exp.* to have a strong desire to snack • *Do we have any food in the house? I've got the munchies;* Do we have any food in the house? I have a strong desire to snack.
▸ NOTE: This expression was originally created by those who found themselves with an intense desire to snack after smoking marijuana.

heave (to) *v.* to vomit • (lit); to throw • *I think I'm gonna heave!;* I think I'm going to vomit!

heifer *n.* fat girl • (lit); a particular breed of cow • *What a heifer!;* What a fat girl!

hit on someone (to) *exp.* to approach someone sexually • *Did he just try to hit on you?;* Did he just try to approach you sexually?

honkin' *adv.* huge • *Can you believe the honkin' amount of homework I have to do?;* Can you believe the huge amount of homework I have to do?
▸ NOTE: Whenever *honkin'* is used, the *-ing* ending is always contracted to *-in'*. *Honking* would actually sound strange to the native speaker's ear.

in a heartbeat *adv.* immediately • *If he treated me like that, I'd leave him in a heartbeat;* If he treated me like that, I'd leave him immediately.

in someone's face (to be) *exp.* to annoy someone • *She's always in my face!;* She always annoys me!
▸ ALSO: **"Get out of my face!"** *exp.* (very popular) "Leave me alone!"

"Isn't that special?" *exp.* a sarcastic phrase said after encountering something bizarre • *Look how those kids are throwing things at their mother! Isn't that special?*
♦ NOTE: This expression comes from the popular television show "Saturday Night Live" where one of the characters repeatedly and sarcastically used this expression.

jam (to) *v.* **1.** to proceed very successfully • *We're almost done with all this work! We're jammin'!;* We're almost done with all this work! We're proceeding very successfully! **2.** to hurry • *The movie starts in five minutes! Let's jam!;* The movie starts in five minutes! Let's hurry! • **3.** to play musical instruments in an impromtu setting • *Wanna jam tonight?;* Do you want to play some music tonight?

jerk someone around (to) *exp.* to mislead someone • *The salesperson jerked me around for an hour!;* The salesperson misled me for an hour!

kick back (to) *exp.* to relax • *I'm just gonna kick back all day;* I'm just going to relax all day.

kinky *adj.* sexually bizarre or deviant • *They're into kinky sex;* They enjoy bizarre sexual acts.

♦ NOTE: In the above sentence, the expression *"to be into something"* was used. This is a common universal expression meaning "to enjoy something."

lightweight *n.* a person with a low tolerance (especially to alcohol) • *He gets drunk on just half a glass of wine. What a lightweight!;* He gets drunk on just half a glass of wine. He has such a low tolerance to alcohol!

major *adj.* extreme • *He's a major dweeb!;* He's a real dweeb!

make a pit stop (to) *exp.* to go to the bathroom • *I have to make a pit stop before we leave;* I have to go to the bathroom before we leave.
♦ NOTE: This expression comes from the sport of race car driving where drivers commonly make a quick stop in the pit for repairs on their cars.

mondo • **1.** *adv.* extremely • *He's mondo cute!;* He's extremely cute! • **2.** *adj.* big • *I've got a mondo headache;* I've got a huge headache.
♦ SYNONYM: **mongo** *adv. & adj.*

no biggie (to be) *exp.* not to be a problem • *I failed my econ test, but no biggie. I can take it again tomorrow;* I failed my economy test, but it's no problem. I can take it again tomorrow.

♦ NOTE: Colloquially, it is more common to say *"It's no biggie"* than *"It's not a biggie."*

nuke (to) *v.* to microwave • *My pizza got cold. I'm gonna nuke it;* My pizza got cold. I'm going to microwave it.

on hit (to be) *exp.* to be exceptional • *That car's on hit!;* That car's fantastic!

on the rag (to be) *exp.* said of a woman who is in a bad mood (due to menstruation) • *You're sure on the rag!;* You're sure in a bad mood!

♦ CAUTION: The noun *"rag"* is a crude yet popular synonym for "sanitary napkin." The expression *"to be on the rag"* is commonly shortened to *"to be O.T.R."*

out of here (to be) *exp.* to be on the verge of leaving • *I'm late! I'm outta here!;* I'm late! I'm leaving now!

party on (to) *exp.* to keep on partying • *Party on!;* Let's keep partying!

♦ NOTE: The noun "party" is commonly used as a verb in slang; *"to party."*

pond scum *exp.* an insult for one who is extremely low and contemptuous • *Why would you want to date him? The guy's nothing but pond scum!;* Why would you want to date him? The guy is contemptuous!

♦ NOTE: The noun "scum" refers to the filthy deposits that accumulate in a stagnant pond. These deposits are usually full of bacteria and oftentimes have a foul odor.

"Psych!" *exclam.* "Fooled you!"

♦ NOTE: A shortened version of the slang expression *"to psych someone out,"* this common exclamation is used to indicate that the speaker has playfully tricked the listener. • *I told her that we were brothers since everyone says we look alike. Then I yelled 'Psych! We're just friends!';* I told her that we were brothers since everyone says we look alike. Then I yelled 'Fooled you! We're just friends!'

pull a _____ (to) *exp.* to act like (name) • *He pulled a Dan and fell asleep in class;* He acted like Dan and fell asleep in class.

pull an all-nighter (to) *exp.* to stay up all night (usually in order to study) • *You look terrible! Did you pull an all-nighter?;* You look terrible! Did you stay up all night?

puppy *n.* thing • *What a great car! This puppy can move!;* What a great car! This thing can move!

rag on (to) *exp.* to criticize • *Every time you come to my house, you rag on me!;* Every time you come to my house, you criticize me!

rip *n.* thievery • *You paid $100 for that? What a rip!;* You paid $100 for that? What thievery!
  ♦ NOTE: This is a shortened version of the popular slang term *"rip-off."*

royal *adj.* extreme • *What a royal jerk!;* What an extreme jerk!

scope [out] (to) *exp.* to observe and examine • *The only reason she came to the party was to scope [out] guys;* The only reason she came to the party was to evaluate guys.

screw someone over (to) *exp.* to deceive or cheat someone • *The guy who sold me my car really screwed me over;* The guy who sold me my car really deceived me.
  ♦ VARIATION: **to screw someone** *exp.* • (lit); to have sexual intercourse with someone • This is a vulgar synonym for the expression *"to screw someone over."* The addition of the preposition *"over"* seems to

soften the vulgarity of the same expression.

scum-sucking pig *exp.* a low and contemptuous person • *What a scum-sucking pig!;* What a low and contemptuous person!

scuz ball *n.* a contemptuous, vulgar, and filthy person • *How can you go out with him? He's such a scuz ball!;* How can you go out with him? He's such a disgusting person!
  ♦ VARIATION (1): **scuz** *n.* • *What a scuz!;* What a disgusting person!
  ♦ VARIATION (2): **scuz bucket** *n.* • *Your sister actually likes that scuz bucket?;* Your sister actually likes that disgusting person?

serious *adj.* intense • *Let's have some serious fun!;* Let's have some intense fun!

"Sure, Bill!" *exclam.* "I don't believe you!" • *You used to date that gorgeous girl? Sure, Bill!;* You used to date that gorgeous girl? I don't believe you!

"Shut up!" *exclam.* "You've got to be kidding!"
  ♦ NOTE: Since the expression *"Shut up!"* also means "Be quiet!" the difference in connotation depends on the delivery of the speaker.

single (to be) *n.* not to be in a relationship • *I prefer being* *single;* I prefer not having a relationship.

sixer *n.* six-pack of beer • *Can you pick up a sixer at the store for me?;* Can you purchase a six-pack of beer at the store for me?

‣ NOTE: The expression *"to pick up"* is commonly used universally to mean **1.** "to purchase" and **2.** "to find someone for a sexual encounter." The difference between definitions **1.** and **2.** depends on the context.

skag *n.* ugly girl • *What a skag!;* What an ugly girl!

sloppy (to be) *adj.* to be drunk due to carelessness • *You got sloppy at her party last night;* You got carelessly drunk at her party last night.

space cadet *exp.* eccentric and flighty person • *She's such a space cadet!;* She's such a flighty person!

‣ SYNONYM (1): **space case** *exp.*
‣ SYNONYM (2): **airhead** *n.*
‣ NOTE: These expressions come from the popular slang adjective *spacy* meaning "in a constant state of bewilderment."

space [out] (to) *v.* **1.** to become temporarily mentally detached due to fatigue or stress • *When*

the professor asked me to give the answer, I totally spaced out!; When the professor asked me to give the answer, my mind went blank! • **2.** to be dazed • *You look totally spaced [out]. What's wrong?;* You look totally dazed. What's wrong? • **3.** to relax • *I can't wait for the weekend to just sit at home and space [out]!;* I can't wait for the weekend to just sit at home and relax! • **4.** to be oblivious due to drugs • *I can't believe he still does drugs. Look at him over there spacing [out]!;* I can't believe he still takes hallucinogens. Look at him over there being oblivious!

‣ NOTE: The expression *"to do drugs"* is commonly used to mean "to consume drugs for recreational use only," whereas the phrase "to take drugs" is used to mean both "to consume drugs for medical purposes or recreational use" depending on the context.

spaz [out] (to) *exp.* to lose control of one's emotions • (lit); to become spastic • *Don't spaz [out] on me!;* Don't lose control of your emotions with me!

‣ ALSO (1): **spaz** *n.* one who loses control of his/her emotions.
‣ ALSO (2): **spaz attack** *exp.* a loss of control of one's emotions • *Don't have a spaz attack!;* Don't have an emotional attack!

studly *adv.* manly • *He's so studly!;*
He's so manly!
♦ NOTE: This comes from the
slang term *stud* meaning a
"masculine man" or literally "a
male horse."

suck up to someone (to) *exp.* to
flatter someone in order to get in
one's good graces • *The way she*
sucks up to the teacher makes me
sick!; The way she flatters the
teacher in order to get in her good
graces makes me sick!

"Take a picture, it lasts longer!"
exp. humorous expression yelled
to someone who is staring.
♦ VARIATION: **"Take a picture!"**

take cuts (to) *exp.* to break into a
line of people rather than queuing
up at the end • *That's the guy*
who took cuts in front of me at
the movies!; That's the guy who
broke into the line in front of me
at the movies!
♦ ALSO: **to give someone cuts**
exp. to allow someone to break
into the line • *She always gives*
cuts to her friends; She always
lets her friends break into the line.

"Take it easy!" *exp.* **1.** "Good-
bye!" • **2.** "Don't get so upset!"
♦ NOTE: The difference in
connotation between **1.** and **2.**
depends on the context.

talk to Ralph/Huey on the big
white phone (to) *exp.*
(humorous) to vomit • *I spent the*
whole night talking to
Ralph/Huey on the big white
phone; I spent the whole night
vomiting.
♦ NOTE: **1.** The verb *"to Ralph"* is
commonly used to mean "to
vomit." • **2.** *"Huey"* is close to
the sound that one would make
while vomiting. • **3.** The
expression *"big white phone"*
refers to the "toilet" because of
its shape when the lid is lifted.

there (to be) *exp.* to plan on being
in a certain location • *I just found*
out that my favorite music group
is performing at the
amphitheater! I'm there!; I just
found out that my favorite music
group is performing at the
amphitheater! I'm going to be
there!

trashed (to be) *adj.* **1.** to be
exhausted • *I'm going to bed. I'm*
trashed; I'm going to bed. I'm
exhausted. • **2.** to be intoxicated
• *He got trashed at the party last*
night; He got intoxicated at the
party last night.
♦ ALSO: **trash (to)** *v.* to criticize
unmercifully • *As soon as he*
walked in, she started trashing
him; As soon as he walked in,
she started criticizing him
unmercifully.

throw attitude (to) *exp.* to act arrogant • *She sure does throw attitude all the time!;* She sure is arrogant all the time!
♦ VARIATION: **to throw tude** *exp.*
♦ NOTE: For more common abbreviations used by teenagers, see page 163.

toss one's cookies (to) *exp.* to vomit • *Every time I go sailing, I toss my cookies;* Every time I go sailing, I vomit.

veg [out] (to) *exp.* to relax and do nothing • *I'm gonna stay home and veg [out];* I'm going to stay home and relax.
♦ NOTE: In this expression, *"veg"* refers to "vegetable" since vegetables stay planted in one position.

wacked [out] (to be) *exp.* to be crazy • *Aren't you scared to be in a room alone with him? He's wacked [out]!;* Aren't you scared to be in a room alone with him? He's crazy!

wasted (to be) *adj.* **1.** to be drunk • **2.** to be intoxicated from drugs *He got wasted last night;* He got drunk/intoxicated from drugs last night.
♦ NOTE: The difference in connotation between definitions **1.** and **2.** depends on the context.

wig [out] (to) *exp.* to lose control of one's emotions • *She wigged [out] when she found out her car was stolen;* She became hysterical when she found out her car was stolen.

wimpy (to be) *adj.* to be helpless, ineffectual or frail • *He's so wimpy. I bet he's never exercised in his life;* He's so frail. I bet he's never exercised in his life.
♦ ALSO: **wimp** *n.* one who is helpless, ineffectual or weak.

wired (to be) *adj.* to be hyperactive • *Coffee makes me wired;* Coffee makes me hyper.

wuss *n.* coward, weakling • *Why are you so scared to tell her you're angry? Don't be such a wuss!;* Why are you so scared to tell her you're angry? Don't be such a coward!

wussy (to be) *adj.* to be spineless or cowardly • *He's so wussy he'll never go camping with you;* He's such a sissy he'll never go camping with you.

yack *v.* to vomit • *If I eat one more bite, I'm gonna yack!;* If I eat one more bite, I'm going to vomit!

PRACTICE USING COMMON TEEN AND COLLEGE SLANG

[Answers on p. 217]

**A. Choose the correct definition of the words in boldface.
    NOTE: There is more than one possible answer for each.**

1. **to leave:**   a. to bolt   b. to space out
                           c. to boogie   d. to book

2. **extreme:**   a. studly   b. major
                           c. mondo   d. royal

3. **terrific:**   a. kinky   b. fly
                           c. dope   d. fresh

4. **fool:**   a. dode   b. dork
                           c. geek   d. puppy

5. **drunk:**   a. lame   b. faced
                           c. fried   d. hammered

6. **to vomit:**   a. to take cuts   b. to blow chow
                           c. to toss one's cookies d. to heave

7. **exhausted:**   a. burnt [out]   b. trashed
                           c. serious   d. mondo

8. **to sleep:**   a. to throw tude   b. to crash
                           c. to catch some Zs   d. to spew

9. **to drink:**   a. to veg [out]   b. to crash
                           c. to chug   d. to down

10. **to get upset:**   a. to spaz [out]   b. to wig [out]
                           c. to veg [out]   d. to freak [out]

A CLOSER LOOK (2):
Common Abbreviations Used by Teenagers

As seen in **STREET TALK -1**, it is very common for all age groups to use acronyms–

> ➤ *Get a **B.L.T.** and an **O.J.** for the **V.P. A.S.A.P. O.K**?;*

> ➤ Get a bacon, lettuce, and tomato sandwich and an orange juice for the vice president as soon as possible, all right?

and abbreviations–

> ➤ *I have a week of **comp** time for vacation coming to me;*

> ➤ I have a week of compensation time for vacation coming to me.

For teens and college students, using these shortcuts gives them a sense of being *cool* or contemporary since the surest way to be ostracized from one's peers is to wear clothing and use language which is outdated.

The following list represents some of the most popular abbreviations used primarily by the younger generation unless otherwise noted.

Beemer *n.* BMW • *I got a Beemer for my birthday!;* I got a BMW for my birthday!

Benz *n.* Mercedes Benz • *I can't believe your father let you drive his new Benz yesterday;* I can't believe your father let you drive his new Mercedes Benz yesterday.
♦ NOTE: This is used by all age groups.

Benz-O *n.* Mercedes Benz • *How much did you pay for your Benz-O?* How much did you pay for your Mercedes Benz?

Caddy *n.* Cadillac • *Have you seen the new Caddy I just bought?*

Have you seen the new Cadillac I just bought?
♦ NOTE: This is used by all age groups.

cas *adj.* casual • *It's easy to feel relaxed with your parents because they're so cas;* It's easy to feel relaxed with your parents because they're so casual.
♦ NOTE (1): The abbreviation *"cas"* is pronounced "caj" like the first three letters of the word "casual."
♦ NOTE (2): The term *"cas"* is oftentimes used by the older generation as well.

def *adj.* **1.** definitely • *Do I think he's cute? Def!;* Do I think he's cute? Definitely! • **2.** fantastic • *That dress is def!;* That dress is fantastic!

do *n.* hairdo • *What do you think of my new do?;* What do you think of my new hairdo?

fridge *n.* refrigerator • *There is nothing to eat in the fridge!;* There's nothing to eat in the refrigerator!
◗ NOTE: This is used by all age groups.

hid *adj.* hideous • *Her dress is hid;* Her dress is hideous.

jel *adj.* jealous • *I'm major jel!;* I'm extremely jealous!

legit *adj.* legitimate • *Does his offer sound legit?;* Does his offer sound legitimate?
◗ NOTE: This is used by all age groups.

low pro *exp.* low profile, inconspicuous • *He likes to be low pro;* He likes to be inconspicuous.

mike *n.* microphone • *Is my mike on?;* Is my microphone on?
◗ NOTE: This is used by all age groups.

no comp *exp.* no competition • *This opponent's gonna be no comp for me;* This opponent is going to be no competition for me.

ob *adj.* obvious • *That's ob!;* That's obvious!

preg *adj.* pregnant • *She looks preg to me;* She looks pregnant to me.
◗ SYNONYM (1): **preggo** *adj.*
◗ SYNONYM (2): **preggers** *adj.*

rad *adj.* radical, fantastic • *He's a rad guitar player!;* He's a fantastic guitar player!

rep *n.* reputation • *He has a bad rep around here;* He has a bad reputation around here.
◗ NOTE: This is used by all age groups.

ridic *adj.* ridiculous • *That's ridic!;* That's ridiculous!

rip *n.* rip off (slang for "thievery") • *That's a total rip!;* That's total thievery!

simp *n.* simpleton, fool • *He's such a simp;* He's such a simpleton.

tude *n.* attitude • *She's throwing major tude;* She has a very bad attitude.

vibes *n.* vibrations (slang for "feelings that one gets from another person or place") • *Every time I see her, I always get bad vibes;* Every time I see her, I feel uneasy.

vocab *n.* vocabulary • *We're taking our vocab test in French class today;* We're taking our vocabulary test in French class today.

A CLOSER LOOK (3):
Common Abbreviations for Course Names in School

Students have also developed this technique into a fine art when referring to the names of their classes. The following abbreviations have been used by students for several generations and have still retained their popularity.

anthro *n.* anthropology • *What time do you have anthro?;* What time do you have anthropology class?

A.V. *n.* audio-visual • *I'm majoring in A.V.;* I'm majoring in audio-visual.

bio *n.* biology • *Who's teaching bio this quarter?;* Who's teaching biology class this quarter?
♦ NOTE: The curriculum in many universities is divided into quarters, others are broken into semesters.

biz ad *n.* business administration • *I didn't know you were interested in biz ad!;* I didn't know you were interested in business administration!

calc *n.* calculus • *If I don't pass calc, I'm going to have to take it again in summer school!;* If I don't pass calculus, I'm going to have to take it again in summer school!

chem *n.* chemistry • *My chem teacher's great!;* My chemistry teacher's great!

comp lit *n.* composition literature • *Who sits next to you in comp lit?;* Who sits next to you in composition literature?

econ *n.* economics • *Econ's my best subject;* Economics is my best subject.

English comp *n.* English composition • *Didn't you take English comp last quarter?;* Didn't you take English composition last quarter?

English lit *n.* English literature • *He shined English lit again?;* He didn't go to English literature class again?

home ec *n.* home economics • *My sister hated her home ec class;* My sister hated her home economics class.

improv *n.* improvisation • *Mrs. Berman is teaching improv this quarter;* Mrs. Berman is teaching improvisation this quarter.

info systems *n.* information systems • *There are only three people in my info systems class;* There are only three people in my information systems class.

kinese *n.* kinesiology • *He's a kinese student;* He's a kinesiology student.

math *n.* mathematics • *You actually like math?;* You actually like mathematics?

P.E. *n.* physical education • *I'm glad I have P.E. early in the morning. It helps wake me up;* I'm glad I have physical education class early in the morning. It helps wake me up.

phys ed *n.* physical education • *I hate phys ed 'cause I'm terrible in sports!;* I hate physical education class cause I'm terrible in sports!

poli sci *n.* political science • *I'm changing my major to poli sci;* I'm changing my major to political science.

psych *n.* psychology • *Your psych teacher's so young!;* Your psychology teacher's so young!

soc *n.* sociology • (pronounced: *"soshe"*) • *I aced my soc final!;* I got a high grade on my sociology final!
◗ NOTE: *soc* is also a common abbreviation among the younger generation meaning "sociable." However, when used as an abbreviation, its connotation changes to "excessively sociable" usually due to one trying to be accepted • *She's so soc!;* She's so excessively sociable!

telecom *n.* telecommunications • *I'm taking telecom with Mr. Graul;* I'm taking telecommunications class with Mr. Graul.

trig *n.* trigonometry • *I don't understand trig;* I don't understand trigonometry.

A CLOSER LOOK (4):
Popular Adjectives With Opposite Meanings

Several decades ago, hoodlums used slang in order not to be understood by the authorities, namely the police, or *cops* in slang. When a hoodlum said, *"Let's scram!"* the cops didn't understand that this expression simply meant, "Let's leave!" But it didn't take long for the cops to catch on to this "secret" language, so the hoodlums created pig-latin whereby the syllables are merely reversed and the letter "y" is attached to the end. Now the hoodlums were saying, *"Let's amscray."* As the cops slowly learned the latest slang words, the thugs would simply create new ones.

This holds true for the younger generation of today. Not long ago, teenagers used the adjective *bad* to mean "good" as a way to confuse parents. However, once parents began to understand this, teens changed it. Therefore, if a teenager points to you and says, "What a *stupid* shirt!" don't be offended. You've just been given one of the ultimate compliments. *Bad* is out, *stupid* is in!

➤ NOTE: The difference between definitions **1.** and **2.** below depend on the context and delivery of the speaker.

badass *adj.* **1.** bad and dangerous • *Don't get him mad. That guy is badass!;* Don't get him mad. That guy is bad and dangerous! • **2.** fantastic • *This party is badass!;* This party is fantastic! ◆ CAUTION: Since the adjective *badass* contains the noun *ass,* vulgar for "buttocks", it is considered somewhat vulgar and should only be used with close friends.

heinous *adj.* **1.** fantastic • *What a heinous car!;* What a fantastic car! • **2.** terrible • *Did you hear about the heinous crime she* committed?; Did you hear about the terrible crime she committed?

hell-a-fied *adj.* **1.** fantastic • *She's hell-a-fied!;* She's fantastic! • **2.** terrible • *This class is totally hell-a-fied!;* This class is really terrible!

killer *adj.* **1.** fantastic • *What a killer dress!;* What a fantastic dress! • **2.** extremely difficult • *This is a killer class!;* That's an extremely difficult class!

meanest *adv.* **1.** best • *He plays the meanest piano!;* He plays the best piano! • **2.** worst • *That was the meanest homework assignment!;* That was the worst homework assignment!

nasty *adj.* **1.** fantastic • *She looks nasty today!;* She looks fantastic today! • **2.** extremely difficult • *The professor just gave us some nasty work to do;* The professor just gave us some difficult work to do.

serious *adj.* **1.** intense and fun • *We did some serious partying last night!;* We did some intense and fun partying last night! • **2.** intense and critical • *There was some serious fighting going on at the market today;* There

was some intense fighting going on at the market today.

◗ NOTE: In the drug world, the verb *"to party"* means "to use cocaine." The difference in connotation simply depends on the context.

stupid *adj.* **1.** absurd • *Take off that stupid shirt!;* Take off that absurd shirt! • **2.** fantastic • *That hat is way stupid!;* That hat is really fantastic!

wicked *adj.* **1.** fantastic • *That's a wicked hat!;* That's a fantastic hat! • **2.** extremely difficult • *This work is wicked!;* This work is extremely difficult!

RAP SLANG

– At the Party –

Dialogue In Slang

At the Party

DIALOGUE

Bob and Tom are attending their high school reunion.

Bob: Hey, **homes**! I thought that was you **walling** over here. **Gimme some skin**! **How ya living**?

Tom: **Yo G**! **Good to go**, man. I was just **maxing and relaxing** here. Hey, you're sure **sporting** some **fly gear**. You must be **living large**? You used to tell everyone you were always **tapped out** all the time.

Bob: I just started **minting** last year. I like those **dead presidents**! I just gotta be careful not to get **jacked** when I walk outside!

Tom: You're not just **talking outside your neck**. You know, you're the first person I've recognized since I **fell in** at this reunion and I've been **clocking** everyone for an hour.

Bob: Well, see that **freak** over there **cresting** at you? Remember her? That's Kim. She used to be a real **duck** but now she's **too cold**!

Tom: Yeah, she could really **bust a move**. I don't mean to be **cracking on** her, but every time I tried **jaw jacking** with **Miss Thang**, she got so **frosted** that I finally just **folded**.

Bob: She was **dissing** you bad, homes. I got **benched** by her tonight, too. You know, this party's **played**. I've been waiting for them to **pump it up** for an hour. I'm **breaking out**. **Peace up**!

Lesson Nine - RAP SLANG *(Hip Hop)*

Translation of dialogue in standard English

At the Party

DIALOGUE

Bob and Tom are attending their high school reunion.

Bob: Hey, **friend**! I thought that was you **standing against the wall** over here. **Shake my hand**! **How are you**?

Tom: **Hi**! **Just great**, **friend**. I was just **relaxing** here. Hey, you're sure **wearing** some **nice clothes**. You must be **rich**? You used to tell everyone you were always **destitute** all the time.

Bob: I just started **making money** last year. I like those **dollars**! I just gotta be careful not to get **robbed** when I walk outside!

Tom: You're not **fooling**. You know, you're the first person I've recognized since I **arrived** at this reunion and I've been **watching** everyone for an hour.

Bob: Well, see that **wild woman** over there **smiling** at you? Remember her? That's Kim. She used to be a real **ugly person** but now she's **really attractive**!

Tom: Yes, she could really **dance**. I don't mean to be **criticizing** her, but every time I tried **talking** with that **conceited woman**, she became so **indifferent** that I finally just **gave up**.

Bob: She just **didn't have any respect for you**, friend. I got **rejected** by her tonight, too. You know, this party's **boring**. I've been waiting for them to **increase the volume on the stereo** for an hour. I'm **leaving**. **Good-bye**!

Lesson Nine - RAP SLANG *(Hip Hop)*

Dialogue in slang as it would be heard

At the Party

DIALOGUE

Bob 'n Tom 'r attending their high school reunion.

Bob: Hey, **homes**! I thought that was you **wallin'** over here. **Gimme s'm skin**! **How ya livin'**?

Tom: **Yo G**! **Good ta go**, **man**. I was jus' **maxin' and relaxin'** here. Hey, yer sher **sportin'** s'm **fly gear**. You must be **livin' large**? You used ta tell everyone you were always **tapped oud** all the time.

Bob: I jus' starded **mintin'** last year. I like those **dead presidents**! I jus' gotta be careful not ta get **jacked** when I walk outside!

Tom: You **ain't jus' talkin' outside d'jer neck**. Ya know, yer the first person I've recognized since I **fell in** at this reunion 'n I've been **clockin'** ev'ryone fer 'n hour.

Bob: Well, see that **freak** over there **crestin'** at cha? Remember her? That's Kim. She used ta be a real **duck** but now she's **too cold**!

Tom: Yeah, she could really **bust a move**. I don' mean ta be **crackin' on** 'er, but ev'ry time I tried **jaw jackin'** with **Miss Thang**, she got so **frosted** thad I fin'lly jus' **folded**.

Bob: She was **dissin'** ya bad, homes. I got **benched** by 'er t'night, too. Ya know, this party's **played**. I been waitin' for 'em ta **pump id up** fer an hour. I'm **breakin' out**. **Peace up**!

Vocabulary

(NOTE: In rap, it is extremely common to contract the *-ing* ending to *-in'* as will be demonstrated in this section.)

ain't *v.* used as a replacement for "am not/are not/is not" • *I ain't touchin' that big dog!;* I'm not touching that big dog! • *There ain't no way I'm goin' to that party;* There is no way I'm going to that party.
 ⁌ NOTE: The term *"ain't,"* considered to be inferior grammar, originated in the South by poorly educated people living in the hills. However, to the despair of English teachers nationwide, it is still popular. *"Ain't"* is also commonly used in jest as a way to emphasis a statement: *You can't expect to graduate college if you never study. It ain't gonna happen!;* You can't expect to graduate college if you never study. It's simply not going to happen!

benched (to get) *exp.* to be reprimanded • *I got benched by my girlfriend 'cause I forgot her birthday;* I was reprimanded by my girlfriend because I forgot her birthday.

break out (to) *exp.* to leave • *What time you breakin' out?;* What time are you leaving?
 ⁌ NOTE: It is extremely popular among the younger generation to contract *"are you"* to simply *"you"* as demonstrated in the above sentence: *What time you breakin' out?*
 ⁌ SYNONYM (1): **to eject** *v.* • *I'm bored here. Let's eject;* I'm bored here. Let's leave.
 ⁌ SYNONYM (2): **to roll out** *exp.* • *You rollin' out with me?;* You leaving with me?
 ⁌ SYNONYM (3): **to jet** *v.* • *I gotta jet!;* I have to leave!

bust a move (to) *exp.* to dance • *I didn't know you could bust a move like that!;* I didn't know you could dance like that!
 ⁌ SYNONYM: **to kick stomp** *exp.* • *Wanna go kick stompin' tonight?;* Do you want to go dancing tonight?

clock (to) *v.* to watch • *Who's that guy clockin' you over there?;* Who's that guy watching you over there?

cold (to be) *exp.* to be attractive • *She's too cold!;* She's pretty!
> ◗ SYNONYM (1): **to be too cold** *exp.*
> ◗ SYNONYM (2): **to be clean** *exp.*
> ◗ SYNONYM (3): **to be cookin'** *exp.*
> ◗ SYNONYM (4): **to be smokin'** *exp.*

crack on someone (to) *exp.* to criticize someone • *Quit crackin' on me!;* Quit criticizing me!
> ◗ SYNONYM (1): **to rank on someone** *exp.* • *Who are you two rankin' on this time?;* Who are you two criticizing this time?
> ◗ SYNONYM (2): **to snap on someone** *exp.* • *If you're gonna start snappin' on me again, I'm breakin' out;* If you're going to start criticizing me again, I'm leaving.

crest (to) *v.* to smile • *I think she's crestin' at you!;* I think she's smiling at you!
> ◗ NOTE: This humorous term comes from a brand of toothpaste by the same name and was simply turned into a verb.

dead presidents *exp.* money • *Look at all those dead presidents!;* Look at all that money!

dis someone (to) *v.* to have disrespect for someone • *Don't dis me!;* Don't have disrespect for me!
> ◗ ALSO: **to dis and dismiss** *exp.* to have disrespect for someone and then ask him/her to leave • *When I see her tomorrow, I'm dissin' and dismissin'!;* When I see her tomorrow, I'm letting her know that I don't like her and then I'm telling her to get out of my life!
> ◗ NOTE: A common error which has become universal is to use the noun "disrespect" as a verb: "to disrespect." For example: *Don't disrespect me!;* Don't have disrespect for me! Although this is incorrect usage, it is extremely common.

duck *n.* unattractive female • *What a duck!;* What an ugly female!
> ◗ ALSO: **to duck** *v.* to date ugly women • *That's his girlfriend? There he goes duckin' again;* That's his girlfriend? There he goes dating ugly women again.

fall in (to) *exp.* to arrive • *What time did you fall in at the party?;* What time did you arrive at the party?

fly gear *exp.* exceptional clothing • *Look at that fly gear!;* Look at that exceptional clothing!

♦ NOTE (1): The expression *"fly gear"* is actually a combination of slang and standard English. The term *"fly"* has become one of the most commonly used adjectives among the younger generation: *That's a fly stereo system!;* That's a fantastic stereo system! However, the term *"gear"* meaning "clothing" or "outfit" is simply a standard term commonly used with the adjective *"fly"* when referring to extremely attractive clothing.

♦ NOTE (2): See: **sport (to)**

fold (to) *v.* to quit or surrender • *This work is too hard. I'm foldin';* This work is too hard. I'm quitting.

♦ NOTE: The verb *"to fold"* is an extremely common card-playing term used by participants who cannot continue the round due to inferior cards. When the player calls out *"I fold,"* the hands which are holding the playing cards are closed or *folded* together indicating surrender.

freak *n.* very attractive sexy individual • *I love goin' to parties to check out all the freaks!;* I love going to parties to examine all the attractive people!

♦ NOTE: **to check out** *exp.* to examine, to look at • *Check her out!;* Examine her!

♦ SYNONYM: **freakazoid** *n.* • *What a freakazoid!;* What a gorgeous and sexy person!

frosted (to be) *adj.* cold and emotionless • *I tried talkin' to her but she was frosted;* I tried talking to her but she was cold and emotionless.

♦ NOTE: **frosty** (common slang term among all age groups) • **1.** *n.* abusive term referring to someone who is cold and emotionless • *Hey, frosty!;* Hey, you cold and emotionless person! • **2.** *adj. He was so frosty with you;* He was so cold and emotionless with you.

give someone some skin (to) *exp.* a common greeting and signal of excitement or congratulations.

♦ NOTE: This signal consists of the initiator calling out *"Gimme some skin!"* At this point, he/she extends the hand, palm up, while the other person slaps it. The process is then reversed as the original initiator slaps the hand of the other person. The expression *"Gimme some skin!"* is commonly used among the younger generation as: **1.** a greeting • *Hey, Steve! Gimme some skin!* • **2.** a signal of excitement • *Your birthday is on the same day as mine? All right! Gimme some skin!* • **3.** a signal of congratulations • *I just heard you're gettin' married! Gimme some skin!*

good to go (to be) *exp.* to be going great • *Everything's good to go;* Everything is going great!

hip hop *n.* rap music (an extremely popular style of song where the performer speaks the lyrics in rhythm).

homes *n.* friend • (lit); someone who is from one's hometown • *Hey, homes!;* Hey, friend!
  ‣ SYNONYM: **homey** *n.*
    ⇨ NOTE: As learned in lesson one, *"homey"* is commonly used among teens in daily conversation. However, the shortened version, *"homes,"* is more readily heard in rap music.
  ‣ NOTE: **squad** *n.* a group of friends.

"How ya livin'?" *exp.* How are you doing?
  ‣ NOTE: *"ya"* is an extremely common contraction of *"are you"* and is used by all age groups.

jack someone (to) *v.* to rob someone • *I got jacked in front of my house!;* I got robbed in front of my house!
  ‣ NOTE: This comes from the standard verb *"to hi-jack"* meaning "to force an airplane pilot to deviate from the normal flight pattern by means of gunpoint."
  ‣ ALSO: **jacker** *n.* robber.

jaw jack (to) *exp.* to talk a lot • *We jaw jacked on the phone for an hour;* We talked on the phone for an hour.
  ‣ NOTE: This is a humorous expression based on the noun "jack" which is a device used to raise one end of a car off the ground in order to change a tire. To operate a jack, a long handle is cranked up and down much like one's jaws when speaking.
  ‣ SYNONYM: **to track** *v.* • *You realize we've been trackin' for two hours already?;* Do you realize we've been talking for two hours already?

live large (to) *exp.* to be very successful (and have a lot of money) • *This is your house? You must be livin' large!;* This is your house? You must be very successful!
  ‣ SYNONYM (1): **to be crazy large** *exp.*
  ‣ SYNONYM (2): **to be extra large** *exp.*
  ‣ SYNONYM (3): **to be stupid large** *exp.*

max and relax (to) *exp.* to relax • *I spent four hours maxin' and relaxin' on the beach today;* I spent four hours relaxing on the beach today.
  ‣ SYNONYM (1): **to chill** *v.*
  ‣ SYNONYM (2): **to cold chill** *exp.*
  ‣ SYNONYM (3): **to cool** *v.*

◆ SYNONYM (4): **to cool out** *exp.*
◆ SYNONYM (5): **to limp** *v.*
◆ SYNONYM (6): **to max out** *exp.*

mint (to) *v.* to make a lot of money • *Ever since he got promoted, he's been mintin'!;* Ever since he got promoted, he's been making a lot of money!
◆ NOTE: It is common in slang to transform nouns into verbs, consequently creating somewhat humorous terms. The verb *"to mint"* is a transformation of the noun "The United States Mint" where money is produced.

Miss Thang *exp.* name given to a pretentious woman • *Look at Miss Thang over there!;* Look at that pretentious woman over there!
◆ NOTE: The term *"thang"* is simply "thing" as it is pronounced with a southern accent. In the 1800s, wealthy women of the South were considered to be exceedingly pretentious since they were always seen in public as being coquettish, cultured, excessively charming, overly attentive to men and always dressed in provocative clothing. Due to the thick accent of the region, their accents became equated with wealth and snobbery. Pronouncing the term "thing" as *"thang,"* as it would have been heard articulated by one of these southern women, is an attempt to mock and belittle anyone displaying these kinds of characteristics or affectations. *"Thang"* is possibly just a shortened version of "pretentious little thing."

peace up *exp.* good-bye • *Talk to ya later. Peace up;* Talk to you later. Good-bye.
◆ VARIATION (1): **peace** *n.*
◆ VARIATION (2): **peace out** *exp.*

played (to be) *adj.* said of a party that peaked and has now become boring • *Let's leave. This party's played;* Let's leave. This party has become boring.

pump it up (to) *exp.* • to increase the volume on a stereo system *My mom just left! Pump it up!;* My mom just left! Increase the volume on the stereo!

sport (to) *v.* to wear.
◆ NOTE: The verb *"to sport,"* is **not** a slang term yet a rather formal synonym for the verb "to wear." It is becoming more and more common to use slang terms in conjunction with the more eloquent synonyms of standard terms as seen in the phrase: *to sport some fly gear.* Since the slang adjective *"fly,"* meaning "exceptional," is used in this phrase, it would be considered fine to include more eloquent terms like "to sport" and "gear." However, a teen would surely be ostracized if he/she were to say *"You're sporting some nice*

clothes" since there are no slang terms to offset the formality of the more eloquent terms.

talk outside one's neck (to) *exp.* to lie or tease • *Don't believe him. He's talkin' outside his neck;* Don't believe him. He's lying.

tapped out (to be) *exp.* to be destitute • *I'd lend you some money but I'm tapped out;* I'd lend you some money but I'm destitute.
▸ NOTE: This term originated in the coal mines where a load of ore would be extracted from a mine shaft until the resource was thoroughly depleted or *"tapped out."*

wall (to) *v.* to lean against the wall at a party (instead of dancing) • *Who's that wallin' over there?;* Who's that leaning against the wall over there?
▸ NOTE: This is an updated version of the common expression *"to be a wall flower."*
▸ ALSO: **to play the wall** *exp.*

"Yo G!" *exp.* "Hello!"
▸ NOTE: *"Yo!"* is a common term in the East for "You!" which is used to get one's attention. *"Yo!"* is considered extremely casual and, therefore, acceptable when used with friends. However, if used with strangers or dignitaries, it would be regarded as rude and disrespectful. In these cases, "Excuse me!" would be the more suitable choice.

PRACTICE THE VOCABULARY

[Answers to Lesson Nine, p. 217]

A. Underline the synonym.

1. **to break out:**	a. to enter	b. to leave
2. **to bust a move:**	a. to break a leg	b. to dance
3. **to clock:**	a. to watch	b. to wait
4. **to crest:**	a. to succeed	b. to smile
5. **to fold:**	a. to leave	b. to quit
6. **dead presidents:**	a. money	b. clothes

7. **hip hop:**   a. dancing   b. rap music

8. **homes:**   a. friend   b. enemy

9. **to jack someone:** a. to rob someone   b. to hit someone

10. **to jaw jack:**   a. to yawn   b. to talk a lot

11. **to mint:**   a. to make money   b. to talk a lot

12. **to be played:**   a. to be exciting   b. to be boring

B. Rewrite the following phrases replacing the italicized word(s) with the appropriate slang synonym(s) from the right column.

1. I got *reprimanded* _____ by her.   A. **peace up**

2. If I don't *leave* _____ now, I'm gonna be late.   B. **folded**

3. Stop *criticizing* _____ me!   C. **crackin' on**

4. Who are you *smiling* _____ at?   D. **benched**

5. She *quit* _____ because she said the work was too hard.   E. **livin' large**

6. I love going to the beach to look at all the *attractive people* _____ .   F. **crestin'**

7. Her father's *very successful* _____ .   G. **played**

8. Talk to ya later. *Good-bye* _____ .   H. **freaks**

9. This party's *boring* _____ .   I. **break out**

10. She's *beautiful* _____ !   J. **cold**

C. FIND-THE-WORD-CUBE

Step 1: Fill in the blanks with the correct word using the list below.

Step 2: Find and circle the word in the grid on the opposite page. The first one has been done for you.

Peace	**large**	**played**
duck	**crest**	**presidents**
Thang	**crack**	**bust**
break	**jacked**	**homes**

1. Hey, _____ ! Good to see ya!

2. I'll talk to ya tomorrow. _____ out!

3. I heard you got _____ in front of your house yesterday!

4. Look at the size of your wallet! Where'd you get all those dead _____ ?

5. Stop criticizing her! You really like to _____ on everyone, don't you?

6. This party's _____ . I'm goin' home.

7. Ya know that conceited girl I was telling you about? Well, there she is...Miss _____ !

8. This big house is yours? You must be livin' _____ !

9. Hey, I think she's startin' to _____ at you.

10. She may be a real _____ , but I like her.

11. It's late. I gotta _____ out!

12. Did you see her on the dance floor? She can really _____ a move!

FIND-THE-WORD CUBE

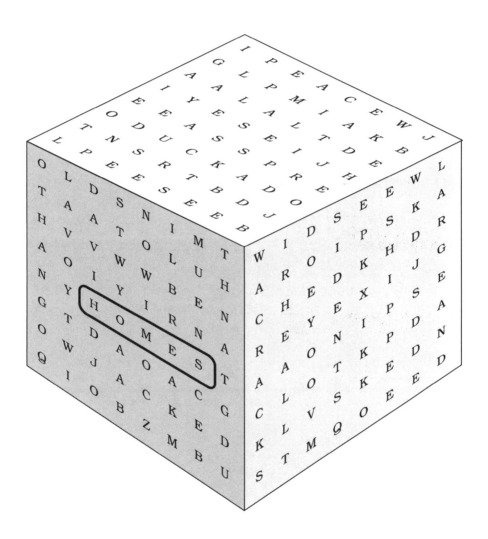

D. **Complete the phrases by choosing the appropriate word(s) from the list below.**

maxin'	Thang	large
played	frosted	fly
skin	go	jacked
jaw	ain't	breakin'

1. Look at Miss _____ who just walked in.

2. I'm _____ out. This party's _____ .

3. You live here? You must be livin' _____ !

4. Congratulations! Gimme some _____ !

5. Good luck tryin' to _____ jack with her. She's _____ .

6. That's some _____ gear you're sportin'!

7. I'm _____ and relaxin' this weekend.

8. Everything is good to _____ today.

9. There _____ no way I'm gonna go with you.

10. I heard you got _____ in broad daylight!

A CLOSER LOOK:
Rap Slang

Rap slang and teen/college slang are very similar since they constantly cross over. However, the main difference is that rap slang is simply newer since it comes from rap music which, compared to the slang that teens have been using for years, is relatively recent.

There is a movement in rap slang to create new and interesting ways of conveying ideas and feelings by actually inventing new terms. Since rap music is heard nationwide, teens began adopting the new lingo into their own vocabulary. This is where the cross-over between rap and teen/college slang begins. In addition, much of the slang that the younger generation currently uses is so expressive and fun that it shows up in rap music. Undoubtedly, there will soon be no difference between the two.

The following is a list of terms derived from rap music, or *"hip hop"* as it is commonly known, that has infiltrated the current slang used by the younger generation.

action *n.* • **1.** fun • *So, where's the action in this city?;* So, where's the fun happening in this city? • **2.** sex • *He went out lookin' for some action;* He went out looking for some sex.
♦ NOTE: The difference in connotation between **1.** and **2.** depends on the context and delivery of the speaker.

baby pop *exp.* young man • *Who's the baby pop you were with last night?;* Who's the young man you were with last night?

bass (to) *v.* • **1.** to play the bass loudly on a stereo system • *We were bassin' so loud last night you could feel the house vibrate;* We were playing the bass so loudly on the stereo system that you could feel the house vibrate. • **2.** to argue • *Look at those two bassin' again;* Look at those two arguing again.

beat boy *n.* rapper • *I didn't know he was a beat boy;* I didn't know

he was a rapper.
♦ VARIATION: **B-boy** *n.*

bomb (to be the) *exp.* to be the best • *She's the bomb!;* She's the best! • *This party's the bomb!;* This party's the best! • *That's the bomb song!;* That's the best song!
♦ NOTE: This expression would thoroughly confuse the average parent since the popular expression *"to be a bomb"* means "to be the worst or a complete failure:" *That movie was a bomb!;* That movie was absolutely terrible!

boom box *exp.* portable stereo • *My mother hates going to the beach because of all the boom boxes everyone has;* My mother hates going to the beach because of all the portable stereos everyone has.

boost (to) *v.* to steal • *Someone boosted my car!;* Someone stole my car!

box *n.* stereo • *Let's hear the new C.D. you bought. Where's your* *box?;* Let's hear the new compact disc recording you bought. Where's your stereo?

to break it down *exp.* to turn down the music • *Could you break it down over there?!;* Could you turn the music down over there?!

broke (to be) *adj.* to be ugly • *I'm not goin' out with her. She's broke!;* I'm not going out with her. She's ugly!
▶ NOTE: In universal slang, *"to be broke"* means "to be poor" which is also in popular use by the younger generation. Teens simply gave this adjective an additional meaning.

brown bag it (to) *exp.* to take one's lunch (to work, to school, etc.) in a brown paper bag instead of eating out • *I'm brown baggin' it today;* I'm bringing my lunch in a brown paper bag today.

bucked (to be) *adj.* get naked •
They got bucked last night and went jogging on the beach!; They got naked last night and went jogging on the beach!
▶ NOTE: This is an updated version of the popular universal expression *"to be buck naked"* meaning "to be completely naked (like a male deer or buck)."

bust a rhyme (to) *exp.* to rap • *That guy can really bust a rhyme;* That guy can really rap.

bust something (to) *exp.* to listen to something • *Bust this tune!;* Listen to this song!

cakes *n.pl.* women or girls • *There are a lot of cakes at your party!;* There are a lot of women at your party!
▶ NOTE: The term *"cakes"* refers to "buttocks."

clout *n.* money • (lit); influence • *Look at all the clout he has in his wallet!;* Look at all the money he has in his wallet!

crank (to) *v.* • **1.** to proceed quickly and smoothly • *I'm crankin' on my homework;* I'm proceeding quickly and smoothly on my homework. • **2.** exceptional • *This music is crankin'!;* This music is great!

creep (to) *v.* to cheat on one's wife or husband • *I heard he's been creepin' at night!;* I heard he's been cheating on his wife at night!

"Do and you're through!" *exp.* "Do it and you're going to be in big trouble with me!"
▶ SEE: Rhyming Slang, p. 131 for additional common rhyming terms.

dressed to impress (to be) *exp.* to be dressed up • *You're dressed to impress tonight!;* You're all dressed up tonight!
▶ SEE: Rhyming Slang, p. 131 for additional common rhyming terms.

Earl (to) *v.* to vomit • *I was so sick, I was Earlin' all over the place!;* I was so sick, I was vomiting all over the place!
♦ SYNONYM (1): **to Ralph** *v.*
♦ SYNONYM (2): **to Rhonda** *v.*

eyes *n.pl.* sunglasses • *Let me just put on my eyes before we go outside;* Let me just put on my sunglasses before we go outside.
♦ SYNONYM: **shades** *n.pl.*

fess with someone (to) *exp.* to annoy someone • *Don't fess with me or do and you're through!;* Don't annoy me or do it and you're going to be in big trouble with me!
♦ NOTE: The term *"fess"* comes from the verbs *"to fool,"* meaning "to jest" and *"to mess,"* meaning "to annoy."

fine as wine (to be) *exp.* to be extremely attractive • *Your boyfriend's fine as wine!;* Your boyfriend's extremely attractive!
♦ SEE: Rhyming Slang, p. 131 for additional common rhyming terms.

funky *adj.* **1.** offensive • *What's that funky smell?;* What's that offensive smell? • **2.** music with a dance beat • *Let's put on some funky music;* Let's put on some music with a good dance beat. • **3.** stylish and offbeat • *That's a funky shirt!;* That's a stylish and offbeat shirt!

get one's boogies on (to) *exp.* to dance hard • *I'm in a dancin' mood. I'm gonna get my boogies on tonight!;* I'm in a dancing mood. I'm going to dance hard tonight!

going on (to have it) *exp.* to be doing well • *She's really got it goin' on;* She's really doing well.

gone (to be) *adj.* to be completely crazy, out of one's mind • *He's gone!;* He's lost his mind!

grill *n.* face • *Nice grill!;* Nice face!
♦ NOTE: This term literally refers to the front end of a car and is consequently used to refer to the "front end of a person," namely "the face."

groove *n.* the bass or driving beat in a song • *This tune's got a great groove;* This song has a great beat.

kickin' (to be) *adj.* to be the best • *This CD is kickin'!;* This compact disc recording is the best!

hearse someone (to) *v.* to kill someone • *He got hearsed last week;* He got killed last week.

honey *n.* young attractive girl • *Let's go to the party and meet some honeys;* Let's go to the party and meet some young attractive girls.

hood *n.* abbreviation for "neighborhood" • *He's not from the hood;* He's not from the neighborhood.

hooptie *n.* old beat up car • *That hooptie just crashed into that wall!;* That old car just crashed into that wall!

hum (to) *v.* to stink • *It's hummin' in this room!;* It stinks in this room!

hut *n.* house • *So, what do you think of my hut?;* So, what do you think of my house?

kick stomp (to) *exp.* to dance • *We're goin' kick stompin' tonight;* We're going dancing tonight.

kicks *n.pl.* shoes • *Where'd you get those cool kicks?;* Where did you get those great shoes?

large and in charge (to be) *exp.* to be the big boss • *Don't fess with him. He's large and in charge!;* Don't annoy him. He's the big boss!

lay something down (to) *exp.* to explain something • *Let me lay it down for you;* Let me explain it to you.

on hit (to be) *exp.* to be very pleasing • *Check him out! He's on hit!;* Observe him! He's very pleasing!

on the flip flop *exp.* later • *Catch ya on the flip flop;* See you later.

out (to be) *adj.* to be crazy • *You're out!;* You're crazy!
♦ NOTE: This is an updated version of the popular expression

"to be out of one's mind" meaning "to be crazy."

rule (to) *v.* to supervise or control • *Why do you always argue with your boss? He's rulin', not you!;* Why do you always argue with your boss? He's the one who makes the decisions, not you!

scan (to) *v.* to observe and examine • *I'm scannin' the room for honeys;* I'm examining the room for attractive girls.

smokin' (to be) *adj.* to be attractive • *She's smokin'!;* She's attractive!

solid (to be) *adj.* to be acceptable • *"I'll pick you up at 3:00, okay?" "Solid;"* "I'll pick you up at 3:00, okay?" "Okay."

souped (to be) *adj.* to be conceited • *She may be too cold but she's souped!;* She may be extremely attractive but she's conceited!

squad *n.* group of friends • *That's my squad over there;* Those are my friends over there.

square *n.* cigarette • *Got an extra square on ya?;* Do you have an extra cigarette on you?

square up (to) *exp.* to calm down • *You better square up or you're gonna get into an accident drivin' like that!;* You'd better calm down or you're going to get into an accident driving like that!

stack (to) *v.* to make a lot of money • *She's stackin' ever since she* *got that promotion;* She's making a lot of money ever since she got that promotion.

step (to) *v.* to dance • *We're goin' steppin' tonight. Wanna come along?;* We're going dancing tonight. Do you want to come along?

suds *n.* beer • *Are those suds you're drinkin'?;* Is that beer you're drinking?

sweat someone (to) *exp.* to bother someone • *Don't sweat me!;* Don't bother me!
  ♦ NOTE: This comes from the common universal expression *"No sweat!"* meaning "No bother!"

take it light (to) *exp.* to calm down • *Take it light and tell me what happened;* Calm down and tell me what happened.

tear it up (to) *exp.* **1.** to have a lot of fun • *We're tearin' it up tonight!;* We're having a lot of fun tonight! • **2.** to dance hard • *I saw you tearin' it up on the dance floor last night!;* I saw

you dancing hard on the dance floor last night!

track (to) *v.* to talk • *We tracked on the phone for an hour;* We talked on the phone for an hour.

trip (to) *exp.* to act irrational • *What are you talkin' about? You're trippin'!;* What are you talking about? You're acting irrational!
  ♦ NOTE: Since the 1960s, this has been a popular term used to describe someone who has taken drugs which causes hallucinations. It is now commonly used to intimate that someone must have taken drugs to become so irrational.

"What up toe?" *exp.* "How are you?"

"Why are you clownin'?" *exp.* "Why are you belittling me?"
  ♦ NOTE: This comes from the popular expression *"to clown around"* meaning "to jest." The expression *"to be clownin'"* is a shortened version of: *"to clown around at someone else's expense."*

JUST FOR FUN

The following is a familiar fairy tale which has been updated using many of the teen/college and rap slang terms that were just learned in the first two chapters.

-Teen/College & Rap Slang-	*-Translation-*
Once upon a time, there was a **bodacious babe** named Cinderella who lived in a **skaggy crib** with her stepmom and two stepsisters, real **ducks**, who **threw major tude** and kept **baggin' on** Cinderella **big time**.	Once upon a time, there was a **beautiful girl** named Cinderella who lived in an **ugly house** with her stepmother and two stepsisters, real **ugly women**, who **were very pretentious** and kept **criticizing** Cinderella **unmercifully**.
One day the King, who was **large and in charge**, decided to **throw a killer bash** in order to **scope out** the **local talent** in the hopes that his son would **kick it** with a **chick** and get **roped**.	One day the King, who was **very powerful**, decided to **have a big party** in order to **research** the local **female possibilities** in the hopes that his son would **spend time** with a **girl** and get **married**.
The day finally came as everyone, except Cinderella, **jetted** to the King's **kegger, party on**! Suddenly a voice from behind her said, "Oh, **don't get all tweaked, girlfriend** and **grow a hair**!" With that, Cinderella found herself **sportin' some fly gear, dressed to impress** and **fine as wine**, wearing a **way stupid** gown and ready to **bail** for the	The day finally came as everyone, except Cinderella, **left** for the King's **party, an exciting party**! Suddenly a voice from behind her said, "Oh, **don't get so upset, my dear** and **be strong**!" With that, Cinderella found herself **wearing some beautiful clothing**, dressed truly **impressively**, looking **ravishing**, wearing a **very lovely** gown and ready to **leave** for the

Castle. But her fairy godmother added, "Just make sure to come home before 12 **AM** or **ASAP, OK**, or I'll be **PO**'d!"

When she **fell in**, everyone was **all** "**Dude! Check out Miss Thang** who's **crestin'** at the prince!" Just then, the prince, who was no **dode** but a **major meatloaf** and a total **babe magnet** who could really **bust a move**, started **clockin'** Cinderella. He immediately gave her **two snaps up** 'cause she was **too cold**. But at midnight, she **booked** outta there and lost one of her glass **spikes**. After **hoofing it** all around the **hood**, he almost **folded** until he **spotted** a **cheeky mama** whose foot fit the **kicker**! At last! He **smoked her out** which **blew his mind** and they were both **fully stoked** happily ever after.

Castle. But her fairy godmother added, "Just make sure to come home before 12 **midnight** or **as soon as possible**, **okay**, or I'll be **very mad**!"

When she **arrived**, everyone **said**, "**Wow! Look at the pretentious girl** who's **smiling** at the prince!" Just then, the prince, who was no **fool** but a **real athlete** and a totally **attractive individual** who could really **dance**, started **gazing at** Cinderella. He immediately gave her **his approval** because she was **so beautiful**. But at midnight, she **dashed** out of there and lost one of her glass **slippers**. After **walking** all around the **neighborhood**, he almost **quit** until he **noticed** an **entrancing girl** whose foot fit the **shoe**! At last! He **found her** which **thrilled him** and they were both **extremely joyous** happily ever after.

SURFER SLANG

– At the Beach –

...I got so **lunched** doin' a **lip floater** on this one **hair ball**, I thought I was gonna **aqua boot!**

Dialogue In Slang

At the Beach

DIALOGUE

Scott and Rick are out surfing.

Scott: The **big mama**'s **fully macking insanely gnarly grinders** with **corduroy to the horizon**. The conditions are **most excellent**!

Rick: I'm with you, **brah**. I was so **amped** this morning that I **busted a few** real early and got so **lunched** doing a **lip floater** on this one **hair ball**, I thought I was gonna **aqua boot**.

Scott: Me, too. As I was **petting the cat** comin' out of the **green room** of this one **clean peeler**, I started **bogulating** and just about **ate the cookie**. I think the **nip factor** got to me. I must have looked like such a **barney** to all the **grommets** out there.

Rick: **Cowabunga**! **Check out** the **gnarlatious betty laceratin'** over there! I'm gonna go **dial in** on her!

Scott: **Gel**, **dude**. I hear she's a total **wilma**... fully **geeklified**. Forget her. What do you say we get some **grunts** and go **scrut** at my house?

Rick: Good idea. This beach is **zooed out** anyway.

Lesson Ten - SURFER SLANG

At the Beach

DIALOGUE

Scott and Rick are out surfing.

Scott: The **ocean** is **really creating incredibly menacing waves** with **one right after the other**. The conditions are **fantastic**!

Rick: I agree, **friend**. I was so **excited** this morning that I went **surfing** real early and got so **jostled** doing a **common manoeuver** on this one **frightening wave**, I thought I was going to **vomit**.

Scott: Me, too. As I was **crouched down** coming out of the **tube** of this one **perfect wave**, I started **surfing badly** and just about **fell off**. I think the **iciness of the water** affected me. I must have looked like such a **fool** to all the **novice surfers** out there.

Rick: **Wow! Observe** the **beautiful girl surfing so well** over there! I'm going to go **talk** to her!

Scott: **Relax, friend**. I hear she's a total **idiot**... completely **moronic**. Forget her. What do you say we get some **food** and go **eat** at my house?

Rick: Good idea. This beach is **overcrowded** anyway.

Dialogue in slang as it would be heard

At the Beach

DIALOGUE

Scott 'n Rick 'r out surfin'.

Scott: The **big mama**'s **fully mackin' insanely gnarly grinders** with **courduroy ta the horizon**. The conditions 'r **most excellent**!

Rick: I'm with ya, **brah**. I was so **amped** this mornin' that I **busted a few** real early 'n got so **lunched** doin' a **lip floader** on this one **hair ball**, I thod I was gonna **aqua boot**.

Scott: Me, too. As I was **pettin' the cat** comin' oud 'a the **green room** 'a this one **clean peeler**, I starded **bogulatin'** 'n just aboud **ate the cookie**. I think the **nip factor** got ta me. I must've looked like such a **barney** ta all the **grommets** out there.

Rick: **Cowabunga! Check out** the **gnarlatious betty laceratin'** over there! I'm gonna go **dial in** on 'er!

Scott: **Gel**, **dude**. I hear she's a todal **wilma**... fully **geeklified**. Ferget 'er. Whatdya say we get s'm **grunts** 'n go **scrut** at my house?

Rick: Good idea. This beach's **zooed out** anyway.

Vocabulary

amped up (to be) *n.* to be extremely excited • *I've never seen you so amped up;* I've never seen you so excited.

aqua boot (to) *exp.* to vomit into the water • *You look terrible! Did you just aqua boot?;* You look terrible? Did you just vomit?
▸ SYNONYM: **to talk to the seals** *exp.*

barney *n.* moron • *Who's the barney out there?;* Who's the moron out there?
▸ ALSO: **to barney** *v.* • Look at that guy barneying out there!; Look at that guy acting like a moron out there!
▸ NOTE: This term is from the animated series "The Flintstones" in which the character Barney is known for being foolish.
▸ SYNONYM (1): **fred** *n.*
▸ SYNONYM (2): **wally** *n.*
▸ SYNONYM (3): **gilligan** *n.*
▸ SYNONYM (4): SEE: **wilma** *n.*

betty *n.* pretty woman or girl • *Lots of bettys out today!;* Lots of pretty women out today!
▸ NOTE: This term is from the animated series "The Flintstones" in which the character Betty is considered, by surfers anyway, as being the pretty one.

big mama (the) *exp.* the ocean • *Hello, big mama!;* Hello, ocean!

bogulate (to) *v.* to surf badly • *I was bogulatin' on that last ride;* I was surfing badly on that last ride.
▸ SYNONYM: **to bog down** *exp.* • *You were boggin' down out there;* You were having trouble surfing out there.

brah *n.* brother, friend • *Where ya goin', brah?;* Where are you going, friend?

bro *n.* shortened version of *brother* meaning "friend" • *Hey, bro!;* Hey, friend!
▸ ALSO: **broly** *adj.* friendly, nice • *How broly of you. Thanks!;* How friendly of you. Thanks! • **non-broly** *adj.* • *Why are you being so non-broly?;* Why are you being so unfriendly?

bust a few (to) *exp.* to surf • *Let's go bust a few after breakfast;* Let's go surfing after breakfast.

check out (to) *exp.* to observe • *Check out this awesome weather!;* Observe this awesome weather!
▸ NOTE: This expression is heard commonly among surfers as well as being very popular among all other groups.

clean peeler *exp.* perfectly formed wave, ideal for riding • *I caught a real clean peeler;* I caught a perfectly formed wave.

corduroy to the horizon *exp.* perfectly aligned waves one after the other like the lines in a pair of corduroy pants • *It was corduroy to the horizon today;* The waves were lined up one after the other today.

"Cowabunga!" *exclam.* exclamation of great excitement.

dial in on someone (to) *exp.* to talk with someone • *Let's go dial in on those girls;* Let's go talk to those girls.

dude *n.* guy, friend • *You really dommo, dude!;* You really dominate when it comes to surfing, friend!
> ♦ NOTE: This term was encountered earlier but it bears repeating since it is constantly used in the surfing (and teen) culture.
> ♦ ALSO: **dudette** *f.* girl • *Hey, dudettes!;* Hey, girls!

eat the cookie (to) *exp.* to get unmercifully tossed around by a wave • *I really ate the cookie;* I really got unmercifully tossed around.

excellent *adj.* terrific • *Excellent wave!;* Terrific wave!
> ♦ NOTE: The standard adjective "excellent" has become so much a part of the surfer's vocabulary (as well as that of teens in general) that it bears mentioning here. To use this term is a sign of being extremely up-to-date. It is additionally popular to use the expression *"most excellent"* when referring to anything that is terrific: *The weather is most excellent today.*

geeklified *adj.* foolish, ridiculous • *That's totally geeklified!;* That's really ridiculous!

gel (to) *v.* to calm down • *Hey, gel dude!;* Hey, calm down, friend!

gnarlatious *adj.* fantastic • *I've never seen such gnarlatious weather!;* I've never seen such fantastic weather!

gnarly *adj.* dangerous and scary • *That wave was gnarly!;* That wave was dangerous!
> ♦ VARIATION: **gnar** *adj.* [pronounced: *nar*]

green room *exp.* tube of a wave • *I must have spent an entire minute in the green room!;* I must have spent an entire minute in the tube!
> ♦ NOTE: The ultimate surfing experience for any surfer is to ride inside the tube of a wave. From the inside, the water looks smooth and shiny with a green tint like melted glass. For this reason, it is oftentimes referred to as the *"green room"* or *"glass house."*

grinder *n.* huge wave • *What a grinder!;* What a huge wave!

grommet *n.* novice surfer • *You're surfin' like a grommet, dude!;* You're surfing like a novice, friend!

grunts *n.pl.* food • *Let's get some grunts;* Let's get some food.
♦ NOTE: This represents the sound of ecstacy a surfer makes when eating after several hours of calorie-burning surfing.

hair ball *exp.* huge wave • *Check out that hair ball!;* Look at that huge wave!

insane *adj.* fantastic • *Did you see the insane grinders out there?;* Did you see the fantastic waves out there?

lacerate (to) *v.* to attack the waves fearlessly • *You were laceratin' those green monsters!;* You were attacking those huge waves!
♦ NOTE: **green monster** *n.* enormous wave with a dark green hue.

lip floater *exp.* a move where the surfer slides over the lip of the wave • *That clean peeler was perfect for doin' a lip floater;* That flawless wave was perfect for gently sliding over the lip.
♦ SYNONYM: **lipper** *n.*

lunched (to get) *exp.* to get thrown around unmercifully by a wave • *I got lunched my first time out;* I got thrown around unmercifully my first time out.

macking (to be) *exp.* said of the ocean that is generating huge waves (the size of Mack trucks • *The ocean's fully mackin' today;* The ocean is really generating huge waves today.

nip factor *exp.* coldness • *What's the nip factor like in the water today?;* How cold is the water today?

pet the cat (to) *exp.* to squat down on the surfboard and slowly move one's arms up and down to keep balance • *We could see you pettin' the cat from the shore;* We could see you squatting and moving your arms up and down from the shore.

scrut (to) *v.* to eat voraciously • *I'm starved! Let's go scrut!;* I'm starved! Let's go eat!

wilma *n.* *n.* female moron • *Did you see that wilma out there?;* Did you see that moronic girl out there?
♦ NOTE: *Wilma* is a cartoon character from the animated series "The Flintstones."

zooed out (to be) *exp.* to be overcrowded • *This beach is zooed out!;* This beach is overcrowded.
♦ NOTE: This is a variation of the popular expression, "to be a zoo:" *It's a zoo here!;* It's overcrowded here!

PRACTICE THE VOCABULARY

[Answers to Lesson Ten, p. 219]

A. **Complete the phrases by choosing the appropriate words from the list below.**

amped	**betty**	**bogulatin'**
peeler	**bust**	**corduroy**
dial	**grommet**	**grunts**
lunched	**nip**	**zooed**

1. He's never surfed before today. He's just a _____ .

2. I can't wait to go surfing! I'm so _____ up!

3. Great wave! That's what you call a real clean _____ .

4. Look at the line of waves out there. Talk about _____ to the horizon!

5. I got fully _____ out there!

6. Grab your board and let's go _____ a few.

7. Look at her! Now, that's a _____ !

8. If you think she's so pretty, why don't you just go _____ in on her?

9. This beach is _____ out. Let's go find a different one.

10. I must be tired or somethin'. I've been _____ all day!

11. Let's get some _____ . I'm starving.

12. After that cold night, I bet the _____ factor in the water is really low.

B. Match the two colums.

☐ 1. You're going to look like a
       total jerk if you wear that to
       the party.

☐ 2. That was real unfriendly of
       him.

☐ 3. I think I'm going to vomit.

☐ 4. I got unmercifully tossed
       around out there.

☐ 5. I must have spent a whole
       minute in the tube of the wave!

☐ 6. Did you see the huge wave out
       there?

☐ 7. You actually like that weird
       girl?

☐ 8. You were really attacking that
       huge wave fearlessly!

☐ 9. That was fantastic!

☐ 10. We could see you squat down
       and move your arms up and
       down from the shore.

☐ 11. I'm starving. Let's go eat.

☐ 12. Hey, friend. Calm down!

A. **I must have spent a whole
    minute in the green room!**

B. **That was real non-broly of
    him.**

C. **We could see you pet the cat
    from the shore.**

D. **I ate the cookie out there.**

E. **You actually like that
    wilma?**

F. **That was insane!**

G. **I'm starving. Let's go scrut.**

H. **Did you see the gnarly
    grinder out there?**

I. **You were really laceratin'
    on that hair ball!**

J. **Hey, brah. Gel!**

K. **You're gonna to look like a
    total barney if you wear
    that to the party.**

L. **I think I'm gonna aqua boot.**

C. Underline the word that best completes each phrase.

   1. The big (**daddy, mamma, brother**)'s really clear today.

   2. Let's go (**bust, break, smash**) a few before lunch.

   3. I caught a real (**dirty, filthy, clean**) peeler!

4. Check out the (**fur, hair, tennis**) ball coming toward us!

5. She's beautiful! What a (**wilma, barney, betty**)!

6. This beach is zooed (**out, in, down**)!

7. The conditions are most (**geeklified, cowabunga, excellent**) today.

8. Look! He's in the (**red, purple, green**) room!

9. This is my first day surfing. But don't tell anyone that I'm just a (**grommet, grinder, barney**), okay?

10. I feel sick. I think I'm gonna aqua (**shoe, sandle, boot**).

11. I can't stand him. He's fully (**gnarly, geeklified, amped up**).

12. Look at the outfit that guy's wearing. What a (**brah, bro, barney**)!

A CLOSER LOOK:
Surfer Slang

Surfer slang has got to be one of the most colorful, whimsical, and entertaining "languages" that our society has yet to encounter. Its melodic delivery makes it unique and somewhat comical. However, to the irritation of surfers everywhere, it is commonly equated with poor education and moronic behavior. This stereotype is frequently played out in television comedies because it is always sure to get a laugh.

Surfer slang is not confined to any one area. This lingo makes its way quickly throughout the world because surfers typically move from place to place, always trying to find the perfect wave or *"clean peeler."*

The true aficionado of the surfing culture can reel off an extensive string of slang words one after the other, forming what may seem like an unintelligible code to the outsider. And that's just the way they want it.

Outsiders, get ready. The following list will surely help you to pass for a local or *"loky."*

▶ NOTE: Surfers tend to use a greal deal of contractions since it is considered "cool" or stylish as will be demonstrated in the next several pages:

abb *n.* abnormal person, jerk • *What an abb!;* What a jerk!

ankle slapper *exp.* a wave too small to ride • *There are nothing but ankle slappers out there;* There are nothing but small waves out there.
 ‣ SYNONYM: **knee slapper** *exp.*

axed (to get) *adj.* to get thrown by a wave • *I got axed out there;* I got thrown off my surfboard out there.

bag (to) *v.* to decline to do something • *I was gonna go party with everyone but I bagged;* I was going to go party with everyone but I declined.

beached (to be) *adj.* to be unable to move due to overeating • *Go without me. I'm beached!;* Go without me. I'm stuffed!

beached whale *n.* derogatory for anyone who is extremely fat • *There are a lot of beached whales out here today;* There are a lot of extremely fat people out here today.

beard *n.* old seasoned surfer • *That beard can really lacerate!;* That old guy can really surf well!

benny *n.* nonsurfer who talks, dresses, and acts like he/she has been surfing for years • *He may look like a surfer, but have you noticed he never goes in the water? What a benny!;* He may look like a surfer, but have you

noticed he never goes in the water? What a fraud!

biffed (to get) *exp.* to get thrown around by a wave • *You really got biffed out there!;* You really got thrown around out there!

big air (to get) *exp.* to get thrown high into the air yet remain standing on the surfboard • *He's gettin' some big air on that wave;* He's getting some incredible altitude on that wave!

blast air (to) *exp.* to take complete control at the top of a wave • *You're really blastin' air today;* You're really in control of those big waves today.

board *n.* shortened version of "surfboard" • *Is that your new board?;* Is that your new surfboard?

boardhead *n.* surfing enthusiast • *All he ever does is talk about surfing. What a boardhead!;* All he ever does is talk about surfing. What surfing enthusiast!

body wompin' *exp.* riding the waves on one's belly without a surfboard, bodysurfing • *We're goin' body wompin' today;* We're going bodysurfing today.
 ‣ NOTE: The term *"bodysurfing"* is commonly used to refer to riding the waves without a surfboard.

bogus *adj.* • **1.** false • *That's just bogus!;* That's just false! • **2.**

rude • *That was really bogus of him to do to you;* That was really rude of him to do to you.
  ♦ ALSO: **bogosity** *n.* rudeness • *That's total bogosity!;* That's total rudeness!

bowl (to) *v.* used to describe an ocean which is producing large tubular waves • *It's bowlin' out there!;* There are a lot of large waves out there!

bucket of nugs *exp.* a lot of waves • *Look at that bucket o'nugs!;* Look at all those waves!

bum (to) *v.* to become angry • *My brother bummed on me 'cause I forgot to pick him up at the airport;* My brother is angry with me because I forgot to pick him up at the airport.

bummer *n.* shame • *What a bummer!;* What a shame!
  ♦ ALSO: **bummer in the summer** *exp.* (See: Rhyming Slang, p. 131) • *Bummer in the summer!* What a huge shame!

bun floss *n.* an extremely small bikini that rides up into the buttocks like a thong • *Look at that bun floss!;* Look at that small bikini that looks like a thong in back!

burly (to be) *adj.* to be extremely cold • *The water's burly today;* The water's freezing today.

butter *n.* girls • *Lots of butter out today;* Lots of girls out today.

  ♦ NOTE: Due to girls' excessive use of cocoa butter to enhance tanning, they have been given the nickname of *"butter."*

carve (to) *v.* to surf extremely well • *She was really carvin' out there;* She was really surfing well out there.

casper *n.* a very pale person on the beach • *What a casper!;* What a pale person!
  ♦ NOTE: This term comes from the television cartoon "Casper, the Friendly Ghost."
  ♦ SYNONYM: **chalk people** *exp.*

choiceamundo *adj.* fantastic • *The weather's choiceamundo today!;* The weather is fantastic today!

comber *n.* wave • *Check out the combers today;* Observe the big waves today.
  ♦ ALSO: **smokin' comber** *n.* huge wave • *There are some smokin' combers out there today;* There are some huge waves out there today.

creamed (to get) *exp.* to get tossed around furiously by a wave • *I got creamed out there;* I got tossed around furiously out there.

da kine *exp.* excellent • *Look at those da kine bettys!;* Look at those beautiful girls!

dealing (to be) *adj.* excellent surfing condition where the waves keep coming one after another (like a card player who deals many cards to each player) • *The waves are dealing today!;* The surfing condition is excellent today!

death *n.* the absolute best • *That girl's death!;* That girl is incredible!

decoy *n.* someone who can't surf • *Lots of decoys out there today!;* Lots of bad surfers out there today!

deep peak takeoff *exp.* mounting of one's surfboard at just the right moment • *I saw you get that deep peak takeoff!* I saw you catch that wave at just the right moment!

dismo *n.* devotee to the surfing culture but never gets his feet wet • *He talks like he's some great surfer but he's nothin' but a dismo;* He talks like he's some great surfer but he doesn't even get near the water.

dommo (to) *v.* to surf extremely well, to "dominate" • *You really dommo out there;* You really dominate out there.

doughnut *n.* extremely round tube • *I lost you in that doughnut for a while!;* I lost you in that tube for a while!

finned (to get) *exp.* to get run over by the fin of another surfboard • *I almost got finned out there;* I almost got run over by another surfer out there.

flail (to) *v.* to make awkward and unsure movements while surfing • *Look at that dude flail on his board!;* Look at that guy make awkward movements on his surfboard!
◗ NOTE: In teen slang, this is used to mean "to fail a test due to being flustered" • fluster + fail = *flail.*

flap (to) *v.* to move one's arm about in a clumsy manner while surfing • *He was flappin'!;* He was making clumsy movements with his arms!

geek-a-mo *n.* fool • *What a geek-a-mo!;* What a fool!

glue foot *exp.* surfer who never falls off the surfboard • *I hear you're a real glue foot;* I hear you never fall off your surfboard.

goob *n.* fool • *What a goob!;* What a fool!
◗ NOTE: This is from the old television series "The Andy Griffith Show" which featured a foolish character named "Goober."

goofy foot *exp.* popular term for a person who rides a surfboard with the right foot forward as opposed to the more common position of the left foot forward • *He's a goofy foot;* He's a surfer who rides with the right foot forward.

green monster *exp.* huge wave • *Did you see the green monsters* *out there?*; Did you see the huge waves out there?

gremlin *n.* novice surfer • *Lots of gremlins out today;* Lots of novice surfers out today.
▶ SYNONYM: **gremmie** *n.*

grind (to) *v.* to surf aggressively • *I was fully grinding before I got biffed;* I was surfing great before I got thrown.

hair *n.* courage • *You've got hair, dude!;* You've got courage, friend!
▶ NOTE: The popular television show "Night Court" borrowed this term to create their own slang expression with, *Oh, grow a hair!* meaning "Oh, don't be so afraid all the time! or more literally, "Oh, get some courage!"

hair out (to) *exp.* to become scared at the last moment • *When I saw that green monster comin', I haired out;* When I saw that huge wave coming, I got scared!

hang five (to) *exp.* to surf toward the front of the surfboard so that the toes of one foot are over the edge • *Check out the grommet hangin' five!;* Look at the novice surfer riding with one foot at the front of the surfboard!

hang ten (to) *exp.* to surf toward the front of the surfboard so that the toes of both feet are over the edge • *Check out the grommet hangin' ten!;* Look at the novice surfer

riding with both feet at the front of the surfboard!

happening *adj.* terrific • *This beach is fully happening;* This beach is really great.

hectic gnarler *exp.* beautiful girl • *Check out the hectic gnarler!;* Look at the beautiful girl!

hit (to) *v.* to satisfy greatly • *This cool breeze is hittin'!;* This cool breeze feels great!

hondo *n.* derogatory term for a person who is not a local resident of the beach community • *Too many hondos at this beach!;* Too many tourists at this beach!

honker *n.* enormous wave • *What a honker!;* What a huge wave!

hot dog (to) *exp.* to show great ability at doing surfing stunts on the board • *He's really hot doggin' it out there;* He's really doing some amazing moves out there!
▶ ALSO: **hot dogger** *n.* a surfer who shows great ability at doing surfing stunts on the surfboard.

in-the-tube forward 360 *exp.* a move where the rider manages to twirl the board completely around while riding the wave • *I saw ya do an awesome in-the-tube forward 360!;* I saw you do a great maneuver where you twirled the board completely around while riding the wave!

kill it (to) *exp.* to surf extremely well • *Your sister was really killin' it this afternoon!;* Your sister was really surfing well this afternoon!

kneebangers *n.* baggy shorts that extend just above the knee • *Cool kneebangers, brah!;* Great shorts, friend!

latronic *n.* later, good-bye • *I gotta jet. Latronic, brah!;* I have to leave. See you later, friend!
  ♦ SYNONYM (1): **late** *n.*
  ♦ SYNONYM (2): **lates** *n.*

liquid smoke *exp.* the long trail of misty spray behind a wave caused by the wind • *Look at that liquid smoke!;* Look at that long trail of mist!

live *adj.* fantastic • *That maneuver was live!;* That maneuver was fantastic!

loomer *n.* a slow ominous wave that seems to get bigger and bigger as it approaches • *Check out the loomer over there;* Look at the ominous wave over there.

mac (to) *v.* to eat voraciously • *Let's go mac. I'm starving!;* Let's go eat a lot. I'm starving!
  ♦ VARIATION: **to mac out** *exp.*
  ♦ NOTE: These expressions were derived from the famous American restaurant chain, *McDonald's.*

macked (to get) *adj.* to get hit hard by a huge wave • *You really got macked out there;* You really got hit hard by a lot of waves out there.

macker *n.* a huge wave (as big as a Mack truck) • *Check out the macker behind you!;* Look at the huge wave behind you!

meat wave *exp.* carload of surfers • *Here comes the meat wave;* Here comes the carload of surfers.

micro *n.* very small wave • *Lots of waves out there but they're all micros!;* Lots of waves out there but they're all little!

milk a wave (to) *exp.* to get all one can from a single wave • *You really milked that macker!;* You really got all you could from that huge wave!

mushburgers *n.pl.* poorly shaped waves with no tube and no power • *This beach has nothin' but mushburgers;* This beach has nothing but bad waves for surfing.
  ♦ SYNONYM: **oatmeals** *n.pl.*

nailed (to get) *adj.* to get pounded by the surf • *That macker nailed me!;* That big wave pounded me!

nectar *adj.* beautiful • *She's nectar!;* She's beautiful!

nose ride *exp.* a common stance where the surfer stands toward the front of the surfboard or "nose" • *That was the first time I didn't get lunched doing a nose ride;* That was the first time I didn't get thrown standing toward the front of the surfboard.

on the die (to be) *exp.* on the verge of getting unmercifully beaten up by a wave • *I swear I was on the die on that one!;* I swear I was on the verge of getting beaten up by that wave!

plugged (to be) *adj.* to be overcrowded • *Let's jet. This beach is plugged;* Let's leave. This beach is overcrowded.
▶ SYNONYM: **to be zooed out** *exp.*

pod (to) *v.* to faint • *I thought I was gonna pod when I saw those smoking combers getting closer;* I thought I was going to faint when I saw those enormous waves getting closer.

pounded (to get) *adj.* to get attacked (by the force of a wave) • *You got pounded brah!;* You got attacked by that wave, friend!

pounder *n.* huge powerful wave • *Did you see that pounder break?;* Did you see that huge powerful wave break?

prosecuted (to get) *adj.* to get completely jostled by a wave • *Are you okay? I saw you get prosecuted out there!;* Are you okay? I saw you get completely thrashed out there!

pump (to) *v.* to generate a constant flow of waves • *It's pumpin' today!;* There are lots of waves out today!

quimby *n.* weakling, jerk • *What a quimby!;* What a jerk!

raw *adj.* fantastic, incredible • *That move was raw!;* That move was incredible!

rig (to) *v.* to talk incessantly • *That dude just won't stop riggin'!;* That guy just won't stop talking!

righteous *adj.* fantastic • *Righteous beach!;* Great beach!

rip it up (to) *exp.* to surf aggressively • *You were rippin' it up today!;* You were surfing aggressively today!
▶ VARIATION: **to rip and tear** *exp.*
▶ ALSO: **ripper** *n.* one who surfs aggressively • *Bro, you're a ripper!;* Friend, you're an aggressive surfer!

scratch over the top (to) *exp.* to just miss catching a wave even after paddling furiously • *Darn! I scratched over the top!;* Darn! I just missed catching the wave!

shaka *n.* an extremely common hand signal among surfers meaning "Everything is cool!" The signal is made by making a fist with the palm facing front, then placing the thumb and little finger against the sides of the hand. The thumb and little finger are then straightened out and held away from each other, forming a "Y." The hand is then twisted back and forth at the wrist.

sharking (to go) *exp.* to go surfing • *We're goin' sharkin' today;* We're going surfing today.

shoot the curl (to) *exp.* to ride all the way through the tube of a wave • *He shot the curl his first time out!;* He rode all the way through the tube of the wave his first time out!

skegging *adj.* extremely fun • *This is a skeggin' party!;* This is a really fun party!

skin it (to) *exp.* to surf without wearing a wetsuit • *Don't you think it's too cold out there to skin it today?;* Don't you think it's too cold out there to surf without a wetsuit today?

slap it off the top (to) *exp.* to surf on the top of a wave and suddenly turn the surfboard in the opposite direction • *Did you see the way I slapped it off the top?;* Did you see the way I suddenly turned my surfboard in the opposite direction?

squid lips *exp.* fool or moron • *Hey, squid lips!;* Hey, you moron!

stacked (to be) *exp.* one practically on top of the other due to overcrowding • *I hate surfing stacked like that!;* I hate surfing with one person practically on top of the other.

stylin' (to be) *adj.* to be doing extremely well • *I was stylin' out*

there today!; I was doing great out there today!

take gas (to) *exp.* to get thrown around unmercifully by a wave • *I really took gas on that wave;* I really got thrown around unmercifully by that wave.

talk to the seals (to) *exp.* to vomit • *I think Bob is sick. He's over there talkin' to the seals;* I think Bob is sick. He's over there vomiting.

taste (to be) *adj.* terrific, beautiful • *Check her out! She's taste!;* Look at her! She's beautiful!

toad (to) *v.* to get thrashed by a wave • *He just toaded out there!;* He just got thrashed by that wave out there!
♦ NOTE: "Toad" is an acronym for "**t**ake-**o**ff **a**nd **d**ie."

tube spit *exp.* the spray of water that can fill the tube of wave • *I got pounded by the tube spit in that wave!;* I got attacked by the spray of water from that wave!

vibe someone out (to) *exp.* to be extremely cold to someone • *Why's she vibing you out, dude?;* Why is she being so cold to you, friend?

wag *n.* moron • *What a wag!;* What a moron!

wax off the top (to) *exp.* to glide across the top of a wave • *That was an insanely smooth ride. Did you see the way I waxed off the* *top?;* That was a really smooth ride. Did you see the way I glided across the top of the wave?

your gnarlyness *exp.* humorous respectful name for a good friend or celebrity • *Be right there, your gnarlyness!;* Be right there, your "fantasticness!"
  ▶ VARIATION: **your gnarlatiousness** *exp.*

ziplocked (to get) *adj.* said of a surfer who is gliding through the tube of a wave when it collapses • *I got ziplocked in that wave!;* I got caught in that wave as it collapsed!
  ▶ NOTE: This humorous term comes from the common

sandwich bag which secures its contents through a special sealing method called "ziplock."

zipper *n.* a wave that comes up quickly and breaks quickly • *That was impossible to ride! That was one gnarly zipper!;* That was impossible to ride! That was one wave that came up fast and broke quickly!

360 curtain floater *exp.* maneuver where the surfer spins the board around in a circle • *That 360 curtain floater you did out there was raw!;* That maneuver where you spun the board around in a circle was incredible!

ANSWERS TO LESSONS 1-10

LESSON ONE - *Slang Used in TV Comedies*

Practice the Vocabulary

A. 1. b
   2. c
   3. a
   4. c
   5. b
   6. c
   7. c
   8. b
   9. b
   10. a
   11. a
   12. b

B. 1. beat
   2. blew
   3. dialogue
   4. flip
   5. faced
   6. goose
   7. block
   8. Mellow
   9. plastered
   10. sound
   11. Yike
   12. tears

C. 1. H   7. L
   2. D   8. B
   3. I   9. E
   4. J   10. G
   5. K   11. C
   6. F   12. A

D. 1. program   7. hang
   2. flip   8. way
   3. faced   9. sound
   4. beat   10. mad
   5. chicken   11. mellow
   6. geeky   12. cookies

"to become extremely angry"

T	O	█	F	L	Y	█	O	F	F
T	H	E	█	H	A	N	D	L	E

LESSON TWO - *More Slang Used in TV Comedies*

Practice the Vocabulary

A. 1. stacked   7. tacks
   2. size   8. knockout
   3. fish   9. turn
   4. guts   10. wall
   5. dirt   11. that won't quit
   6. ice   12. pull

B. 1. trip
   2. easy
   3. guts
   4. down
   5. in
   6. picnic

   7. Cut
   8. land
   9. jock
   10. dirt
   11. lights
   12. stick

C. **CROSSWORD PUZZLE**

	K	N	O	C	K	O	U	T
			F					A
	S		F			C		C
D	I	R	T		J	O	C	K
	Z		H			L		S
	E		E			D		
			W					
	C	R	A	Z	E	D		
	U		L					
	T		L	A	N	D		

D. 1. B
   2. I
   3. H
   4. A
   5. J
   6. E

   7. C
   8. G
   9. K
   10. D
   11. F
   12. L

LESSON THREE - *Slang Used in TV Dramas*

Practice the Vocabulary

A. 1. there
    2. through
    3. whammy
    4. plug
    5. easy
    6. warmed
    7. knocked
    8. swing
    9. break
    10. cookie
    11. clean
    12. soap

B. 1. face
    2. up
    3. coming
    4. on
    5. fling
    6. over
    7. straight
    8. hitched
    9. no
    10. spirits
    11. slut
    12. ticker
    13. hoo
    14. go

C. 1. K
    2. H
    3. I
    4. L
    5. A
    6. F
    7. J
    8. E
    9. B
    10. C
    11. D
    12. G

LESSON FOUR - *Slang Used in T.V. News*

Practice the Vocabulary

A. 1. b
    2. c
    3. a
    4. c
    5. a
    6. c
    7. b
    8. a
    9. c
    10. b
    11. a
    12. c

B. 1. K   7. G
  2. B   8. C
  3. J   9. H
  4. D   10. L
  5. I   11. E
  6. F   12. A

C. 1. a   7. b
  2. b   8. a
  3. b   9. a
  4. a   10. b
  5. b   11. b
  6. a   12. a

LESSON FIVE - *Slang Used in T.V. Sports News*

Practice the Vocabulary

A. 1. D   7. E
  2. H   8. F
  3. L   9. G
  4. B   10. K
  5. C   11. J
  6. A   12. I

B. 1. count   7. draw
  2. hit   8. freethrow
  3. turnover   9. fouled
  4. jam   10. barnburner
  5. stuffed   11. alley-oop
  6. load   12. cut

C.

SCOREBOARD

```
F R E E T H R O W W
J D R A W C U T F H
A F O U L E D F F I
M L O A D C O U N T
F Y S T U F F E D F
A L L E Y O O P F F
B A R N B U R N E R
F F T U R N O V E R
```

LESSON SIX - *Slang Used in T.V. Weather News*

Practice the Vocabulary

A. 1. crisp
   2. twister
   3. buckets
   4. scorcher
   5. wave
   6. kick
   7. flip
   8. rays
   9. doozie
   10. nasty
   11. tap
   12. roll

B. 1. J
   2. A
   3. L
   4. C
   5. H
   6. G
   7. D
   8. I
   9. B
   10. E
   11. K
   12. F

C. 1. a
   2. b
   3. a
   4. b
   5. b
   6. b
   7. b
   8. a
   9. a
   10. a
   11. b
   12. a

D. 1. scorcher
   2. nasty
   3. crisp
   4. doozie
   5. twister
   6. hatches
   7. ridge
   8. call
   9. kick
   10. tap
   11. buckets
   12. wave

FIND-THE-WORD-CUBE

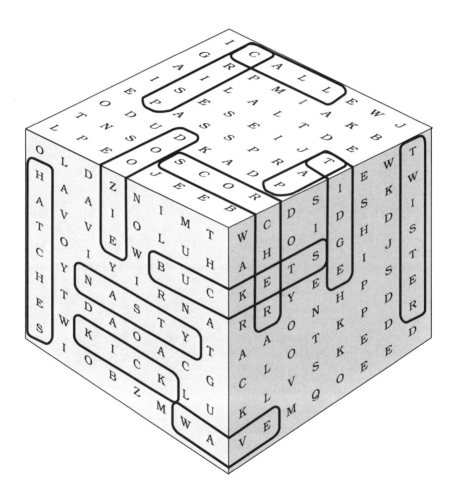

LESSON SEVEN - *Slang Used in Traffic Reports*

Practice the Vocabulary

A. 1. bottleneck
   2. clue
   3. dead
   4. clip
   5. bender
   6. hour
   7. heavy
   8. go
   9. tangle
   10. scene
   11. Heads
   12. rubberneckers

B. 1. D
   2. K
   3. J
   4. A
   5. H
   6. E
   7. C
   8. F
   9. I
   10. B
   11. G
   12. L

C. 1. dead
   2. rush
   3. bottleneck
   4. scene
   5. tabs
   6. break
   7. go
   8. spin
   9. rubbernecker
   10. heavy
   11. Clue
   12. row

LESSON EIGHT - *Teen/College Slang*

Practice the Vocabulary

A. 1. cut
   2. hit
   3. jam
   4. latest
   5. mick
   6. scamming
   7. shining
   8. spew
   9. stoked
   10. tweaked
   11. way
   12. deal

B. 1. H
   2. C
   3. K
   4. B
   5. F
   6. A
   7. G
   8. I
   9. M
   10. E
   11. D
   12. L
   13. J
   14. N

C. **WORD SEARCH**

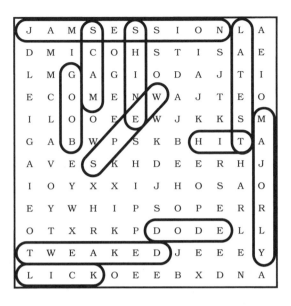

A CLOSER LOOK (1):
Practice Using Common Teen and College Slang

A. 1. a, c, d   6. b, c, d
   2. b, c, d   7. a, b
   3. b, c, d   8. b, c
   4. a, b, c   9. c, d
   5. b, c, d   10. a, b, d

LESSON NINE - *Rap Slang*

Practice the Vocabulary

A. 1. b   7. b
   2. b   8. a
   3. a   9. a
   4. b   10. b
   5. b   11. a
   6. a   12. b

B. 1. D   6. H
    2. I   7. E
    3. C   8. A
    4. F   9. G
    5. B   10. J

C. 1. homes   7. Thang
    2. Peace   8. large
    3. jacked   9. crest
    4. presidents   10. duck
    5. crack   11. break
    6. played   12. bust

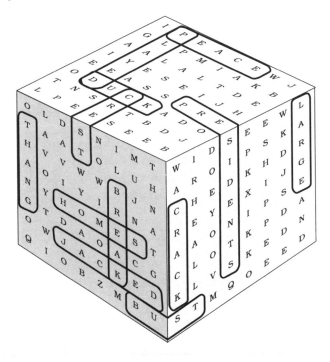

D. 1. Thang   6. fly
    2. breakin', played   7. maxin'
    3. large   8. go
    4. skin   9. ain't
    5. jaw, frosted   10. jacked

LESSON TEN - *Surfer Slang*

Practice the Vocabulary

A. 1. grommet
   2. amped
   3. peeler
   4. corduroy
   5. lunched
   6. bust
   7. betty
   8. dial
   9. zooed
   10. bogulating
   11. grunts
   12. nip

B. 1. K
   2. B
   3. L
   4. D
   5. A
   6. H
   7. E
   8. I
   9. F
   10. C
   11. G
   12. J

C. 1. mamma
   2. bust
   3. clean
   4. hair
   5. betty
   6. out
   7. excellent
   8. green
   9. grommet
   10. boot
   11. geeklified
   12. barney

Glossary

-A-

ace hurler *n.* (baseball) the best pitcher • *Jones is our ace hurler;* Jones is our best pitcher.
♦ ALSO: **ace** *n.* an outstanding player (used by all sports) • *Have you ever seen her play tennis? She's a real ace!;* Have you ever seen her play tennis? She's an outstanding player!

ain't *v.* (rap slang) used as a replacement for "am not/are not/is not" • *I ain't touchin' that big dog!;* I'm not touching that big dog! • *There ain't no way I'm goin' to that party;* There is no way I'm going to that party.
♦ NOTE: The term *"ain't,"* considered to be inferior grammar, originated in the South by poorly educated people living in the hills. However, to the despair of English teachers nationwide, it is still popular. *"Ain't"* is also commonly used in jest as a way to emphasis a statement: *You can't expect to graduate college if you never study. It ain't gonna happen!;* You can't expect to graduate college if you never study. It's simply not going to happen!

alley-oop *n.* (basketball) a shot made whereby a player jumps up next to the basket, catches a pass from another player at the height of the jump, and then stuffs the ball in the basket before hitting the ground • *Magic Johnson was famous for his alley-oop shots;* Magic Johnson was famous for catching passes while in mid air and stuffing the ball in the basket.

along the same lines (to be) *exp.* to pertain to the same subject • *We'll talk about that later. Your subject isn't along the same lines as what we're currently discussing;* We'll talk about that later. Your subject doesn't pertain to what we're currently discussing.

amped up (to be) *n.* (surfer slang) to be extremely excited • *I've never seen you so amped up;* I've never seen you so excited.

aqua boot (to) *exp.* (surfer slang) to vomit into the water • *You look terrible! Did you just aqua boot?;* You look terrible? Did you just vomit?

‣ SYNONYM: **to talk to the seals** *exp.*

at large (to be) *exp.* (said of a criminal who is being pursued by the police) to be among society • *It's frightening to think that the killer has been at large for five years!;* It's frightening to think that the killer has been among society for five years!

‣ NOTE: **to take it on the lam** *exp.* to disappear quickly after committing a crime • *After he robbed the bank, the robber took it on the lam;* After he robbed the bank, the robber disappeared.

-B-

back on the front burner (to be) *exp.* said of an old news story that is noteworthy again • *Problems arising from severe rainstorms are back on the front burner again;* Problems arising from severe rainstorms are noteworthy again.

‣ ALSO: **to put something on the front burner** *exp.* to expedite something that has high priority • *The boss just told me that we have to finish the other project in two hours! We'd better put it on the front burner;* The boss just told me that we have to finish the other project in two hours! We'd better expedite it since it has high priority.

‣ ANTONYM: **to be put on the back burner** *exp.* to take low priority • *Due to the emergency, everything else will have to be put on the back burner for a while;* Due to the emergency, everything else

will have to take low priority for a while. • *I'm going to have to put fixing my car on the back burner for now. I have to leave town suddenly;* I'm going to have to postpone fixing my car for now. I have to leave town suddenly.

‣ NOTE: The term *"burner"* used in these expressions refers to the "burner of a stove." In the culinary world, elements such as gravies, sauces, etc. that aren't used at once are placed on the back burners of the stove where they are allowed to cook slowly or simmer while the chef tends to the more immediate parts of the meal.

backfire (to) *exp.* to have an opposite outcome or effect of what was expected • *I wanted the teacher to like me, so I brought her a small gift and she got mad at me! She accused me of trying to bribe her. That sure backfired on me!;* I wanted the teacher to like me, so I brought her a small gift and she got mad at me! She accused me of trying to bribe her. That sure had the opposite outcome or effect of what I was expecting!

bag on someone (to) *exp.* (teen slang) **1.** to reprimand someone • *My mom bagged on me for coming home late last night;* My mother reprimanded me for coming home late last night. • **2.** to criticize • *My dad keeps baggin' on me about my clothes;* My dad keeps criticizing me about my clothes.

‣ SYNONYM: **to rag on someone** *exp.* • *My girlfriend ragged on me for an hour 'cause I forgot our* *date;* My girlfriend reprimanded me for an hour because I forgot our date. • *My mom always bags on me about my taste in music;* My mother always criticizes me about my taste in music.

bank job (to pull a) *exp.* to execute a bank robbery • *The last time they tried to pull a bank job, they got arrested;* The last time they tried to execute a bank robbery, they got arrested.

barnburner *n.* (used by all sports) an exciting game • *What a barnburner! That was the best soccer game I've ever seen!;* What an exciting game! That was best soccer game I've ever seen!

barney *n.* (surfer slang) moron • *Who's the barney out there?;* Who's the moron out there?
▶ ALSO: **to barney** *v.* • Look at that guy barneying out there!; Look at that guy acting like a moron out there!
▶ NOTE: This term is from the animated series "The Flintstones" in which the character Barney is known for being foolish.
▶ SYNONYM (1): **fred** *n.*
▶ SYNONYM (2): **wally** *n.*
▶ SYNONYM (3): **gilligan** *n.*
▶ SYNONYM (4): SEE: **wilma** *n.*

batten down the hatches (to) *exp.* to secure one's home by making it watertight • (lit); (nautical expression) to make the hatch of a ship watertight by sealing it with a wooden plank or batten • *Batten down the hatches! We have rough seas ahead!;* Make the hatch

watertight! We have rough seas ahead!

beat it (to) *exp.* to leave • *We'd better beat it before they come home;* We'd better leave before they come home.
▶ SYNONYM: **to scram** *exp.* • *Let's scram!;* Let's leave!

behind bars (to be) *exp.* to be in jail • *You can relax now. He's behind bars;* You can relax now. He's in jail.
▶ SYNONYM: **to be in the slammer** *n.* • *It's very simple. If you steal, you'll end up in the slammer;* It's very simple. If you steal, you'll end up in jail.
⇨ NOTE: The term *"slammer"* is an onomatopoeia for the slamming sound made by a closing jail door. The term comes from gangster lingo and is used by the toughest of gangsters and detectives. For this reason, when *"slammer"* is used by anyone else, it would usually be in jest only. In fact, this kind of language has been used in countless comedies as a way to get a laugh by having a sweet old grandmother-type unexpectedly use this "tough" gangster lingo.

benched (to get) *exp.* (rap slang) to be reprimanded • *I got benched by my girlfriend 'cause I forgot her birthday;* I was reprimanded by my girlfriend because I forgot her birthday.

betty *n.* (surfer slang) pretty woman or girl • *Lots of bettys out today!;* Lots of pretty women out today!
▶ NOTE: This term is from the

animated series "The Flintstones" in which the character Betty is considered, by surfers anyway, as being the pretty one.

big mama (the) *exp.* (surfer slang) the ocean • *Hello, big mama!;* Hello, ocean!

big rig *n.* a large commercial multi-wheeled truck that carries a trailer • *Your mother drives a big rig?;* Your mother drives a large commercial truck?

bio *n.* (teen slang) common abbreviation for "biology" • *She's the best student in bio class;* She's the best student in biology class.
♦ NOTE: For additional common abbreviations used in school, refer to page 163.

blast the stereo (to) *exp.* (teen slang) to turn the volume up loudly on the stereo • *I can't believe she blasts the stereo at midnight!;* I can't believe she turns the volume up loudly on the stereo at midnight!
♦ SYNONYM (1): **to crank up the stereo** *exp.* • *Let's crank up the stereo and party!;* Let's turn up the volume on the stereo and have a party!

blow someone off (to) *exp.* to jilt someone • *Did you hear that Jim just blew off his girlfriend?;* Did you hear that Jim just jilted his girlfriend?
♦ SYNONYM: **to shine someone** *exp.* • *He shined his girlfriend;* He jilted his girlfriend.

blow someone off the face of the earth (to) *exp.* • **1.** to shoot someone with extreme force • *I'm gonna get my gun and blow him off the face of the earth!;* I'm going to get my gun and shoot him! • **2.** to reprimand someone severely • *I can't believe my sister lied to me! When I see her again, I'm gonna blow her off the face of the earth!;* I can't believe my sister lied to me! When I see her again, I'm going to reprimand her severely!
♦ NOTE: The difference between **1.** and **2.** depends on the context.
♦ VARIATION: **to blow someone away** *exp.* • *The robber blew the bank teller away in broad daylight!* The robber shot the bank teller in broad daylight!
♦ SYNONYM: **to waste someone** *exp.* (gangster lingo) • *Let's waste him!;* Let's kill him!

bogulate (to) *v.* (surfer slang) to surf badly • *I was bogulatin' on that last ride;* I was surfing badly on that last ride.
♦ SYNONYM: **to bog down** *exp.* • *You were boggin' down out there;* You were having trouble surfing out there.

bottleneck *n.* traffic congestion due to a sudden decrease in lanes • *There's always a bottleneck on this part of the highway because it decreases from four lanes to two;* There's always congestion on this part of the highway because it decreases from four lanes to two.
♦ NOTE: The shape of a bottle is similar to the shape of a roadway that decreases in the number of

lanes, becoming increasingly narrow at one end.

brah *n.* (surfer slang) brother, friend • *Where ya goin', brah?;* Where are you going, friend?

break out (to) *exp.* (rap slang) to leave • *What time you breakin' out?;* What time are you leaving?
♦ NOTE: It is extremely popular among the younger generation to contract *"are you"* to simply *"you"* as demonstrated in the above sentence: *What time you breakin' out?*
♦ SYNONYM (1): **to eject** *v.* • *I'm bored here. Let's eject;* I'm bored here. Let's leave.
♦ SYNONYM (2): **to roll out** *exp.* • *You rollin' out with me?;* You leaving with me?
♦ SYNONYM (3): **to jet** *v.* • *I gotta jet!;* I have to leave!

break something to someone (to) *exp.* to disclose information of an emotional nature to someone • *I just don't know how I'm going to be able to break the news to her;* I just don't know how I'm going to be able to disclose this kind of emotional information to her.

break the ice (to) *exp.* to make the first move in establishing communication • *I'm going to break the ice with the new employee;* I'm going to make the first move in establishing communication with the new employee.

break up (to) *exp.* (of traffic) to decrease in congestion • *I can't believe all this congestion. Hopefully, it'll break up after the construction work on the highway;* I can't believe all this congestion. Hopefully, it'll decrease after the construction work on the highway.

bro *n.* (surfer slang) shortened version of *brother* meaning "friend" • *Hey, bro!;* Hey, friend!
♦ ALSO: **broly** *adj.* friendly, nice • *How broly of you. Thanks!;* How friendly of you. Thanks! • **non-broly** *adj.* • *Why are you being so non-broly?;* Why are you being so unfriendly?

buff • **1.** *n.* devotee, fanatic • *Tom's a real music buff;* Tom's a real devotee of music. • **2.** *adj.* muscular • *Your brother's buff!;* Your brother's muscular! • buffed, buffed out *adj.* muscular.
♦ SYNONYM: **freak** *n.* • *He's a real movie freak;* He's a real movie enthusiast.

bullet *n.* (football) an extremely fast pass • *Did you see the bullet he threw? I could hardly follow it!;* Did you see the fast pass he threw? I could hardly follow it!

bunch-up *n.* sudden traffic congestion • *Slow down! There's a bunch-up ahead!;* Slow down! There's some sudden traffic congestion ahead!
♦ NOTE: It is very common to say either *"Slow down!"* or *"Slow up!"* to advise someone to decrease his/her speed. Both expressions are identical and may be used interchangeably.

burnt/burned to a crisp (to get) *exp.* to get extremely sunburned • *Make sure to cover yourself or you're gonna get burnt/burned to a crisp;* Make sure to cover yourself or you're going to get extremely burnt/burned by the sun's rays.
▶ NOTE: The past tense of the verb *"to burn"* is "burnt" and "burned."
▶ SYNONYM: **to get fried** *exp.*

bust a few (to) *exp.* (surfer slang) to surf • *Let's go bust a few after breakfast;* Let's go surfing after breakfast.

bust a move (to) *exp.* (rap slang) to dance • *I didn't know you could bust a move like that!;* I didn't know you could dance like that!
▶ SYNONYM: **to kick stomp** *exp.* • *Wanna go kick stompin' tonight?;* Do you want to go dancing tonight?

-C-

C.D. *n.* (teen slang) (used by all ages) common abbreviation for "compact disc" • *My parents bought me a new C.D. player for my birthday;* My parents bought me a new compact disc player for my birthday.

call for (to) *exp.* to predict • *The weather report is calling for rain today;* The weather report is predicting rain today.
▶ NOTE: This expression is used primarily in reference to the weather.

Capitol Hill *exp.* Congress • *Ever since the war began last week, there has been a lot of activity on Capitol Hill;* Ever since the war began last

week, there has been a lot of activity in Congress.
▶ NOTE: *"Capitol Hill"* also stands for the "hill" where the Capitol stands and is commonly used to refer to Washington, D.C. in general.

carry out something (to) *exp.* to execute something • *He carried out the chief's orders;* He executed the chief's orders.

catch someone or something later (to) *exp.* to see someone or something later • *I'll catch you later;* I'll see you later. • *I'll catch the movie next week;* I'll see the movie next week.

cheap seats *exp.* (baseball) the least desirable seats in the ball park located at the other end of the ball park where the view is poor • *I couldn't believe how far the batter hit the ball. It went all the way into the cheap seats!;* I couldn't believe how far the batter hit the ball. It went all the way into the seats at the other end of the ball park!

check out (to) *exp.* (surfer slang) to observe • *Check out this awsome weather!;* Observe this awsome weather!
▶ NOTE: This expression is heard commonly among surfers as well as being very popular among all other groups.

check up on someone (to) *exp.* to verify the condition of someone • *I'll be right back. I'm gonna go check up on the baby;* I'll be right back. I'm going to go verify the condition of the baby.

chicken out (to) *exp.* to become scared • *I was going to ask her out but I chickened out at the last minute;* I was going to ask her out but I got scared at the last minute.
♦ SYNONYM: **to wuss out** *exp.* • *He was going to ask his boss for a raise but he wussed out;* He was going to ask his boss for a raise but he got scared.

clean peeler *exp.* (surfer slang) perfectly formed wave, ideal for riding • *I caught a real clean peeler;* I caught a perfectly formed wave.

clear shot *n.* an unobstructed passage • *After all that traffic, it's finally nice to have a clear shot the rest of the way;* After all that traffic, it's finally nice to have an unobstructed passage the rest of the way.

clip *n.* speed • *Your boat is really powerful. We're moving at quite a fast clip!;* Your boat is really powerful. We're moving at quite a fast speed!

clock (to) *v.* (rap slang) to watch • *Who's that guy clockin' you over there?;* Who's that guy watching you over there?

clue someone in on something (to) *exp.* to inform someone of something • *Let me clue you in on what's been going on while you've been on vacation;* Let me inform you of what's been going on while you've been on vacation.

cold (to be) *exp.* (rap slang) to be attractive • *She's too cold!;* She's pretty!
♦ SYNONYM (1): **to be too cold** *exp.*
♦ SYNONYM (2): **to be clean** *exp.*
♦ SYNONYM (3): **to be cookin'** *exp.*
♦ SYNONYM (4): **to be smokin'** *exp.*

cold fish (to be a) *exp.* to be an unfriendly person • *How can she be such a cold fish when her parents are so friendly?;* How can she be such an unfriendly person when her parents are so friendly?

come clean with someone (to) *exp.* to tell someone the entire story • *You're not coming clean with me. What really happened?;* You're not telling me the entire story. What really happened?

come forward (to) *exp.* to identify oneself • *He came forward and admitted committing the crime;* He identified himself as having committed the crime.

come on the heels of something (to) *exp.* said of an event that follows directly behind another • *The earthquake comes on the heels of the fire that engulfed the city last week;* The earthquake follows directly behind the fire that engulfed the city last week.

come to (to) *exp.* to revive • *Look! She's coming to!;* Look! She's reviving!
♦ SYNONYM: **to snap out of it** *exp.* • *He just fainted but I think he'll snap out of it in just a moment;* He just fainted but I think he'll revive in just a moment.

corduroy to the horizon *exp.* (surfer slang) perfectly aligned waves one after the other like the lines in a pair of corduroy pants • *It was corduroy to the horizon today;* The waves were lined up one after the other today.

"Cowabunga!" *exclam.* (surfer slang) exclamation of great excitement.

crackdown *n.* a rigorous attack • *The police force has implemented a crackdown on gang violence;* The police force has implemented a rigorous attack on gang violence.

crack on someone (to) *exp.* (rap slang) to criticize someone • *Quit crackin' on me!;* Quit criticizing me!
 ♦ SYNONYM (1): **to rank on someone** *exp.* • *Who are you two rankin' on this time?;* Who are you two criticizing this time?
 ♦ SYNONYM (2): **to snap on someone** *exp.* • *If you're gonna start snappin' on me again, I'm breakin' out;* If you're going to start criticizing me again, I'm leaving.

crazed (to be) *adj.* to be agitated as a result of being very busy • *I have so much work to do today, I'm a little crazed;* I have so much work to do today, I'm a little agitated.
 ♦ NOTE: This adjective comes from the expression *"to be going crazy."*
 ♦ SYNONYM: **to be bouncing off the walls** *exp.* to be so busy and moving that it appears that one is literally propelling from one end of the room to the other.

crest (to) *v.* (rap slang) to smile • *I think she's crestin' at you!;* I think she's smiling at you!
 ♦ NOTE: This humorous term comes from a brand of toothpaste by the same name and was simply turned into a verb.

crook *n.* criminal • *Two crooks robbed our house yesterday;* Two criminals robbed our house yesterday.
 ♦ NOTE: The term *"crook"* is also commonly used figuratively to mean "one who cheats people of money." For example: *How can you trust him? The guy's a crook!;* How can you trust him? The guy's dishonest!

crossing pattern *exp.* (football) a strategy whereby the receiver of the ball runs diagonally from one side of the field to the other in an effort to evade the other team's defenders while trying to approach the goal • *The only way he's gonna be able to avoid getting stopped by the other team is to perform a crossing pattern;* The only way he's going to be able to avoid getting stopped by the other team is to run diagonally from one side of the field to the other.

cut [a record, a C.D., an album, etc.] (to) *exp.* (teen slang) to record • *Did you hear that Nancy was just hired to cut an album?;* Did you hear that Nancy was just hired to record an album?
 ♦ ALSO (1): **cut** *n.* **1.** song from a recording • *I like the first cut on that album;* I like the first song on that album. • **2.** share of profits •

My cut is 70%, yours is 30%; My share of the profits is 70%, yours is 30%. • **3.** elimination round in a contest • *Congratulations! You made the first cut!;* Congratulations! You avoided getting eliminated in the first round!
▸ ALSO (2): **to lay down tracks** *exp.* • This is a common expression in the music industry referring to recording on multi-track tape. Each track contains a different musical line either instrumental or vocal. When all tracks are played at the same time, a complete song is produced.

cut the lead (to) *exp.* (used in all sports) to reduce the difference in scores late in the game • *With moments left in the game, the losing team suddenly cut the lead;* With moments left in the game, the losing team suddenly reduced the lead.

cut to the chase (to) *exp.* to go directly to the most essential part or culmination of a story • *I don't care about the details. Just cut to the chase. Are they really going to get a divorce?;* I don't care about the details. Just go directly to the culmination of the story. Are they really going to get a divorce?
▸ NOTE: This expression was derived from the movie industry. Audiences used to commonly fill the theaters to watch westerns which would typically culminate in an exciting chase scene. If a director felt that it was taking too long to get to this part of the movie, he would instruct the editor to "cut to the chase" to keep the viewers from

getting bored.
▸ SYNONYM: **cut to the juicy part** *exp.*
⇨ NOTE: **the juicy part** *exp.* the most interesting, and usually shocking, part of a story.

cutback *n.* reduction in spending • *Since we're over-budget this month, we're going to have to make some cutbacks immediately;* Since we're over-budget this month, we're going to have to make some reductions in spending immediately.
▸ SEE: **deep cuts** *exp.*

-D-

dead presidents *exp.* (rap slang) money • *Look at all those dead presidents!;* Look at all that money!

dead stop *n.* complete stop • *We were at a dead stop for an entire hour on the highway!;* We were at a complete stop for an entire hour on the highway!
▸ ALSO: **to stop dead** *exp.* to stop completely and suddenly • *When I saw the snake, I stopped dead in my tracks;* When I saw the snake, I stopped completely and suddenly.

deadly *adj.* (teen slang) **1.** excellent • *That group plays the most deadly music;* That group plays the best music. • **2.** extremely difficult • *The math final was deadly;* The math final was extremely difficult.
▸ NOTE: For additional popular adjectives with opposite meanings, refer to page 167.

death warmed over (to look like) *exp.* to look very sick and close to death, pale, exhausted • *I haven't slept in three days because the baby keeps crying. I must look like death warmed over;* I haven't slept in three days because the baby keeps crying. I must look very sick and close to death.

▶ SYNONYM: **to look like something the cat dragged in** *exp.* to look terrible • *What happened to you? You look like something the cat dragged in!;* What happened to you? You look terrible!

deep cuts *exp.* severe reductions in spending • *Deep cuts were made in the school's budget this year;* Severe reductions were made in the school's budget this year.

deep left center *n.* (baseball) the portion of the ball park between left and center field. This part of the playing field is often called *"the power alleys"* since a ball hit in these poorly guarded areas is not likely to be retrieved quickly • *Look who's coming up to bat! We'd better cover deep left center since he always aims for the power alleys!;* Look who's coming up to bat! We'd better cover the area between left and center field since he always aims for this part of the playing field!

dial in on someone (to) *exp.* (surfer slang) to talk with someone • *Let's go dial in on those girls;* Let's go talk to those girls.

dialogue someone (to) *exp.* to talk to someone • *There's my favorite movie star! I'm gonna go dialogue her;* There's my favorite

movie star! I'm gonna go talk to her.

▶ SYNONYM: **to chew the fat with someone** *exp.* to chat with someone • *We chewed the fat for an hour;* We chatted for an hour.

dirt *n.* • **1.** gossip, scandal • *Got any new dirt to tell me?;* Do you have any new gossip to tell me? • **2.** material which causes corruption, pornography • *What is this dirt you're reading?;* What is this corruption you're reading?

▶ ALSO: **dirty** *adj.* pornographic, obscene • *I found my little brother looking at dirty magazines!;* I found my little brother looking at pornographic magazines! • *My parents don't tolerate dirty language spoken in their home;* My parents don't tolerate obscene language spoken in their home.

dis someone (to) *v.* (rap slang) to have disrespect for someone • *Don't dis me!;* Don't have disrespect for me!

▶ ALSO: **to dis and dismiss** *exp.* to have disrespect for someone and then ask him/her to leave • *When I see her tomorrow, I'm dissin' and dismissin'!;* When I see her tomorrow, I'm letting her know that I don't like her and then I'm telling her to get out of my life!

▶ NOTE: A common error which has become universal is to use the noun "disrespect" as a verb: "to disrespect." For example: *Don't disrespect me!;* Don't have disrespect for me! Although this is incorrect usage, it is extremely common.

do the trick (to) *exp.* to have a positive effect • *I'm sorry you don't feel well. Here, drink this tonic. It'll do the trick;* I'm sorry you don't feel well. Here, drink this tonic. It'll have a positive effect.

doc *n.* abbreviation for "doctor" • *Hey, doc! Good to see you!;* Hey, doctor! Good to see you!
♦ NOTE: The usage of *"doc"* is extremely familiar.

dode *n.* (teen slang) fool • *Our new teacher is the biggest dode!;* Our new teacher is the biggest fool!
♦ SYNONYM: **dork** *n.* • *What a dork!;* What a fool!
♦ NOTE: **dode** = *dork + dude*

doozie (to be a) *adj.* to be impressive • *Did you see the black eye he got? What a doozie!;* Did you see the black eye he got? It's impressive!
♦ NOTE: This adjective comes from one of the most admired cars of the mid 1920's; the *"Deusenberg."*
♦ SYNONYM: **humdinger** *n.*

double whammy *exp.* one shocking event right after another • *It was a shock to her when she found out that she was pregnant. But it was a double whammy when the doctor told her that she was going to have triplets!;* It was a shock to her when she found out that she was pregnant. But it was a double shock when the doctor told her that she was going to have triplets!

drag on (to) *exp.* to prolong • *This meeting is dragging on!;* This meeting is too prolonged!

draw play *exp.* (football) a strategy whereby a player pretends to hand off the ball to another player in order to divert the other team. This *"draws"* the defenders toward the wrong player while the player who actually has the ball runs freely toward the goal • *That draw play was executed perfectly!;* That fake handoff was executed perfectly!

drive a three-two fastball (to) *exp.* (baseball) to hit a fast pitch thrown to the batter when he has three balls and two strikes against him.
♦ NOTE (1): **drive (to)** *v.* to project a ball with great force.
♦ NOTE (2): Once the batter has missed three balls that were legally thrown from the pitcher (*"strikes"*), the batter loses his turn. If the batter misses four balls that were illegally or incorrectly thrown from the pitcher (*"balls"*), the batter is allowed to advance freely to first base. When the batter has three balls and two strikes against him, this is called a *"full count."* This is a crucial moment in the game since the next pitch is especially important; one more ball, the batter advances — one more strike, the batter is *"out."*

duck *n.* (rap slang) unattractive female • *What a duck!;* What an ugly female!
♦ ALSO: **to duck** *v.* to date ugly women • *That's his girlfriend? There he goes duckin' again;* That's

his girlfriend? There he goes dating ugly women again.

dude *n.* (surfer slang) guy, friend • *You really dommo, dude!;* You really dominate when it comes to surfing, friend!
♦ NOTE: This term was encountered earlier but it bears repeating since it is constantly used in the surfing (and teen) culture.
♦ ALSO: **dudette** *f.* girl • *Hey, dudettes!;* Hey, girls!

dumped (to get) *exp.* to get rejected or abandoned • *I got dumped by my boyfriend;* I got rejected by my boyfriend. • *Your girlfriend isn't very nice to you. Why don't you just dump her?;* Your girlfriend isn't very nice to you. Why don't you just abandon her?
♦ ALSO: **to get dumped on** *exp.* to be deceived • *I got dumped on by my best friend;* I got deceived by my best friend.

-E-

eat the cookie (to) *exp.* (surfer slang) to get unmercifully tossed around by a wave • *I really ate the cookie;* I really got unmercifully tossed around.

excellent *adj.* (surfer slang) terrific • *Excellent wave!;* Terrific wave!
♦ NOTE: The standard adjective "excellent" has become so much a part of the surfer's vocabulary (as well as that of teens in general) that it bears mentioning here. To use this term is a sign of being extremely up-to-date. It is additionally popular

to use the expression *"most excellent"* when referring to anything that is terrific: *The weather is most excellent today.*

-F-

face up to (to) *exp.* to confront • *You have to face up to what you've done;* You have to confront what you've done.

fake a handoff (to) *exp.* (football) to pretend to pass the ball in order to dupe the other players into thinking that another player has the ball. This technique enables the player with the ball to run freely toward the goal • *Did you see how he just faked a handoff to the other player?;* Did you see how he just pretended to give the ball to the other player?
♦ SEE: **draw play** *exp.*

fall in (to) *exp.* (rap slang) to arrive • *What time did you fall in at the party?;* What time did you arrive at the party?

fender-bender *exp.* a minor traffic accident without any casualties • *I got into a little fender-bender on the way to work today;* I got into a minor traffic accident on the way to work today.
♦ NOTE (1): This expression is part of the extensive world of *Rhyming Slang.*
♦ NOTE (2): For additional rhyming slang, see page 131.

fling *n.* a love affair • *Didn't he know that his wife would probably find out about his fling sooner or later?;*

Didn't he know that his wife would probably find out about his love affair sooner or later?

flip [out] (to) *exp.* to become uncontrollably upset • *My mother flipped [out] when I wrecked her car;* My mother became uncontrollably upset when I wrecked her car.
‣ SYNONYM: **to wig [out]** *exp.* • *She wigged [out] when I told her the news;* She became uncontrollably upset when I told her the news.

fly gear *exp.* (rap slang) exceptional clothing • *Look at that fly gear!;* Look at that exceptional clothing!
‣ NOTE (1): The expression *"fly gear"* is actually a combination of slang and standard English. The term *"fly"* has become one of the most commonly used adjectives among the younger generation: *That's a fly stereo system!;* That's a fantastic stereo system! However, the term *"gear"* meaning "clothing" or "outfit" is simply a standard term commonly used with the adjective *"fly"* when referring to extremely attractive clothing.
‣ NOTE (2): See: **sport (to)**

fold (to) *v.* (rap slang) to quit or surrender • *This work is too hard. I'm foldin';* This work is too hard. I'm quitting.
‣ NOTE: The verb *"to fold"* is an extremely common card-playing term used by participants who cannot continue the round due to inferior cards. When the player calls out *"I fold,"* the hands which are holding the playing cards are closed

or *folded* together indicating surrender.

foul (to) *v.* (used in all sports) to commit a violation against another player • *Thompson got fouled for pushing another player;* Thompson was penalized for pushing another player.

freak *n.* (rap slang) very attractive sexy individual • *I love goin' to parties to check out all the freaks!;* I love going to parties to examine all the attractive people!
‣ NOTE: **to check out** *exp.* to examine, to look at • *Check her out!;* Examine her!
‣ SYNONYM: **freakazoid** *n.* • *What a freakazoid!;* What a gorgeous and sexy person!

freethrow *n.* (basketball) an unobstructed toss at the basket, made from a specific line, awarded a team due to a foul being committed by the opposing side • *Our team won because we were awarded two freethrows;* Our team won because we were awarded two unobstructed tosses at the basket because the other side committed fouls against us.

frosted (to be) *adj.* (rap slang) cold and emotionless • *I tried talkin' to her but she was frosted;* I tried talking to her but she was cold and emotionless.
‣ NOTE: **frosty** (common slang term among all age groups) • **1.** *n.* abusive term referring to someone who is cold and emotionless • *Hey, frosty!;* Hey, you cold and emotionless person! • **2.** *adj. He*

was so frosty with you; He was so cold and emotionless with you.

-G-

geeklified *adj.* (surfer slang) foolish, ridiculous • *That's totally geeklified!;* That's really ridiculous!

geeky *adj.* foolish • *Why are you wearing that geeky hat?;* Why are you wearing that foolish hat?
  ♦ ALSO: **to be geeked out** *exp.* to be foolish looking • *Do I look geeked out in this dress?;* Do I look foolish in this dress?
  ♦ SYNONYM: **nerdy** *adj.* • *Those glasses are really nerdy;* Those glasses are really foolish looking.

gel (to) *v.* (surfer slang) to calm down • *Hey, gel dude!;* Hey, calm down, friend!

get down to brass tacks (to) *exp.* to discuss the prevailing essential matters • *I would love to continue talking about my vacation but we really should get down to brass tacks;* I would love to continue talking about my vacation but we really should discuss the prevailing essential matters.

get faced (to) *exp.* to get extremely intoxicated • *We got faced at the party;* We got extremely intoxicated at the party.
  ♦ NOTE: This expression is a euphemistic and shortened version of *"to be shitfaced."*

get over something (not to be able to) *exp.* to be unable to rid oneself of the shock about something • *I just can't get over how he could lie that way;* I just can't stop being astonished about how he could lie that way.

get with the program (to) *exp.* to become aware, to become current • *Didn't you know this was a formal dinner? Get with the program!;* Didn't you know this was a formal dinner? Get current!
  ♦ SYNONYM: **to get a clue** *exp.*

getup *n.* clothing, outfit • *What kind of getup is she wearing?;* What kind of outfit is she wearing?
  ♦ NOTE: The term *"getup"* may be used both derogatorily and favorably, depending on the context and delivery of the speaker: *Nice getup!;* Nice outfit!

gig *n.* (teen slang) musical performance • *I was asked to perform tomorrow but the gig doesn't pay enough!;* I was asked to perform tomorrow but the performance doesn't pay enough!

give it to someone straight (to) *exp.* to disclose something to someone in a very direct way • *Give it to me straight. I can take it;* Be frank with me. I can endure it.
  ♦ SYNONYM: **to tell someone something point blank** *exp.* • *He told me point blank that if I didn't start working harder, I'd be fired;* He told me frankly that if I didn't start working harder, I'd be fired.

give someone some skin (to) *exp.* (rap slang) a common greeting and signal of excitement or congratulations.

◗ NOTE: This signal consists of the initiator calling out *"Gimme some skin!"* At this point, he/she extends the hand, palm up, while the other person slaps it. The process is then reversed as the original initiator slaps the hand of the other person. The expression *"Gimme some skin!"* is commonly used among the younger generation as: **1.** a greeting • *Hey, Steve! Gimme some skin!* • **2.** a signal of excitement • *Your birthday is on the same day as mine? All right! Gimme some skin!* • **3.** a signal of congratulations • *I just heard you're gettin' married! Gimme some skin!*

give someone the eye (to) *exp.* to look at someone with romantic interest • *I think that guy is giving you the eye;* I think that guy is looking at you with romantic interest.
　◗ SYNONYM: **to check someone out** *exp.* • *She's been checking you out ever since you came in;* She's been looking at you romantically ever since you came in.

gnarlatious *adj.* (surfer slang) fantastic • *I've never seen such gnarlatious weather!;* I've never seen such fantastic weather!

gnarly *adj.* (surfer slang) dangerous and scary • *That wave was gnarly!;* That wave was dangerous!
　◗ VARIATION: **gnar** *adj.* [pronounced: *nar*]

go easy on someone (to) *exp.* to be lenient with someone • *I don't know why the judge went so easy on the criminal;* I don't know why the

judge was so lenient with the criminal.
　◗ ANTONYM (1): **to throw the book at someone** *exp.* to give someone the maximum punishment (said only of the court system) • *The judge really threw the book at him!;* The judge really gave him the maximum punishment!
　◗ ANTONYM (2): **to come down on someone** *exp.* to criticize someone severely • *Her parents are always coming down on her;* Her parents are always criticizing her.

goob *n.* (teen slang) fool • *What a goob!;* What a fool!
　◗ NOTE: This term comes from the old television series "The Andy Griffith Show" which featured a foolish character named "Goober."

good to go (to be) *exp.* (rap slang) to be going great • *Everything's good to go;* Everything is going great!

goose cooked (to have one's) *exp.* to be in severe trouble • *If I forget her birthday again this year, my goose is cooked;* If I forget her birthday again this year, I'm going to be in severe trouble.
　◗ SYNONYM: **to have one's butt in a sling** *exp.* • *My butt's gonna be in a sling if I don't get home by 9:00;* I'm going to be in severe trouble if I don't get home by 9:00.

grand slam *exp.* (baseball) a home run with three runners on base, resulting in four home runs • *He hit a grand slam!;* He hit a home run with a player on each base!
　◗ SEE: **load the bases (to)** *exp.*

♦ ALSO: **grand slam home run** *exp.*
♦ VARIATION: **grand slammer** *exp.*

green room *exp.* (surfer slang) tube of a wave • *I must have spent an entire minute in the green room!;* I must have spent an entire minute in the tube!
♦ NOTE: The ultimate surfing experience for any surfer is to ride inside the tube of a wave. From the inside, the water looks smooth and shiny with a green tint like melted glass. For this reason, it is oftentimes referred to as the *"green room"* or *"glass house."*

grinder *n.* (surfer slang) huge wave • *What a grinder!;* What a huge wave!

grommet *n.* (surfer slang) novice surfer • *You're surfin' like a grommet, dude!;* You're surfing like a novice, friend!

grunts *n.pl.* (surfer slang) food • *Let's get some grunts;* Let's get some food.
♦ NOTE: This represents the sound of ecstacy a surfer makes when eating after several hours of calorie-burning surfing.

-H-

hair ball *exp.* (surfer slang) huge wave • *Check out that hair ball!;* Look at that huge wave!

half court *n.* (basketball) the halfway point on a basketball court • *He made a shot into the basket all the way from half court!;* He threw the ball into the basket all the way from the halfway point on the basketball court!

hang (to) *v.* to pass the time idly • *Let's hang here for a while until it stops raining;* Let's just pass the time here for a while until it stops raining.
♦ NOTE: This is a common shortened version of the expression *"to hang out."*
♦ SYNONYM: **to kick back** *exp.* • *Let's kick back at my house;* Let's pass the time idly at my house.

hang with someone (to) *exp.* (teen slang) to spend time with someone (and do nothing in particular), to socialize with someone • *She likes hanging with her friends in the park;* She likes socializing with her friends in the park.
♦ SYNONYM: **to kick it with someone** *exp.* • *I'm going to Bob's house to kick it for a while;* I'm going to Bob's house to socialize for a while.
♦ NOTE: The expression *"to hang with someone"* is a shortened version of *"to hang out with someone."* It is extremely popular among teens to drop the preposition *"out"* from commonly used expressions. For example:
  to freak out (to lose control of one's emotions) = *to freak;*
  to chill out (to relax) = *to chill;*
  to space out (to become forgetful) = *to space;* etc.

hard pack *n.* snow that has been packed down due to traffic • *I don't like skiing on hard pack because I have trouble stopping!;* I don't like skiing on snow that's packed down because I have trouble stopping!

hate one's guts (to) *exp.* to despise someone intensely right down to the core of his/her being • *I hate his guts!;* I despise him right down to the core of his being!

"Heads up!" *exp.* "Be alert and look up!"
♦ NOTE: This is a common cry to warn people that something is flying through the air and could potentially cause harm on its way down.

heat wave *n.* continuous high temperatures • *We're having a heat wave in the middle of the winter!;* We're having continuous high temperatures in the middle of the winter!

heavy *adj.* (of traffic) dense • *Traffic was heavy all the way home;* Traffic was dense all the way home.

heist *n.* armed robbery • *That's the guy I saw commit the heist today!;* That's the guy I saw commit the armed robbery today!
♦ SYNONYM: **stickup** *n.* • *Did you hear about the stickup today at the bank?;* Did you hear about the armed robbery today at the bank?

"Hello!" *exclam.* (teen slang) "Become realistic!" • *You just got a job as a Spanish translator? Hello! You don't speak Spanish!;* You just got a job as a Spanish translator? Get realistic! You don't speak Spanish!
♦ NOTE: *"Hello!"* is a humorous exclamation commonly used in

response to a ridiculous comment.
♦ SYNONYM: **"Have you lost it?"** *exp.* • *You're going skydiving? Have you lost it?;* You're going skydiving? Have you lost touch with reality?

"Hi there!" *exp.* "Hi!"
♦ NOTE: This is a very casual greeting that should only be used in informal situations.

high *exp.* • high pressure area in the atmosphere which results in clear skies • *There's been a high sitting over the city for the past week which is why the weather's been so beautiful;* There's been a high pressure area in the atmosphere sitting over the city for the past week which is why the weather has been so beautiful.

hinge on something (to) *exp.* to depend on something • *Whether or not we get the big contract hinges on your dinner tonight with the client;* Whether or not we get the big contract depends on your dinner tonight with the client.

hip hop *n.* (rap slang) rap music (an extremely popular style of song where the performer speaks the lyrics in rhythm).

hit (to) *v.* (football) to complete a pass to a receiver • *Although he got tackled in the process, Hirsch managed to hit his receiver;* Although he got tackled in the process, Hirsch managed to complete a pass to his receiver.

hit (to) *v.* (teen slang) (used by all ages) to go to • *Wanna hit the stores with me?;* Do you want to go to the stores with me? • *Did you hit the concert last night?;* Did you go to the concert last night?

hit *n.* (teen slang) (used by all ages) popular song, movie, play, person, etc. • *My brother just wrote a song that I know is going to be a hit;* My brother just wrote a song that I know is going to be popular. • *You're going to be a big hit at the party;* You're going to be very popular at the party.
◗ ALSO: **smash hit** *exp.* very popular song, movie, play, person, etc.
◗ ANTONYM: **bomb** *n.* unsuccessful song, movie, play, person, etc. • *That movie is going to be a big bomb;* That movie is going to be a big failure.

hitched (to get) *exp.* (humorous) to get married • (lit); to get fastened together • *So, when are you two finally gonna get hitched?;* So, when are you two finally going to get married?

hold on (to) *exp.* to wait • *Hold on! Don't go without me!;* Wait! Don't go without me!
◗ SYNONYM: **to hold the phone** *exp.* • *Hold the phone! That was a really mean thing you just said;* Wait! That was a really mean thing you just said.

homes *n.* (rap slang) friend • (lit); someone who is from one's hometown • *Hey, homes!;* Hey, friend!

◗ SYNONYM: **homey** *n.*
⇨ NOTE: As learned in lesson one, *"homey"* is commonly used among teens in daily conversation. However, the shortened version, *"homes,"* is more readily heard in rap music.
◗ NOTE: **squad** *n.* a group of friends.

homey *n.* (teen slang) close friend, pal • *Have you met Jeff? He's been my homey for the past 10 years;* Have you met Jeff? He's been my close friend for the past 10 years.
◗ SYNONYM: **goomba** *n.* • *Hey, my goomba! Can I borrow five dollars?;* Hey, good friend! Can I borrow five dollars?

hook *n.* (teen slang) the part of the song which is the most memorable, whether it be the lyrics or melody • *This song has the greatest hook. I keep singing it all day!;* This song has the most memorable section. I keep singing it all day!

hoopla *n.* commotion • *Why is there so much hoopla about his visit? Who is he, anyway?;* Why is there so much commotion about his visit? Who is he, anyway?

"How does that sound?" *exp.* "Does that appeal to you?"
◗ SYNONYM: **"How does that grab you?"** *exp.*

"How ya livin'?" *exp.* (rap slang) How are you doing?
◗ NOTE: *"ya"* is an extremely common contraction of *"are you"* and is by all age groups.

hunk *n.* an extremely muscular and virile man • *What a hunk!;* What an extremely muscular and virile man! ♦ ALSO: **hunky** *adj.* extremely muscular and virile • *Your brother's so hunky!;* Your brother's so muscular and virile!

-I-

"I'll say" *exp.* "Absolutely!"
♦ SYNONYM: **"You said it!"** *exp.*
♦ ANTONYM: **"No way!"** *exp.* "Absolutely not!"

I *n.* an extremely common abbreviation for "interstate" • *I-10 is one of the few interstate highways that stretches all the way across the United States;* Interstate 10 is one of the few interstate highways that stretches all the way across the United States.

in broad daylight *exp.* in the middle of the day • *My car was stolen in broad daylight!;* My car was stolen in the middle of the day! ♦ ANTONYM: **in the dead of night** *exp.* in the middle of the night • *Why were you out in the dead of night?;* Why were you out in the middle of the night?

in full swing (to be) *exp.* • **1.** to be fully operational • *The airport is back in full swing;* The airport is back to being fully operational. • **2.** to be completely underway • *The party's in full swing;* The party is completely underway.

in no time *adv.* quickly • *He figured out the math problem in no time;* He figured out the math

problem quickly.
♦ VARIATION (1): **in no time flat** *adv.*
♦ VARIATION (2): **in no time at all** *adv.*

infield hit *exp.* (baseball) a hit made by a batter where the ball does not leave the part of the field enclosed by the three bases and home plate, also referred to as the *"diamond"* • *He made a clean infield hit and got to first base;* He made a perfect hit inside the diamond-shaped playing field and got to first base.

insane *adj.* (surfer slang) fantastic • *Did you see the insane grinders out there?;* Did you see the fantastic waves out there?

-J-

jack someone (to) *v.* (rap slang) to rob someone • *I got jacked in front of my house!;* I got robbed in front of my house! ♦ NOTE: This comes from the standard verb *"to hi-jack"* meaning "to force an airplane pilot to deviate from the normal flight pattern by means of gunpoint." ♦ ALSO: **jacker** *n.* robber.

jam session *exp.* (teen slang) a meeting of musicians who come together to do musical improvisations • *I couldn't sleep 'cause my brother's group had a jam session in his bedroom all night!;* I couldn't sleep because my brother's group got together and did musical improvisations in his bedroom all night!

jam *n.* (basketball) the act of pushing or *"dunking"* the ball through the hoop • *With seconds to spare, Olson made the jam!;* With seconds to spare, Olson pushed the ball through the hoop!

‣ ALSO: **to jam** *v.* to push or *"dunk"* the ball through the hoop.

jaw jack (to) *exp.* (rap slang) to talk a lot • *We jaw jacked on the phone for an hour;* We talked on the phone for an hour.

‣ NOTE: This is a humorous expression based on the noun "jack" which is a device used to raise one end of a car off the ground in order to change a tire. To operate a jack, a long handle is cranked up and down much like one's jaws when speaking.

‣ SYNONYM: **to track** *v.* • *You realize we've been trackin' for two hours already?;* Do you realize we've been talking for two hours already?

jock *n.* athlete • *My father used to be a real jock when he was in school;* My father used to be a real athlete when he was in school.

jump-start (to) *exp.* to start something suddenly that was completely lifeless • (lit); to restart a dead car battery • *We have to do something to jump-start the economy before it's too late!;* We have to do something to start the economy quickly before it's too late!

-K-

keep tabs on something for someone (to) *exp.* to keep a close surveillance on something for someone • *While I'm on vacation, will you keep tabs on any new developments at work for me?;* While I'm on vacation, will you keep a close surveillance on any new developments at work for me?

kick up (to) *exp.* (said of wind, dust, pollen, etc.) to begin to blow around in the air • *The dust is really kicking up all of a sudden;* The dust is really blowing around suddenly.

knock off something (to) *exp.* to rob something • *Where did you get all that money? What did you do…knock off a bank?;* Where did you get all that money? What did you do…rob a bank?;

‣ SYNONYM: **to hold up something** *exp.* • *I just overheard that man say he's gonna hold up the bank!;* I just overheard that man say he's going to rob the bank!

knock someone up (to) *exp.* to get someone pregnant • *If she doesn't stop sleeping around, she's gonna get herself knocked up;* If she doesn't stop sleeping around, she's going to get herself pregnant.

‣ NOTE: This expression is considered to be extremely casual language and should only be used with friends and family.

knock someone's block off (to) *exp.* to punch someone in the face • *If you don't give me that, I'm gonna knock your block off!;* If you don't give me that, I'm going to punch you in the face!

‣ NOTE: **block** *n.* face, head.

‣ SYNONYM: **to punch someone's**

lights out exp. • *She punched his lights out in front of everyone!;* She knocked him unconscious in front of everyone!

knockout (to be a) adj. to be a stunning beauty • *Your mother's a knockout!;* Your mother is a stunning beauty!
♦ SYNONYM: **to be a ten** exp. to be rated the highest on a scale of 1-10.

knotted (to be) v. (used in all sports) to be tied (said of the score) • *The score's been knotted for the past half hour!;* The score has been tied for the past half hour!

-L-

lacerate (to) v. (surfer slang) to attack the waves fearlessly • *You were laceratin' those green monsters!;* You were attacking those huge waves!
♦ NOTE: **green monster** n. enormous wave with a dark green hue.

lame adj. (teen slang) **1.** stupid, moronic • *He's so lame;* He's so moronic. • **2.** mediocre • *I can't believe how lame the new teacher is;* I can't believe how mediocre the new teacher is.
♦ ANTONYM: **dope** adj. excellent • *You look dope, today!;* You look great today!

land oneself something (to) exp. • to acquire something after a great deal of effort • *I heard you just landed yourself a great job!;* I heard you just acquired a great job! • *I just landed a big contract with a national company!;* I just acquired a big contract with a national company!
♦ NOTE: The verb "to land" is commonly used in regards to fishing: *to land a fish;* to catch a fish and bring it to shore.

latest adj. (teen slang) (used by all ages) newest, most recent • *Her dress is the latest fashion from Paris;* Her dress is the newest fashion from Paris.

lay-up n. (basketball) the act of dribbling the ball toward the goal, bringing the ball up with one hand and gently placing the ball either directly in the basket or off the backboard into the basket.
♦ VARIATION: **lay-in** n.

lick n. (teen slang) musical phrase • *That lick is too complicated for me to play on the guitar;* That musical phrase is too complicated for me to play on the guitar.

lie in wait (to) exp. said of an animal who hides and waits patiently and silently for its prey to arrive • *I know you want to catch the robber, but you can't just lie in wait for him. That could take days!;* I know you want to catch the robber, but you can't just wait for him. That could take days!

lift one's spirits (to) exp. to make one feel more cheerful • *I think a nice walk outside will lift your spirits;* I think a nice walk outside will make you feel more cheerful.

lip floater *exp.* (surfer slang) a move where the surfer slides over the lip of the wave • *That clean peeler was perfect for doin' a lip floater;* That flawless wave was perfect for gently sliding over the lip.
 ‣ SYNONYM: **lipper** *n.*

live large (to) *exp.* (rap slang) to be very successful (and have a lot of money) • *This is your house? You must be livin' large!;* This is your house? You must be very successful!
 ‣ SYNONYM (1): **to be crazy large** *exp.*
 ‣ SYNONYM (2): **to be extra large** *exp.*
 ‣ SYNONYM (3): **to be stupid large** *exp.*

load the bases (to) *exp.* (baseball) to successfully get a player on each base • *The bases are loaded. If he hits a home run now, they'll get four runs and win!;* Each base has a player on it. If he hits a home run now, they'll get four points and win!
 ‣ NOTE: **run** *n.* a point made by a player who has successfully run around the entire diamond, hitting all three bases and home plate.

lunched (to get) *exp.* (surfer slang) to get thrown around unmercifully by a wave • *I got lunched my first time out;* I got thrown around unmercifully my first time out.

-M-

macking (to be) *exp.* (surfer slang) said of the ocean that is generating huge waves (the size of Mack trucks • *The ocean's fully mackin' today;*

The ocean is really generating huge waves today.

mad crush on someone (to have a) *exp.* to have great romantic interest in someone • *I can't believe she has a mad crush on me!;* I can't believe she has romantic interest in me!
 ‣ NOTE: In this expression, the adjective *"mad"* which literally means "angry," takes on the slang meaning of "intense," having nothing to do at all with anger.
 ‣ SYNONYM: **to have the hots for someone** *exp.*

majorly *adv.* (teen slang) extremely • *He's majorly weird!;* He's extremely weird!
 ‣ SYNONYM: **mega** *adv.* • *He's mega hot!;* He's extremely sexy!

max and relax (to) *exp.* (rap slang) to relax • *I spent four hours maxin' and relaxin' on the beach today;* I spent four hours relaxing on the beach today.
 ‣ SYNONYM (1): **to chill** *v.*
 ‣ SYNONYM (2): **to cold chill** *exp.*
 ‣ SYNONYM (3): **to cool** *v.*
 ‣ SYNONYM (4): **to cool out** *exp.*
 ‣ SYNONYM (5): **to limp** *v.*
 ‣ SYNONYM (6): **to max out** *exp.*

meanest *adv.* (teen slang) **1.** best • *That's the meanest car I've ever driven!;* That's the best car I've ever driven! • **2.** most difficult • *This is the meanest homework assignment we've ever had!;* This is the hardest homework assignment we've ever had!
 ‣ ALSO: **mean** *adj.* (used by all ages) **1.** menacing • *The weather*

looks mean today; The weather
looks menacing today. • **2.** great •
She's a mean cook!; She's a great
cook!
♦ NOTE: For additional popular
adjectives with opposite meanings,
refer to page 167.

mellow out (to) *exp.* to calm down
• *Would you mellow out? There's
no need to get so upset!;* Would you
calm down? There's no need to get
so upset!
♦ SYNONYM: **to chill [out]** *exp.*

mercury *n.* temperature • (lit); the
metallic liquid in thermometers
which rises in hot temperatures and
drops in cold temperatures •
Where's the mercury today?;
What's the temperature today? •
The mercury's rising; The
temperature's rising.

mick class *exp.* (teen slang) easy
class • *What a mick class!;* What an
easy class!
♦ NOTE: This is a shortened version
of the expression: **Mickey Mouse
class.**
♦ ALSO: *This class is really mick!*
[or] *This class is really Mickey
Mouse!;* This class is really easy!

mint (to) *v.* (rap slang) to make a lot
of money • *Ever since he got
promoted, he's been mintin'!;* Ever
since he got promoted, he's been
making a lot of money!
♦ NOTE: It is common in slang to
transform nouns into verbs,
consequently creating somewhat
humorous terms. The verb *"to
mint"* is a transformation of the

noun "The United States Mint"
where money is produced.

Miss Thang *exp.* (rap slang) name
given to a pretentious woman •
Look at Miss Thang over there!;
Look at that pretentious woman
over there!
♦ NOTE: The term *"thang"* is
simply "thing" as it is pronounced
with a southern accent. In the
1800s, wealthy women of the South
were considered to be exceedingly
pretentious since they were always
seen in public as being coquettish,
cultured, excessively charming,
overly attentive to men and always
dressed in provocative clothing.
Due to the thick accent of the
region, their accents became
equated with wealth and snobbery.
Pronouncing the term "thing" as
"thang," as it would have been
heard articulated by one of these
southern women, is an attempt to
mock and belittle anyone displaying
these kinds of characteristics or
affectations. *"Thang"* is possibly
just a shortened version of
"pretentious little thing."

move in (to) *exp.* **1.** to approach •
We better get home. The clouds are
really moving in fast!;* We had
better get home. The clouds are
really approaching fast! • **2.** to
relocate to a new home • *When are
you planning on moving in?;* When
are you planning on relocating to
your new home?
♦ NOTE: In the first sentence, *We
better get home,* the verb "to have"
is purposely missing: *We **had** better
get home.* Although incorrect in

standard English, it is extremely common in colloquial speech to omit "had" before "better."

-N-

nab (to) *v.* to apprehend • *The cops nabbed the guy who stole my wallet!;* The police officers apprehended the guy who stole my wallet!
▸ SYNONYM: **to bust** *v.* • *They busted the robber just as he was leaving the bank;* They apprehended the robber just as he was leaving the bank.

nasty (to be) *adj.* said of severe weather • (lit); to be extremely unpleasant • *Have you ever seen such nasty weather?;* Have you ever seen such unpleasant weather?

nip factor *exp.* (surfer slang) coldness • *What's the nip factor like in the water today?;* How cold is the water today?

"No biggy!" *exp.* "No problem!"

"No way, José!" *exp.* "Absolutely not!"

not *exclam.* (teen slang) not really, just kidding • *That's such a beautiful jacket you're wearing! Not!;* That's such a beautiful jacket you're wearing! Not really!
▸ NOTE: This exclamation has become extremely popular among teenagers. It is used humorously to turn a positive statement or compliment into an insult.

-O-

O.R. *n.* abbreviation for: operating room • *You're wanted in O.R. immediately!;* You're wanted in the operating room immediately!
▸ NOTE: When "operating room" is abbreviated to *"O.R.,"* the definite article "the" is usually dropped as demonstrated in the above example. Oddly enough, this abbreviation is commonly heard on television yet rarely, if ever, used within the medical community.

off-the-wall (to be) *adj.* to be highly unusual and bizarre • *You really like him? He's so off-the-wall;* You really like him? He's so unusual and bizarre. • *Her sense of humor is really off-the-wall;* Her sense of humor is really bizarre.
▸ SYNONYM: **to be out there** *exp.* • *She's really out there!;* She's really bizarre!
⇨ NOTE: The expression *"to be out there"* refers to "out there in space" or "in another world."

on shaky ground (to be) *exp.* to be unsure • *Ever since our fight, we've been on shaky ground;* Ever since our fight, we've been on uncertain terms with each other.

on tap (to be) *exp.* to be pending • (lit); (bar slang) said of various beverages (beer, sodas, etc.) which are discharged through spigots on the bar • *We have good weather on tap for tomorrow;* We have good weather pending for tomorrow.

on the flip side *exp.* conversely •
(lit); on the reverse side of the
record • *If our plan succeeds, we
could earn thousands of dollars. On
the flip side, if we fail, we could lose
everything;* If our plan succeeds, we
could earn thousands of dollars.
Conversely, if we fail, we could
lose everything.

on the floor (to be) *exp.* said of a
proposal to be considered by an
assembly • *We have a motion on the
floor to increase taxes;* We have a
motion to be considered for
discussion to increase taxes.
♦ ALSO (1): **the floor** *n.* members of
an assembly • *The chairman took
questions from the floor;* The
chairman took questions from the
assembly.
♦ ALSO (2): **to have the floor** *exp.* to
have one's turn to speak before an
assembly • *The senator from
California has the floor;* The
senator from California may now
speak.

-P-

PAT *exp.* (football) an abbreviation for
"point after touchdown" which
refers to a team's chance to get
another point by kicking the ball
over the goalpost • *The PAT
brought the score up to 15 to 13;*
The extra point made by kicking the
ball over the goalpost brought the
score up to 15 to 13.

peace up *exp.* (rap slang) good-bye •
Talk to ya later. Peace up; Talk to
you later. Good-bye.

♦ VARIATION (1): **peace** *n.*
♦ VARIATION (2): **peace out** *exp.*

peek one's head in (to) *exp.* to
visit someone without ceremony
and briefly • *I don't want to disturb
her. Well, I'll just peek my head in
and say hello;* I don't want to
disturb her. Well, I'll just visit her
briefly.

pet the cat (to) *exp.* (surfer slang)
to squat down on the surfboard and
slowly move one's arms up and
down to keep balance • *We could
see you pettin' the cat from the
shore;* We could see you squatting
and moving your arms up and down
from the shore.

pick up chicks (to) *exp.* to look
for girls for romantic encounters •
*This bar is great for pickin' up
chicks;* This bar is great for finding
girls for romantic encounters.
♦ SYNONYM: **to cruise chicks** *exp.*

pick up speed (to) *exp.* to increase
in speed • *Our sled started picking
up speed as we went down the hill;*
Our sled started increasing in speed
as we went down the hill.

pickup *n.* a popular abbreviation of
"pickup truck" • *I've always wanted
to buy a pickup because I like
driving high off the ground;* I've
always wanted to buy a pickup
truck because I like driving high off
the ground.

picnic (to be a) *adj.* enjoyable
experience (usually used in the
negative *"to be no picnic"*) • *You
think I like having to tell him he's*

fired? Believe me. This is no picnic for me; You think I like having to tell him he's fired? Believe me. This is not an enjoyable task for me.
♦ SYNONYM: **to be a snap** *exp.* • *The math homework was a snap;* The math homework was extremely easy.

plastered (to be) *adj.* to be extremely intoxicated • *Don't let her drive. She's plastered!;* Don't let her drive. She's extremely drunk!
♦ SYNONYM: **to be blitzed** *adj.*

played (to be) *adj.* (rap slang) said of a party that peaked and has now become boring • *Let's leave. This party's played;* Let's leave. This party has become boring.

pop in (to) *exp.* to arrive without notice • *I wish she wouldn't just pop in on us all the time. Why doesn't she ever call us first?;* I wish she wouldn't just arrive at our house without notice all the time. Why doesn't she ever call us first?
♦ ALSO: **to pop over** *exp.* to arrive unceremoniously (or without notice) • *Why don't you pop over after the movie?;* Why don't you come over after the movie?
♦ SYNONYM: **to drop in** *exp.* • *You'll never believe who dropped in today!;* You'll never believe who arrived without notice today!

powder *n.* fresh light powdery snow • *Skiing on powder requires a different technique than skiing on hard pack;* Skiing on fresh light powdery snow requires a different technique than skiing on hard packed snow.

powers that be (the) *exp.* the people in charge • *I'd like to allow you to come in but I didn't make up the rules...the powers that be did!;* I'd like to allow you to come in but I didn't make up the rules...the people in charge did!

private eye *n.* private investigator • *My father's training me to be a private eye;* My father is training me to be a private investigator.
♦ NOTE: This is actually a shortened and humorous version of "private investigator" which may be abbreviated to: *"P.I."* or *"private I."* However, since comic books depict private investigators as hunters with one huge eye enlarged by the magnifying glass they use to track foot prints, the letter "I" in *"private I"* was replaced with its homonym: *"eye."*

pull down the rebound (to) *exp.* (basketball) to seize a missed ball that has bounced off the backboard or the basket • *Robinson pulled down the rebound and ended up scoring two points for his side!;* Robinson seized the ball from the other team as it bounced off the backboard and ended up scoring two points for his side!

pull it together (to) *exp.* to become organized • *How am I possibly going to be able to pull it together before they arrive?;* How am I possibly going to be able to get organized before they arrive? • *How'd you pull the dinner together so fast?;* How did you organize the dinner so fast?

♦ VARIATION: **to get it together** *exp.*

pull the plug (to) *exp.* • **1.** to disconnect the life support of someone who has a critical illness • *Since there was no cure for him, the doctor thought it would be best to pull the plug and not let him suffer any longer;* Since there was no cure for him, the doctor thought it would be best to disconnect the life support and not let him suffer any longer. • **2.** to cancel permanently • *The sponsors pulled the plug on the project;* The sponsors canceled the project permanently.

pull through (to) *exp.* to survive a difficult illness or situation • *College was very difficult but I managed to pull through;* College was very difficult but I managed to survive.
♦ SYNONYM: **to make it** *exp.* • *It was a severe illness, but she's gonna make it;* It was a severe illness, but she's going to survive.

pump it up (to) *exp.* (rap slang) • to increase the volume on a stereo system *My mom just left! Pump it up!;* My mom just left! Increase the volume on the stereo!

put someone or something down (to) *exp.* to criticize someone • *Why do you put me down for everything I do?;* Why do you criticize me for everything I do? • *Stop putting down her performance! I thought it was terrific;* Stop criticizing her performance! I thought it was terrific.
♦ SYNONYM: **to jump all over someone** *exp.* • *Quit jumping all over me about it!;* Quit criticizing me about it!

-R-

rain buckets (to) *exp.* to rain heavily • *It's really raining buckets outside today!;* It's really raining heavily outside today!
♦ SYNONYM: **to rain cats and dogs** *exp.*

ridge *n.* (meteorology term) a high pressure area characterized by clear skies • *We have clear skies today due to a ridge that's sitting above the city;* We have clear skies today due to a high pressure area that's sitting above the city.

rocks (on the) *adv.* served with ice • *Would you like your drink on the rocks?;* Would you like your drink served with ice?

roll in (to) *exp.* • **1.** to approach in a rolling motion • *Look at those clouds roll in;* Look at those clouds approach. • **2.** to arrive casually • *She rolled into work an hour late!;* She casually arrived at work an hour late!

rubbernecker *n.* gawker, one who cranes his/her neck (as if it were made of rubber) in order to observe a traffic accident or unusual occurrence on the road • *On my way home, I was behind a rubbernecker who kept slowing down every time we passed a traffic accident;* On my way home, I was behind a gawker who kept slowing down every time we passed a traffic accident.

♦ NOTE: **to rubberneck** *v.* to gawk • *Stop rubbernecking and drive!;* Stop gawking and drive!

running play *exp.* (football) a play where an attempt is made to advance the football toward the goal by running with it as opposed to passing it through the air • *He tried twice to make a running play but he kept getting tackled;* He tried twice to run with the ball but he kept getting tackled.

rush hour *exp.* period of heavy traffic due to the close of business at the end of the day • *If we go to the movies now, we're going to hit rush hour;* If we go to the movies now, we're going to be on the roads when traffic is heaviest.

-S-

scam (to) *v.* (teen slang) to scrutinize people in the hopes of a possible sexual encounter • *He always goes to bars to scam on chicks;* He always goes to bars to scrutinize girls for possible sexual encounters. ♦ SYNONYM: **to cruise** *v.* • *I think that guy is cruising me;* I think that guy is scrutinizing me for a possible sexual encounter.

scene *n.* (of police) the exact place where an incident took place • *The police arrived at the scene of the crime;* The police arrived at the exact place where the crime took place.

scorcher *n.* an extremely hot day (which leaves everything scorched by the heat) • *It's a real scorcher today! I'm going swimming;* It's an extremely hot day today! I'm going swimming.

scrut (to) *v.* to eat voraciously • *I'm starved! Let's go scrut!;* I'm starved! Let's go eat!

shine something (to) *exp.* (teen slang) to exclude something from one's plans • *He didn't feel like going to work today, so he just shined it;* He didn't feel like going to work today, so he just excluded it from his plans. ♦ SYNONYM: **to blow something off** *exp.* • **1.** to exclude something from one's plans • *I'm blowing off my classes today;* I'm not going to my classes today. • **2.** to ignore something or someone • *Just blow it off!;* Just ignore it!

shoot [some] hoop (to) *exp.* (basketball) to play basketball (since the goal of the game is to shoot the ball through the hoop) • *Wanna come over and shoot [some] hoop today?;* Do you want to come over and play some basketball today? ♦ VARIATION: **to shoot some hoops** *exp.*

shoot down (to) *exp.* to reject unanimously • *The committee shot down my proposal;* The committee unanimously rejected my proposal. ♦ SYNONYM: **to steam-roll** *exp.* • *They all steam-rolled my decision;* They all rejected my decision.

shoulder *n.* the edge of the roadway where a car may park without obstructing traffic • *I had to pull off* *onto the right shoulder to change my tire;* I had to take my car off to the side of the road to change my tire.

sideline route *n.* (football) a common route taken by a receiver as he runs with the football along the edge of the field as opposed to running down the middle of the field.

size someone or something up (to) *exp.* to evaluate someone or something • *I sized him up and just don't like him;* I evaluated him and just don't like him. • *After sizing up the situation, I don't think we should proceed any further;* After evaluating the situation, I don't think we should proceed any further.

slow and go *exp.* braking and accelerating • *There's a lot of slow and go on the road right now due to rush hour;* There's a lot of braking and accelerating on the road right now due to everyone leaving work at the same time.
  ♦ ALSO: **stop and go** *exp.* stopping and accelerating.

slut *n.* girl with loose morals • (lit); prostitute • *She's had sex with every guy in school. I'm telling you, she's a real slut!;* She's had sex with every guy in school. I'm telling you, she's like a prostitute!
  ♦ NOTE: This term is a crude and derogatory synonym for "prostitute."

soak up the rays (to) *exp.* to sunbathe • (lit); to absorb the rays of the sun • *I'm gonna go lie by the*

pool and soak up the rays; I'm going to go lie by the pool and absorb the rays of the sun.
  ♦ NOTE: As seen in lesson one, teens have modified this expression to: *"to bag some rays."*
  ♦ VARIATION (1): **to soak up some rays** *exp.*
  ♦ VARIATION (2): **to catch some rays** *exp.*

soap *n.* daytime serial drama • *My mother loves watching soaps every afternoon;* My mother loves watching daytime serial dramas every afternoon.
  ♦ NOTE: These daytime serial dramas were nicknamed *"soap operas"* or simply *soaps* since their backers were primarily soap sponsors.

spew (to) *v.* (teen slang) to vomit • (lit); to spout or gush • *If I eat that, I'll spew!;* If I eat that, I'll vomit!
  ♦ SYNONYM (1): **to blow chow** *exp.* • *Her little brother got sick at the dinner table and blew chow;* Her little brother got sick at the dinner table and vomited.
  ♦ SYNONYM (2): **to blow chunks** *exp.*

spin out (to) *exp.* said of a car that is out of control and begins to spin due to slippery roads, applying the brakes suddenly, a flat tire, etc. • *I was driving on the highway and I suddenly got a flat tire which made the car spin out. Luckily, there was no one else on the road at the time;* I was driving on the highway and I suddenly got a flat tire which made the car spin from the loss of control.

Luckily, there was no one else on the road at the time.

sport (to) *v.* (rap slang) to wear.
‣ NOTE: The verb *"to sport,"* is **not** a slang term yet a rather formal synonym for the verb "to wear." It is becoming more and more common to use slang terms in conjunction with the more eloquent synonyms of standard terms as seen in the phrase: *to sport some fly gear.* Since the slang adjective *"fly,"* meaning "exceptional," is used in this phrase, it would be considered fine to include more eloquent terms like "to sport" and "gear." However, a teen would surely be ostracized if he/she were to say *"You're sporting some nice clothes"* since there are no slang terms to offset the formality of the more eloquent terms.

spot someone (to) *v.* to find someone • *I had trouble spotting you in this crowd;* I had trouble finding you in this crowd.

stacked (to be) *exp.* to have large breasts • *She says she doesn't like being stacked because it puts too much weight on her shoulders;* She says she doesn't like having such large breasts because it puts too much weight on her shoulders.

State Pen *exp.* a common abbreviation for the "State Penitentiary" • *It's practically impossible to escape from the State Pen;* It's practically impossible to escape from the State Penitentiary.

steal *n.* (basketball) the act of snatching the ball away from another player.
‣ ALSO: **to steal** *v.* to snatch the ball away from another player • *Just as Adams was about to shoot, Beaver stole the ball;* Just as Adams was about to throw the ball into the basket, Beaver snatched the ball away.

stick around (to) *exp.* to stay • *Stick around. The fun is about to begin!;* Stay here. The fun is about to begin!

stick of furniture *n.* single piece of furniture • *After the fire, they don't have a stick of furniture left;* After the fire, they don't have a single piece of furniture left.

stoked (to be) *adj.* (teen slang) to be excited • (lit); to be fueled (as in a furnace) • *I passed the final! I'm stoked!;* I passed the final! I'm excited!
‣ SYNONYM: **to be jazzed** *exp.* • *Tomorrow's a holiday! I'm jazzed!;* Tomorrow's a holiday! I'm excited!

stop by (to) *exp.* to visit unceremoniously • *Why don't you just stop by after dinner and we'll watch some television together?;* Why don't you just come over here casually after dinner and we'll watch some television together?
‣ SYNONYM: **to pop in** *exp.* • *Pop in any time!;* Come over casually any time!

straight up *adv.* pure and undiluted (said of alcoholic drinks) • *I had a hard day today. I think I need a* *vodka straight up;* I had a hard day today. I think I need some undiluted vodka.

stud *n.* (teen slang) a muscular and virile man • (lit); a male animal • *That's your brother? What a stud!;* That's your brother? What a muscular and virile man!
♦ ALSO: **studmuffin** *n. What a studmuffin!;* What a muscular and virile man!
♦ SYNONYM: **babe** *n.* any sexually attractive person • *He/She is a major babe!;* He/She is a real sexy person!
♦ NOTE: In the opening dialogue, the definite article "the" was used in front of *stud* instead of the usual indefinite article "a": *That guy is such **the** stud!* This construction is extremely popular with the younger generation.

stuffed (to get) *exp.* (football) to halt a play by the opposing team preventing the ball from advancing • *The receiver tried running with the ball but kept getting stuffed;* The receiver tried running with the ball but kept getting halted.

-T-

take it easy (to) *exp.* to relax • *The doctor said you have to take it easy for a week. So, get back to bed!;* The doctor said you have to relax for a week. So, get back to bed!
♦ SYNONYM: **to mellow out** *exp.* • *I'm just gonna stay here all day and mellow out;* I'm just going to stay here all day and relax.

"Take it from me" *exp.* "Believe me."

talk outside one's neck (to) *exp.* (rap slang) to lie or tease • *Don't believe him. He's talkin' outside his neck;* Don't believe him. He's lying.

tangle *n.* a traffic accident where two or more cars have collided • *Did you see the tangle on the highway today?;* Did you see the traffic accident on the highway today?

tapped out (to be) *exp.* (rap slang) to be poor • *I'd be glad to lend you some money but I'm tapped out;* I'd be glad to lend you some money but I'm poor.
♦ NOTE: This term originated in the coal mines where a load of ore would be extracted from a mine shaft until the resource was thoroughly depleted or *"tapped out."*

teed off (to be) *exp.* to be angry • *He got teed off at me 'cause I was 20 minutes late;* He got angry at me because I was 20 minutes late.
♦ NOTE: This is a common shortened version of *"to be ticked off."*
♦ VARIATION: **to be T'd off.**

"That tears it!" *exp.* "That's all I can tolerate!"
♦ VARIATION: **"That rips it!"** *exp.*

"That's a load off my mind" *exp.* "That's a relief!" • *It's a real load off my mind to know that you'll be baby sitting the kids tonight;* It's a real relief to me to know that you'll be baby sitting the kids tonight.

"...that won't quit" *exp.* "...that is exceptional" • *She has a face that won't quit! She has a beautiful face!"*
  ‣ SYNONYM: **for days** *exp.* • *He has a body for days!;* He has a fantastic body!

"The lights are on but nobody's home" *exp.* said of someone who appears to be awake yet is hopelessly oblivious and slow.
  ‣ SYNONYM (1): **not to be cooking on all four burners** *exp.* not to be using one's entire brain.
  ‣ SYNONYM (2): **not to have both oars in the water** *exp.*
  ‣ SYNONYM (3): **"The elevator doesn't go all the way to the top"** *exp.*

"There's no getting around it" *exp.* "There is no way to evade the issue."

ticker *n.* heart • *He has a strong ticker because he jogs every day;* He has a strong heart because he jogs every day.

tight (to get) *adj.* **1.** said of money that is hard to acquire • *Money is getting tighter and tighter these days;* Money is getting harder and harder to acquire these days. • **2.** to get intoxicated • *I think I'd better stop drinking. I'm starting to get tight;* I think I'd better stop drinking. I'm starting to get intoxicated.
  ‣ ALSO: **to be tight with money** *exp.* to be miserly with money •

She's so tight with her money; She's so miserly with her money.

top of the seventh *exp.* (baseball) the first part of the seventh inning.
  ‣ ANTONYM: **bottom of the seventh** *exp.* the second part of the seventh inning.
  ‣ NOTE: Baseball games are divided into nine innings. Each inning is then separated into two parts; the first part or *"top"* where one team is allowed to bat and the second part or *"bottom"* where the opposing team gets a chance at bat. Both expressions *"top of the..."* and *"bottom of the..."* can be used with any inning.

toss one's cookies (to) *exp.* to vomit • *He tossed his cookies in the bus;* He vomited in the bus.
  ‣ SYNONYM: **to blow chunks** *exp.*

touch and go (to be) *exp.* to be unpredictable • *I didn't know if the car would make it up the hill. It was touch and go for a while;* I didn't know if the car would make it up the hill. It was unpredictable for a while.

🖉 **tough cookie (to be a)** *exp.* • **1.** to be strong and robust • *My father pulled through beautifully after the operation. He's one tough cookie;* My father pulled through beautifully after the operation. He's really strong and robust. • **2.** to be uncompromising • *I don't think you'll get the boss to let you go on vacation early. He's one tough cookie;* I don't think you'll get the boss to let you go on vacation early. He's very uncompromising.

tough row to hoe (to be a) *exp.*
to be a difficult job to accomplish •
(lit); to be a difficult row of crop to
hoe • *If he doesn't learn how to be
independent, he's going to have a
tough row to hoe;* If he doesn't
learn how to be independent, he's
going to have difficulty in life.

trip (to be a) *exp.* to be rather
strange • *I've never met anyone so
bizarre. She really is a trip!;* I've
never met anyone so bizarre. She
really is strange.
♦ SYNONYM: **to be screwy** *exp.* •
He's screwy!; He's crazy!

trough *n.* (meteorology term) a low
pressure area characterized by
cloudy skies or even rain • *We're
going to have cloudy skies
tomorrow due to a trough that's
moving in from the west;* We're
going to have cloudy skies
tomorrow due to a low pressure area
that's moving in from the west.

turn out (to) *exp.* to conclude •
They turned out to be great friends;
They concluded by being great
friends.
♦ SYNONYM: **to end up** *exp.* • *They
ended up by compromising;* They
concluded by compromising.

turnover *n.* (basketball) the act of a
team losing possession of the ball •
*Just as the team was going to score,
there was an unexpected turnover;*
Just as the team was going to score,
they unexpectedly lost possession of
the ball.
♦ ALSO: **to turnover** *v.* to lose
possession of the ball.

tweaked [out] (to be) *exp.* (teen
slang) **1.** to be in a state of disarray
• *My hair is all tweaked [out]
today;* My hair is in a state of
disarray today. • **2.** to be
unresponsive and lethargic • *After
seeing the car accident, I feel sort of
tweaked [out];* After seeing the car
accident, I feel sort of unresponsive.
• **3.** to be defective • *This computer
is all tweaked [out]. I can't get it to
work right;* This computer is
completely defective. I can't get it
to work right.

twister *n.* tornado • *The twister
picked up our house and dropped it
two blocks away!;* The tornado
picked up our house and dropped it
two blocks away!

-U-

underway (to be/get) *exp.* to
begin the first step of a process •
The plan is underway; The plan has
just begun.

upshot *n.* outcome • *What was the
upshot of the meeting with the new
president?;* What was the outcome
of the meeting with the new
president?

-W-

walk (to) *v.* (baseball) to be allowed
to walk freely to the next base due
to four unsatisfactory balls being
thrown by the pitcher • *Since the
bases are loaded, if the next batter
gets to walk, the team will score one
more run;* Since there is a player on
each base, if the next batter gets to

walk freely to the next base due to four unsatisfactory balls being thrown by the pitcher, the team will score one more point.

wall (to) *v.* (rap slang) to lean against the wall at a party (instead of dancing) • *Who's that wallin' over there?;* Who's that leaning against the wall over there?
‣ NOTE: This is an updated version of the common expression *"to be a wall flower."*
‣ ALSO: **to play the wall** *exp.*

wash *n.* (used in all sports) a one-sided game • *Let's leave. This game looks like it's gonna be a wash;* Let's leave. This game looks like it's going to be one-sided.
‣ VARIATION: **washout** *n.* • **1.** a boring game • **2.** rained out • *We got washed out today;* We were unable to play today due to rain.

way *adv.* (teen slang) very • *He's way handsome!;* He's very handsome!
‣ SYNONYM: **fully** *adv.* • *"Do you like him?" "Fully!";* "Do you like him?" "Very much!"

"What is your/his/her/their deal?" *exp.* (teen slang) "What is your/his/her/their problem?" • *I don't know what her deal is but she's always angry;* I don't know what her problem is but she's always angry.
‣ ALSO: **"What's the deal?"** *exp.* "What's the problem?"

wide receiver *n.* (football) a player who generally runs down the field with the intention of receiving passes • *In order to be a wide receiver, you have to be fast!;* In order to be the player who receives passes while running down the field, you have to be fast!

wilma *n.* (surfer slang) *n.* female moron • *Did you see that wilma out there?;* Did you see that moronic girl out there?
‣ NOTE: *Wilma* is a cartoon character from the animated series "The Flintstones."

work a pitcher to a full count (to) *exp.* (baseball) said of a batter who has received three balls and two strikes from the pitcher. The next throw from the pitcher is now critical in determining whether or not the batter will be allowed to walk to the next base or be eliminated.

work one's way down/through/over/etc. (to) *exp.* to approach a destination laboriously • *As you work your way down the mountain, be sure to take the time to rest;* As you slowly descend the mountain, be sure to take the time to rest.

-Y-

"Yike!" *exclam.* exclamation denoting surprise • *Yike! What was that?!*
‣ VARIATION: **Yikes!**

"Yo G!" *exp.* (rap slang) "Hello!"
‣ NOTE: *"Yo!"* is a common term in the East for "You!" which is used to get one's attention. *"Yo!"* is considered extremely casual and, therefore, acceptable when used

with friends. However, if used with strangers or dignitaries, it would be regarded as rude and disrespectful. In these cases, "Excuse me!" would be the more suitable choice.

"Yoo hoo!" *exclam.* an exclamation to get someone's attention • *Yoo hoo! Nancy! I'm over here!*

-Z-

zip *n.* (used in all sports) • *The score is 3 to zip;* The score is 3 to zero.

zooed out (to be) *exp.* (surfer slang) to be overcrowded • *This beach is zooed out!;* This beach is overcrowded.
  ♦ NOTE: This is a variation of the popular expression, "to be a zoo:" *It's a zoo here!;* It's overcrowded here!

Learn slang while you drive!

Tel: 1-800-23-SLANG

International Orders call 818-981-3090 or Fax: 818-981-3868

VISA • MasterCard

TITLES	BOOK	CASSETTE
STREET TALK -1- . . . . *How to Speak and Understand American Slang*	$14.95	$12.50
STREET TALK -2- . . . . *Slang Used in Popular American Television Shows (plus lingo used by Teens, Rappers, & Surfers)*	$14.95	$12.50
BIZ TALK -1- . . . . *American Business Slang & Jargon*	$14.95	$12.50
STREET FRENCH . . . . *How to Speak and Understand French Slang*	$14.95	$12.50
MORE STREET FRENCH . . . . *Slang, Idioms, & Popular Expletives*	$14.95	$12.50
STREET SPANISH . . . . *How to Speak and Understand Spanish Slang*	$14.95	$12.50
BLEEP! . . . . *A Guide to Popular American Obscenities*	$12.95	$12.50

Domestic orders, add $4 shipping/handling for the first item – add $1 for each additional item.
California residents, please add applicable sales tax.
Street address must be used - U.P.S. can not deliver to post office box.
International orders, add $5 shipping/handling for the first item – add $2 for each additional item.
(International orders - approximately 6 weeks delivery. For special shipping, please call 818-981-3090)

OR SEND YOUR ORDER AND CHECK TO:

OPTIMA BOOKS • 270 N. Canon Drive, Suite 1270 • Beverly Hills, CA 90210 • USA

For international orders, please send an International Money Order.
(prices subject to change)

✂ -

Please send me _____ book(s) and _____ cassette(s) for *Street Talk -1-*
Please send me _____ book(s) and _____ cassette(s) for *Street Talk -2-*
Please send me _____ book(s) and _____ cassette(s) for *Biz Talk -1-*
Please send me _____ book(s) and _____ cassette(s) for *Street French*
Please send me _____ book(s) and _____ cassette(s) for *MORE Street French*
Please send me _____ book(s) and _____ cassette(s) for *Street Spanish*
Please send me _____ book(s) and _____ cassette(s) for *Bleep!*

NAME _____

ADDRESS _____

_____

CITY _____ STATE/PROVINCE _____